PORTRAIT OF
BATH

By the same author
Portrait of Avon

Portrait of
BATH

by

John Haddon

ROBERT HALE · LONDON

© *John Haddon 1982*
First published in Great Britain 1982

ISBN 0 7091 9883 3

Robert Hale Limited
Clerkenwell House
Clerkenwell Green
London EC1R 0HT

Photoset by
Kelly Typesetting Limited
Bradford-on-Avon, Wiltshire
Printed in Great Britain by
St Edmundsbury Press
Bury St Edmunds, Suffolk
Bound by Woolnough Bookbinding Ltd

Contents

Illustrations

PICTURE CREDITS

All photographs by the author except the following: 1, 2, 18, Brian Davis, Bath City Council; 48, Bath University.

MAPS

The maps are based upon the Ordnance Survey map with the permission of the Controller of Her Majesty's Stationery Office. Crown Copyright Reserved.

Introduction

There is a not unnatural tendency for non-residents to think of Bath solely in terms of Roman baths and Georgian architecture and this aspect is of some importance to the city in relation to the tourist trade—from April 1980 to March 1981, for example, over six hundred and ninety thousand people visited the Roman Baths and Pump Room, bringing in over six hundred and twenty-seven thousand pounds, and over a hundred and seventy thousand went to the Assembly Rooms and Museum of Costume, creating a revenue of a hundred and fifteen thousand pounds. Some nine thousand people attended the walking tours of the city conducted by the Mayor's honorary guides. Coaches roll in daily, disgorging their human load for a quick look round the city, and there is a brisk trade in hotel rooms, souvenirs, and other tourist requirements. It is therefore proper that this book should include details of the Roman occupation, the eighteenth-century development, and Georgian architecture.

This is by no means the whole story and if a portrait of this city is to have any claim to completeness it must take into account the considerable amount of development that has taken place in the nineteenth and twentieth centuries such as the provision of modern amenities, the conversion of one-time family houses to flats or offices, the addition (some would say intrusion) of modern architecture, the development of industry, and the expansion of suburbs. Bathonians work in a whole variety of jobs in offices, shops, factories, hospitals, services, and educational establishments, and they look to the future rather than the past.

In 1888 the British Association produced a *Handbook of Bath* for its meeting in the city and in the section on the nineteenth century Austin J. King wrote, "The idea of many hundreds of gaily-dressed ladies and gentlemen sauntering through life, bathing, promenading, and dancing within the city, and forming themselves into Watteau-like groups on the slopes of the hills, all under the paternal despotism of an *Arbiter Elegan-tarium*, is not one we can connect with stability." Stability, however, is not something we can expect of a living city for cities, like people, are at the same time in a state of being and a state of becoming, and although a ghost from the eighteenth century would recognize many of the buildings he would find much of the social behaviour and work activity incomprehensible. A city without people is dead and undeserving of the name, for buildings are fabricated to fulfil human dreams and needs; they are built for use and without it they are reduced to scenery for a play which is never performed.

This portrait is not, therefore, a snapshot of a city frozen at a single moment of time but a series of accounts of various cities of Bath which have existed, each with their own particular characteristics, in different periods of time, which have in their different ways helped to fashion the Bath of today. Much of this will be expressed in terms of the built environment for this is the visible expression of the needs and fashions of its time. The Roman baths, the medieval abbey, the Georgian new towns, the Victorian railway station and the new shopping precinct are all part of present-day Bath yet each was the product of a different society with different life styles, different fashions, and different technology, and although there is much which is special to Bath the city still typifies a principle of change which applies to all living urban areas.

Because of this principle of change, planning must adjust itself as time goes on and planners are coming to realize that in spite of the vociferous conservationist groups, whose value is not to be underestimated, a large number of citizens are concerned with more mundane things such as getting, and keeping, a job, finding suitable accommodation at an affordable price, getting the right kind of shopping, education, and entertainment facilities, and moving about easily in the city. In 1981, the council canvassed the public for their views on the present and future with such questions as "Are you getting the shops you need?", "Should new roads be built?", "Should more industry be encouraged?", "Should the City promote itself as a centre for the new technology?", "Should more sports and entertainment facilities be provided, and where?", "Should we be doing more to help youth organizations?", "Where could we put a campsite?", "Is there a preoccupation with attracting visitors?" and "Should we pursue a policy of restoring historic buildings at all costs or be selective in those we retain?" The proposal is now to plan for the whole city, not for selected parts, and, as their pamphlet says, "it is hoped that the City Plan will reach those parts of the City which other plans have failed to reach".

Another interesting proposal comes from a feasibility study conducted in co-operation with the council by a team of Italian, British, and French experts under the consortium company EPDG Project Development Group (Europe) Ltd, and it argues for a revival of Bath as a spa and treatment centre using the thermal water, the bottling and sale of the mineral water, and the use of the hot water for a geothermal project to heat the spa hotels and public buildings. It proposes a 'two-pole' development. One pole would be the traditional centre around the Pump Room and Bath Street with a new 90-bedroom Royal Bath Hotel and the reopening of bathing facilities at the Beau Street and Cross Baths, and the other would be developed around the site of the Bath Spa Nurses' Home at the bottom of North Road, where there would be a 200-bedroom Bath Spa Hotel and treatment centre. Conference facilities would be included, there would be treatment facilities for up to 40,000 people a year, and the cost is estimated at £15 million at current prices. The proposed charges for full board are £50 a day at the Royal Bath and £39 at the Bath Spa!

They point out that spas are now big business in Europe with some 7 million customers in Eastern Europe and 8 million in Western Europe, and that from Britain some 1.6 million visitors travel abroad on spa holidays each year. They say that the amoeba or 'bug' problem of Bath spa water, mentioned later in this book, can be solved and that there is sufficient thermal water to support a new spa development. The project began when Lord Selsdon of the Midland Bank suggested that the spa might be revitalized and much of the detailed advice has come from the Italian spa company Terme di Porretta who operate the successful Roman spa at Porretta Terme established some 100 years ago.

The city council has expressed considerable interest in this scheme but obviously in the present state of local authority finances it cannot go it alone and the possibility of starting the scheme will depend on finding a partnership with a major private investor. It is calculated that if a private investor can be found the council's contribution to the first stage, lasting six to nine months, would be up to £50,000.

It is an attractive and imaginative scheme and providing that
financial backing can be obtained it will restore to Bath something on which the city's reputation was founded for centuries—
the use of its thermal waters.

1

Overview

Our point of view, in several senses of the phrase, determines what we see. When I was small my parents sometimes took me to Bath on a real puffing, clanking train and my first impression of the city was a message in huge white letters which said "We Have Redemption Through His Blood" and changed, as we drew into the station, to "Christ Died For Our Sins". I was greatly impressed at being addressed in this way from what I now know to be the roof of an Ebenezer chapel and I would probably have been even more affected if I could have seen the roofs on the other side which change from information to admonition—"Ye Must Be Born Again" and "Prepare To Meet Thy God". I did not really understand the message but it gave me the impression that Bath was a pretty stern place which shouted at you from the roof-tops. The only other thing I remember is that the water in the Roman baths looked like thin soup.

Today I drive in from the west along the Upper Bristol Road and used to be presented with a different piece of information. By the side of the road were two poles bearing three boards. The top one said, "Bath, the Georgian City", the middle one was a grey blank which might well have represented the Middle Ages, and the bottom, narrow one said, "The Aquae Sulis of the Romans". This is an archaeologically correct sequence but it suggests that nothing has happened since Georgian times whereas in fact a great deal of Bath is Victorian all-sorts and there is a not inconsiderable amount of inter-war neo-Georgian and post-war shoe-box, as well as council and private housing put up between the wars and since 1945. Indeed, past the board you drive down Newbridge Road which did not exist before the 1820s when John Loudon McAdam engineered it for the Bath Turnpike Trust and which is bordered on one side by Victorian villas and on the other by inter-war semis. From then on it is mostly Victorian terraces until you top a rise and enter John Wood's Queen Square of the 1730s—Georgian Bath at last!

If however you go in along the *Lower* Bristol Road, Bath appears as an industrial city for here, squeezed between road and river, is a collection of factories, while the other side of the road is lined with Brunel's railway embankment and rows of Victorian terraces. It is a motley collection of enterprises— crane hire ("Sparrows lift everything"), Stothert and Pitt's engineering works (George Stothert started with an iron- monger's shop in Southgate Street in 1785, although it was then confusingly called Horse Street), Charles Bayer's corsets (Court Royal Foundations), Arkana cabinet works in an old vertical factory and Herman Miller's in a large horizontal box, Peter Simper who makes juke-boxes, and so on. This is not the tourist image of Bath but it is vital to the city's economy as over twenty per cent of workers in Bath are employed in industry and ware- housing.

The eastern approach along the London Road is more impres- sively Georgian and gives a better introduction to the archi- tectural treasures of eighteenth-century Bath but it breaks down as the city centre approaches and, indeed, none of the valley-way routes offers a view of the city as a whole. For a general impression you need to look out from the steep roads which descend the hills from north and south and see the build- ings spreading like a large grey, ribbed scarf draped over the hillsides and valley bottoms. It is this—the greyness, the ribbing, the undulations, the green hills above—which provides the basis for a portrait of Bath.

What we have here is a layer-cake in which the layers are rock strata through which from east to west has been gouged an asymmetrical V-shaped trench, the valley of the Avon, its flanks deeply grooved by tributary streams. On the sides of the valley the strata were exposed but, owing to the steepness and the presence of slippery clays, slumping occurred in the distant past and the junction of the different beds is often impossible to identify. The most recent slip, a small one, was in the late nineteenth century when a row of buildings was so badly affected that the area was not rebuilt but cleared and turned into Hedgemead Park, a pleasant open green space with trees beside the London Road. Back in 1788 they were constructing Camden Crescent on an arched platform out from the hillside up above Hedgemead when the end started slipping and the four last houses were never built. It must be stressed that these were isolated incidents, that the slopes are now generally stable, and that Bath is not destined to slide down the hillside and pile up in the valley bottom.

The top layer of rock forms plateaux north and south of Bath. In the north lies Lansdown (the long hill) where in 1643 Parliamentarians and Royalists fought each other to a stand-still and which today has rather different contests on the race-horse track and the windy soccer fields. On the west it descends to the Weston Brook and on the east is separated by the Swainswick Brook from Charmy Down (a wartime airfield) whose southern end, isolated by the stream valley of Chilcombe Bottom, forms the Little Solsbury Hill, triangular in shape and crowned by an Iron Age fort of modest scale but singular attrac-tiveness. This is beyond the city boundaries but to complete the picture we can move across the narrow, steep-sided valley in which is crammed the village of Batheaston and up beyond to Banner Down along whose top stretches a ruler-straight Roman road, the Fosse Way, running from Aquae Sulis to Corinium (Cirencester), Ratae (Leicester), and Lindum (Lincoln). East-ward the wider valley of the By or Box Brook, followed by the A4, separates Banner Down from the north–south plateau which stretches from Bathford to Bradford-on-Avon.

The peculiar course of the Avon which here runs from south to north in a valley of great beauty, separates this plateau from its westward continuation which forms a bulwark to the south of Bath. Here the north-running valleys are shorter and less strongly formed so that the plateau top is a continuous stretch. One result is that the built-up area created by the expansion of a string of villages south of the crest—Southdown, Odd Down, Combe Down—forms a suburban ring invisible from the rest of the city so that while the map shows that Bath is as wide from north to south as from east to west (about five kilometres) the visual impression is that it is a linear city running east–west. Indeed these southern villages were not administratively part of Bath until the twentieth century and those on the north-facing slope, Lyncombe and Widcombe were not incorporated until the Municipal Corporations Reform Act of 1835.

The southern plateau also includes, at its eastern end, the most extensive open space inside the city bounds. This consists of Claverton Down at whose northern end, over the city bound-ary, lies Bathampton Down with its Iron Age encampment. At the north end of Claverton Down the city playing-fields were handed over in 1965, not without some local protest, for the building of Bath University which crouches fairly unobtrusively on the skyline. "The site which it [the City] has given the University," wrote the Mayor, Councillor Mrs Elsie Hanna, "is wholly within the City boundary, is one of great natural beauty, and offers the University an opportunity for development and expansion such as few Universities enjoy anywhere in the world."

The streams whose valleys wrinkle the north-facing slopes are now mainly culverted but the topography they created influenced the creation of villages. As the Avon swings towards the base of the hill two tributary valleys come together as sites for the settlements of Widcombe (wide valley) and Lyncombe (torrent valley). To their west rises one of the notable features of Bath, tree-clad Beechen Cliff, beyond which to the west another valley, followed by the old Holloway down which came the Fosse, separates it from Twerton (Two-Ford), itself split by a valley into South Twerton and Twerton which is curious, because they ought to be East and West. Finally, the Newton Brook in its lower reach forms the western boundary of the city. South of the various Downs the land drops steeply to the Englishcombe Brook, Horsecombe Vale, and the Midford Brook.

The southern plateau is of more than topographical significance for although the hills both north and south are capped with the type of stone from which Bath was built it was only in the southern region that it was quarried. This stone is the great oolite of the Jurassic period and was laid down in a warm, shallow sea some 150 million years ago, a distance of time impossible to conceive but quite recent in geological terms. It is, in its most perfect form, a granular limestone which to imaginative eyes resembled fish eggs and was therefore called roestone, a term which geologists transformed into "oolite", from the Greek for egg (*oon*) and stone (*Lithos*), thus making it academically respectable.

The grains were formed by the deposition of lime on small fragments as they rolled about in the sea and these were then bound together by more lime. There were, however, times when conditions were not right for this and bands of the finer building stone are separated by layers of shelly or rubbly limestone which, unlike the best oolite, cannot be cut into large smooth-faced blocks (ashlar) or carved into decorative forms. The eighteenth-century quarries of Combe Down were mostly open but in later stone workings, especially to the east, the good stone had to be followed into the hillside creating a maze of underground galleries.

The oolite is a freestone, meaning that it can be cut in any direction, but to get the best resistance to weathering it should be 'laid in its bed', that is it should be built into a wall the same way as it lay in the ground. This also applies to stacking the blocks, which has to be done for some time to allow the water, or 'quarry sap', to drain out and the rock to harden, for when it is first cut it is quite soft and over-hasty use can cause considerable weathering problems.

The ashlar slabs, 6–8 inches thick, were used for facing walls which were mostly constructed of the poorer rubbly limestone although in the nineteenth century they were often used to cover brick and in some of the poorer dwellings were used without any backing, which made for a weak wall. In some cases money was saved by simply facing the front walls and a sneaky look round the back may well reveal rubble or, in later buildings, brick.

When it is first used the Bath stone is almost white and during the eighteenth century there were some who complained of the glare from the new buildings, but after a while atmospheric weathering turns it grey or black and rots the surface, particularly in the carvings. This is because rain-water is made mildly acidic by dissolved carbon dioxide and the calcium carbonate (lime) reacts with it to form a soluble bicarbonate. Even more destructive is dissolved sulphur, mainly from coal fires, which converts the lime into calcium sulphate, softer, spongier, and bulkier than the original. Thus either the outside rots away or else the water gets below the surface and blisters are formed which eventually break open and cause pitting. The rate at which the rotted stone is removed depends upon the amount of exposure to rainwash and so buildings can become streaked. Moreover, the stone seems to have a remarkable affinity for soot which clings tightly and forms a hard black scale.

These disadvantages are part of the reason why the eighteenth-century quarry owner and local plutocrat, Ralph Allen, had difficulty in selling his stone to London which preferred a more resistant version of the oolite, Portland stone, which in any case could be imported by the cheaper sea route. Other coloration of the stone comes from the growth of lichens which have a liking for lime. Lichen, sulphur, rain and soot—this is why Bath is a grey city. Contrary to what some have said, it was never golden—but what's wrong with grey?

Gentle, venerable, sitting quietly against the greens of the countryside the greying stone has a quiet attraction—but not for some. In the nineteenth century there began a taste for painting the stonework and in several places this may still be seen, often with fading lettering advertising some library, shop or factory. This is not a very attractive treatment and today the aim is to make Bath, or rather its major architectural features, white again. Bath has a "town scheme" for cleaning groups of buildings by assisting house owners with local and Government grants, and newly cleaned groups of buildings can be seen in, for example, the Circus and Pulteney Street. The Pump Room has also been cleaned. Cleaning is done by washing with water, other methods being considered too harsh, and rotted carvings are replaced by facsimiles. It is an expensive business and there is little hope that the majority of Bath will ever be anything other than grey. Where it does take place the results are startling.

Bath stone is now too expensive to use but since the Bath Act of 1925 new buildings must be faced with a suitable substitute and so we get artificial Bath stone based on crushed limestone poured into moulds and sometimes bonded on to breeze blocks. It has a resemblance to the original but it stains instead of weathering and while in some ways more efficient than Bath stone it has nowhere near the same visual quality. There are incongruous patches of red-brick housing which crept in before the Act was passed and quite a bit of dark Pennant sandstone in Victorian buildings. The Act has, however, saved the city from the brutalist horrors of exposed concrete.

One other thing may be noticed in examining Bath stone and that is that it often has veins. These are of crystalline limestone, or calcite, deposited by water forcing its way slowly through weaknesses in the rock. These veins tend to be more resistant than the oolite and therefore often protrude slightly from the surface.

Oolite 'tiles' were used for roofing in the eighteenth century, although they had to be brought from further north in the Cotswolds, but these have mainly been replaced by slate, made available after the coming of the railway in the 1840s, and later buildings have clay or concrete tiles in varying shades of red. One housing development, Snow Hill beside the London Road, has green roofs resulting from the oxidation of the copper cover and some of the post-war buildings sit under black hats of painted metal.

Hampton Down quarries got a fresh lease of life when they supplied stone for the Kennet and Avon Canal which opened in 1810 and a tramway was built down the side of the hill, crossing the main road on an arch which has since been demolished. The big expansion of the nineteenth century was over in Wiltshire at Box and Corsham and started with the cutting of Box Tunnel in 1836–41.

Below the great oolite are successive strata of fuller's earth rock and clay, inferior (i.e. lower) oolite, and the Upper, Middle, and Lower Lias. Inferior oolite is mainly limestone, Upper Lias contains the Midford Sands, and Lower Lias consists of bands of limestone, much used as building material in the surrounding villages, and clay. Fuller's earth clay has been of particular importance as it was used for removing grease from woollen cloth and its presence contributed to the local late-medieval textile industry—hence the number of tucking mills, tucking being another word for fulling. Until recently fuller's earth was mined just south of Bath by the Fosse Way but the works are now closed. Inferior oolite varies in character from place to place but produced a good building stone at Dundry Hill south of Bristol and at Doulting on the southern fringe of Mendip whence it was carried to build Wells Cathedral.

Bath's cradling hills are environmentally significant in three ways. Firstly, they provide a pleasant rural back-drop of hedged green fields to the highly sophisticated townscape of the city, a city which is small enough to give many glimpses of the hills through gaps between the buildings. This green hill setting has to a large extent been preserved by the city planners between the wars and since. Secondly, the steep slopes of the lower edges necessitated a street pattern dominated by orientation along the contours—hence the appearance of horizontal ribbing. Thirdly, there is a climatic, or rather micro-climatic, effect in that air tends to stagnate in the bottom of the valley creating a somewhat warm, moist, and enervating atmosphere which has been commented on, sometimes favourably ("balmy Bath") but more often with distaste. Pope called it "a sulphurous pit" and Mrs Piozzi, enjoying a bracing holiday at Weston-super-Mare in the late eighteenth century, wrote that the bottom of Bath was like a stew-pot. It is not, however, as bad as all that.

This takes us down to the other major element in what we might call "landshape", the valley bottom. The Avon comes up, as we have seen, from the south before swinging westward along the edge of a broad plain of pasture. From here it slides along south-west towards the heart of the city, passes under the Cleveland Bridge and strides south to Dolemeads and Beechen Cliff from which point it heads westward out of the city. It was in the angle between the north–south and east–west stretches that the ancient walled city—Roman, Saxon, and medieval—was sited. The reason for this was that the river, having filled the bottom of the valley with sands and gravels proceeded to cut into them, leaving the remains as river terraces or benches. In Bath most of these terraces are very narrow and are used mainly for roads but inside the angle the old floor was wider and formed a well-drained level surface sufficiently high to be above flood level.

Yet it was not dry, for coming up through it from possibly two and a half miles below the surface, hot water, at a temperature of 48°C, emerged through two springs at the rate of a quarter of a million gallons a day. Recent excavations have shown that in the Iron Age a wall was constructed round the chief spring, under the present King's Bath, but it was not until the Romans encapsulated the spring in concrete, making a reservoir, that the ground could be drained adequately to form the foundations for a city, a city some fifteen feet below the present ground level—which is why you have to go downstairs to visit the Roman baths. The heating of the water is due to the normal increase in temperature below the Earth's surface and Bath is *not* sitting on a volcano.

Hot water forcing its way up through the Earth's crust under pressure is bound to acquire a mineral content and an analysis in 1961 detected forty-three separate items although most of these were mere traces and the only ones in quantity were calcium, magnesium, sodium, sulphate, and chloride (see *Bath: Some Encounters with Science*, Williams and Stoddard, 1978). Even then there is sixteen times as much dissolved material in an equivalent volume of sea-water. In 1901 the Hon. R. W. Strutt discovered helium in the gases emitted by the baths and in 1903 he reported that there was radium in the water. This was confirmed in 1912 by Sir William Ramsay and aroused great interest, Bath producing an advertisement in which the city was seen to be radiating waves of energy. The amount of radium is, in fact, negligible, and there is no danger of people

becoming irradiated. More serious has been the recent discovery that the bath waters have become the home of an amoeba
dangerous to human health.

On the north–south stretch the terrace lies about half a kilo-
metre to the east of the river leaving a low-lying flood plain
which is liable to inundation. Until 1774 this was undeveloped
except for a pleasure-ground known as Spring Gardens but in
that year Pulteney Bridge was completed and in 1758 a city
extension in Bathwick, centred on Great Pulteney Street, was
started on a masonry platform which raised it above flood level.
To the south of this the land remained open and is now occupied
by a cricket ground, recreation ground, and sports centre. The
southern tip of the flood plain, known as Dolemeads, was
developed with cheap housing after the opening of the Kennet
and Avon Canal which here descends to the Avon in a short
flight of locks. The area became a slum and was cleared in 1900
and replaced by rows of red-brick houses, the first council
housing in Bath. It is on the edge of this that we find the
battlemented Ebenezer chapel of 1820 with its roof-top
messages.

Only in the short section below Pulteney Bridge does the
Avon make any really significant contribution to the urban
scene and this is largely due to late nineteenth-century developments which cleared a clutter of market buildings, set a Grand
Parade on columns, and created the riverside Parade Gardens.
It is here, on the Grand Parade, that visitors gather to lean on
the stone balustrade and admire Adam's Pulteney Bridge and
the river with its U-shaped weir. A bit further up you can hire a
boat and get a view of Bath from the bottom up, an interesting
experience.

The planners, dreaming of riverside amenity, have made
some effort with walkways and landscaping but the results are
lacking in charm and the sight of the river is not improved by
the necessary sheet-steel piling of the banksides designed to
send flood water hurrying out of the city to make itself a
nuisance further downstream. The water is a good deal cleaner
than it was in the eighteenth and early nineteenth centuries
when the stream was an open sewer; fish may be caught and
swans may be seen, but in general the town turns a not very
attractive backside to the river and crowds it too closely for
comfort. The days are long gone when beyond the city walls
meadows and orchards sloped gently down to the river bank in

the Abbey Orchard, the Ham, the Ambry and Great Kingsmead. Indeed, it is more pleasant, and in some ways more rural, to walk along the banks of the canal rescued from dereliction by the voluntary workers of the Kennet and Avon Canal Trust.

The landshape is important in determining the pattern of Bath and the green hills are a blessing, but this is secondary to the strong yet subtle attractiveness of the built environment. Bath is a city which inspires affection, not awe, for although it has its fine set pieces of Circus, crescents, and squares, everything is on a human scale, manageable to the eye, not neck-breaking, although in places wearying to the legs. Moreover there is no Grand Plan, for the city grew piecemeal as individual developers got to work in response to market demand, and it is full of visual surprises—surprises but not shocks, for the use of a common stone and a common scale, respected even after the Palladian rules of the early eighteenth century had lost their hold, gives a comforting homogeneity which binds the contrasts into a whole—it is not therefore surprising that much of the city is now designated as a conservation area in one large block. It is a city for living in, a city for people, and you can love it, as most do, without being able to tell Corinthian from Ionic or a triglyph from a Vitruvian scroll. On the other hand people are well aware that the peculiar quality of built Bath makes it very sensitive to unneighbourly architectural intrusions or additions and the pages of the local newspaper reverberate with protest against the activities of post-war developers. This is not new—the Society for the Preservation of Old Bath was formed in 1908.

A city without people is not a city, and the citizens of Bath are people of today, so Bath is modern. Dickens saw the place as peopled with ghosts of the eighteenth century but he was a literary gent, and most of today's inhabitants go about their business of coping with the trials and tribulations and joys of living their own lives without seeing Beau Nash or Jane Austen at every corner as they shop in a supermarket, go dancing at Tiffany's, have a pint in a pub, a meal in a restaurant, or an argument with a traffic warden; many of these people are young—any image of Bath streets being full of old ladies being towed about in Bath chairs should be instantly dispelled. And it is the needs and expectations of the people of the Bath of today which create the problems of adapting a city, Georgian and Victorian, which was built to meet demands which either no longer exist or have been modified almost beyond recognition. The tall family house with a kitchen in the basement, servants' bedrooms in the attic, coal fires in the family rooms, and no bathrooms is an anachronism, unacceptable today. Streets which were adequate for sedan-chairs and carriages cannot cope with mass motor traffic. In the eighteenth century there was no call for bus stations, car-parks, garages, railway stations, office blocks, cinemas, supermarkets, hotels, large factories, or small semi-detached houses.

The challenge of change is no new thing, and certainly not in Bath. The Romans built a spa which fell into ruins and over it a Saxon monastic town arose, owing nothing to the Roman street pattern or building style. In Norman times Bath became a cathedral city and in the Middle Ages it developed as a woollen town and market centre. With the surrender of the monastery to Henry VIII's commissioners buildings began to go up on the old monastic land. After the Civil War there was considerable building activity controlled by some rudimentary planning restrictions as council minutes show, so that when Pepys visited it he found a tidy town with good stone buildings—buildings which, as contemporary drawings show, had gables and mullioned windows, often set in bays or oriels. A few gables remain but most of the city was refaced in the new fashion of the Palladian style in the eighteenth century while in the green fields outside the walls developers set up a new town in the Roman Classical style, then the latest fashion. For the new social needs of the town they provided Assembly Rooms, a Pump Room, a theatre, pleasure gardens, broad walks, and proprietary chapels, while old buildings were turned into lodging-houses, coffee-houses, libraries, and shops. In the back streets they built mews for stabling horses, and rows of minor dwellings to house the workers.

The Victorians set about hauling Bath into the modern world, giving the city a water supply and sewerage, gas, electricity, trams, public parks, new schools, and three railways, two of which, the Somerset and Dorset and the LMS amalgamated in 1875. They built two railway stations, one Jacobean, one Greek Revival. Baroque extensions to the Guildhall housed the new bureaucracy, a secondary school, and an art gallery. The Pump Room got a concert hall and the new-found Roman baths were given a pillared surround with statues of Roman emperors. New streets were cut and corners heightened and made more ostentatious. The ground floors of Georgian buildings were given large sheets of plate glass for the new department stores and many a pub got a mahogany-and-cut-glass treatment. Georgian houses were knocked together to make hotels and new hotels were built, notably the Grand Spa in Second Empire style, and the Empire which is Jacobean up to the roof where it goes crazy. They added a second Palladian block to the eighteenth-century hospital (now the Royal Mineral Water Hospital) and built a new Greek Revival Royal United Hospital on whose extension can still just be seen in faded letters the legend "Albert the Good" (it would be nice to have this refreshed). In the suburbs rose the villas, Italianate and Gothic, and acre upon acre of by-law terraced housing. They built a new theatre, and then rebuilt it after it caught fire, and they erected a music-hall opposite. They provided two new swimming-baths and a new treatment centre by the Pump Room. They built half a dozen new bridges over the river to improve access, and new churches, Grecian, Gothic and Byzantine, to improve people's chances of salvation.

They also found themselves with some rather unpleasant slums down towards the river and Avon Street, one of the first pieces of Georgian development descended from its early respectability to become a byword for roughness, with its doss-houses, prostitutes, and thieves, although it did have a propor-tion of respectable poor. A newspaper report of an election meeting in Bath in 1880 noted that "The harmony of the pro-ceedings was, however, a little marred by the arrival of a con-tingent of some twenty or thirty Avon Street roughs, armed with thick sticks. Their arrival was greeted with overpowering groans. Several sharp scrimmages occurred."

Groaning at Avon Street became a popular pastime with the council but nothing positive was done whereas in "the filthy, odious Dolemeads" with its "very poor description of houses" the land was cleared, as we have seen, for council housing. Other degraded areas were Holloway, at one side of Beechen Cliff, noted for its beggars, thieves, and "dreary pot-houses", and the Morford Street, Ballance Street, Lampard's Buildings, region up behind the prestigious Circus; Lampard's Buildings got its improvement scheme in 1902.

On the whole the major Victorian building sits quite well in the Georgian matrix. Much of it showed a Classical neighbour-liness and a respect for the general scale of the place (it was bigger, but not excessively so, except in the Empire Hotel) and it was still in Bath stone. Less happy were the changes made to individual houses—the removal of glazing bars and substitution of plate glass, the cutting down of window bottoms thus altering their proportions, the addition of iron balconies and of boxes for exterior blinds, and in some shopping streets the addition of a multiplicity of hanging signs.

The pace of change slowed down in the inter-war period but activity by no means ceased. For example Bath got, all in neo-Georgian style, a Forum Cinema (and two others in a less self-consciously eighteenth-century garb), a new post office, a large Co-op., a Woolworth's, and electricity offices. A new Royal United Hospital was built on a green site in Combe Park where there had been a wartime hospital, the old one became a technical college, and new secondary schools were built away from the city centre. Council estates appeared and workers' flats replaced a small slum area in Kingsmead (near Avon Street). Meanwhile many of the old Georgian family houses sprouted rows of bellpushes or brass plates as they became divided into flats or were taken over by doctors, dentists, solicitors and the like. The Assembly Rooms lost their former glory and in 1921 the ballroom became a cinema and the tea-room a salesroom. From this they were rescued in 1931 by a Mr Cork who presented them to the National Trust. Restored, they were re-opened in 1938 by the Duchess of Kent. The Bath Royal Literary and Scientific Institution building, with its noble Grecian portico, was pulled down and the institute moved in 1932 to new buildings in Queen Square, now the reference library. South of the abbey the single-storey Kingston Baths of 1763–6 were finally demolished and the present paved courtyard substituted.

Much of this change resulted from the Bath Act of 1925 which the corporation put up after holding a referendum amongst the citizens. Other results of the Act were the rebuilding of corners in Kingsmead Square, the cutting of a new thoroughfare from St James's Parade to Southgate Street, and the purchase of river bridges to free them from tolls. The economic situation, however, prevented the realization of a planned riverside development. A second Act in 1937 would have moved the Royal Mineral Water Hospital (its name changed in 1935 to the Royal National Hospital for Rheumatic Diseases) and made changes to Walcot Street, opposition to which resulted in another referendum, but its intentions were frustrated by the onset of war.

One pioneer provision was the listing of pre-1820 buildings which could not then be altered without corporation agreement.

During the Second World War little building took place apart from batches of brick hutments on Lansdown, Combe Down (Foxhill), and between the canal and the Warminster Road. These were put up by the Ministry of Works for the considerable portion of the Admiralty which had been evacuated to Bath in 1939 and started off by occupying hotels (including the Empire), the technical college, the domestic science college, Kingswood School, and the Royal School. Much of the Admiralty work at Bath was in design and it was here that were designed the last RN battleship, HMS *Vanguard*, the last two aircraft carriers, *Eagle* and *Ark Royal*, submarines, including midgets, and the floating Mulberry Harbour and PLUTO (Pipe Line Under the Ocean) for the Normandy invasion. The Navy, now called less gloriously the Ministry of Defence (Navy) is still a major employer in Bath and post-war Bath projects included the Polaris submarine.

On the nights of Saturday and Sunday 25th and 26th April 1942 came the 'Baedeker' air raids on Bath which destroyed or damaged over 1,900 buildings, killed over 400 people, and injured hundreds more. It was a hard, sad night borne with fortitude, and over eighty per cent of the city was affected in one way or another. In the Georgian set pieces there was damage to Queen Square, the Circus, the Crescent, the Paragon, and Somerset Place. The recently restored Assembly Rooms were gutted by fire and St James's at the bottom of Stall Street and Holy Trinity, Monmouth Street, were reduced to shells. The west wing of the Royal Hospital had a direct hit and the eastern range of the V-shaped Green Park was destroyed. Small areas were flattened, one north of the Circus in Julian Road, the others in the south at Kingsmead and Holloway, but there were no large areas of devastated land open for development as at Bristol, say, or Plymouth, or Coventry.

When building recommenced the Georgian buildings were restored with facsimile façades—nearly half of the Francis Hotel in the south side of Queen Square is a replacement and Somerset Place was almost entirely rebuilt behind its restored façade as accommodation for the domestic science college. In the Julian Road area neo-Georgian flats and a modernistic church were put up. The bombed Kingsmead area was filled, however, with a foretaste of the future—offices and flats in a boxy, rectilinear style, faced with artificial stone—and by the London Road were built the Snow Hill council flats, tall and thin, with balconies and copper roofs and Bath's one high-rise residential block. The grey buildings of Holloway were later to be completely demolished and replaced by a private development of conspicuous, dark-topped, white-faced cuboid houses.

Bath would have developed differently if the council had adopted the Abercrombie Plan which they commissioned in 1943, the year after the raids and published in 1945, the year the war ended. In Abercrombie's Bath, Kingsmead became a shopping precinct with a new technical college nearby and not far away a new Royal Hospital. The riverside at Walcot was opened up and there was a lido in the recreation ground and five new bridges over the Avon. The suburbs were to be developed as fourteen "neighbourhoods". From the railway station was a view over an open plaza to new hotels and a grand concert room. Abercrombie was ambivalent about the style for the new buildings but in his drawings they come out as neo-Georgian. A great deal of work had gone into the plan, it was readable and persuasive, and it was greeted with enthusiasm, but it was not to be implemented.

Tidying up began under the 'Blitz and Blight' Act of 1944, and then in 1947 came the Town and Country Planning Act which made Bath a planning authority and required it to produce a town map and written statement containing proposals for development for the next twenty years, with provision for reassessment every five. Bath had already some experience in city planning, with her Acts and the collaboration between Professor Abercrombie, the City Engineer, Mr John Owens, and the Planning Officer, Mr Anthony Mealand, but there was still a lot of work to be done and the new plan, which owed something, although not a lot, to previous proposals, was not ready until 1952, by which time there was a new Planning Officer, Mr J. C. Wilkinson. It was submitted to the Minister in 1952 but was not approved until 1955, or finally published until 1958, eleven years after the Act by which it was required. During this lengthy period there was not only a brake on new work in the city but also some changes in the proposals. The Royal Hospital was going to be moved, as in the 1938 Act, to a site on Avon Street where piling had been put in before the war, and the technical college was to be put into Norfolk Crescent along with a county college, an abortive proposal of the 1944 Education

Act, but it was decided to put the Tech. on Avon Street and leave the hospital where it was. The hospital was reopened by Princess Marina in 1965.

Although the war had been over for some years there were still many gaps left by the bombing and most of the rebuilding we have already noted had to wait for the new plan to be put into effect. This included the Snow Hill flats, a large council estate at Whiteway on the hill above Twerton, the Ballance Street/ Morford Street area (developed 1969), and numerous other patches of housing, council or private. Other plans which have been realized were for a bus station opposite Bath Spa railway station (ex-GWR); flats, Government offices, and a telephone exchange in the Kingsmead area, a number of new secondary schools, and a new domestic science college at Sion Hill. St John's Church was demolished to make way for a new Woolworth's and Marks and Spencer's. If British Rail had stuck to their original intentions the two stations, Bath Spa and Green Park, would have been amalgamated, the former becoming the passenger station and the latter the central goods depot, but this proposal was abandoned. The old LMS line and Green Park station were closed in 1966 and the latter was bought by the corporation in 1972 since when it has been sadly derelict and only in 1981 was work begun on developing the site—for a supermarket.

Things moved along rather slowly in the fifties but problems, particularly over traffic, were increasing and in 1964 the city council commissioned Colin Buchanan and Partners to make a report which was issued in the following year as "A Planning and Transport Study of Bath" and was taken as the basis for further planning. It was concerned principally with taking east–west traffic through Bath as painlessly as possible for the historic fabric by running it through twin tunnels under the north central part, fed by a new road along the riverside, entering at lower Walcot, and emerging from Victoria Park to join the Upper Bristol Road at a large interchange. Additional relief was to be provided by a road in a trench, the New Bond Street Cut. Much of the central area was to be pedestrianized, with peripheral depots from which the shops could be serviced by trolley, and some penetration by buses would be permitted. The consultants were also commissioned to make a study of conservation problems and their report came out in 1969 along with similar studies of Chester, York, and Chichester. These were all instigated by the Ministry of Housing and Local Government which was at last coming to realize how rapidly the best bits of Britain were disappearing.

Given the pounding and shaking that Georgian Bath was getting from the ever-increasing traffic, the great inconvenience to pedestrians, and the impossibility of constructing an adequate bypass in the constricted valley, the Buchanan tunnel seemed a reasonable solution to many people including myself, the majority on the council, Whitehall (1967), and the architectural correspondent to the *Bath Chronicle* whose articles ranged from "On just the right line, by George!" in 1969 to "Sorry—Buchanan's still best for Bath" in 1971. Opposition from conservationists, who were particularly incensed by the amount of demolition required to provide the approach roads and intersections, was slow to start but soon accelerated into a major row which was taken up in the national Press.

It was not just Buchanan who excited opposition, for along with the road schemes the council proposed and were beginning to put into effect a number of CDAs (Comprehensive Development Areas) which were destroying acres of minor Georgian buildings and replacing them with buildings that were arousing no one's admiration; "crass monstrosities", wrote Colin Amery and Dan Cruikshank in *The Rape of Britain* (1975), "in violent discord with the character of what remains". Castigating the council became a popular local sport, vigorously assisted by the *Chronicle* which was always happy to print protest letters or to photograph protesters, particularly if they were young, female and photogenic—which several of them were. The delicate drawings in Peter Coard's *Vanishing Bath* of 1971 which showed that much that was graceful had been lost, and the swingeing attack by Adam Fergusson in *The Sack of Bath* (1973) lent weight to the movement. The city's Chief Planning Officer, yet another one, made the reasonable statement, in effect, that retaining Georgian artisan dwelling would be all right if we had Georgian artisans to put in them. After all, today's artisans are likely to require rather more in terms of mod. cons., although Fergusson argued that, "those who live in and enjoy the beauties of an eighteenth-century town should not expect the amenities of Harlow New Town or Hemel Hempstead." What people *ought* to expect, in somebody else's opinion, is not necessarily what they *do* expect, and the majority of Bath's citizens were silent during the Great Controversy.

The minority made up for this. There were letters to the paper and telegrams to the Minister; cars said "Save Bath" on their back windows and posters appeared on houses; there were processions with banners and there were meetings in the Abbey Churchyard and outside the Guildhall; there were clashes of opinion within the Preservation Trust which resulted in resignations; pamphlets were published by university students and the Young Liberals; there was a Bath Action Group started by an ex-model, her daughter, and another lady who sold musical instruments, and a Bath Environment Campaign founded by a Research and Development Manager and the owner of a high-class toy shop, and a Bath Amenity and Transport Association. Amongst the rebels were business and professional people, students, housewives, an ex-Harvard American, an ex-city councillor, and the retired City Engineer who had been part-author of the Abercrombie plan and considered it adequate. The youngest of the leaders was twenty-two, the oldest seventy-eight. The Environment Campaign and the Preservation Trust both commissioned reports which were highly critical of the Buchanan proposals. Meanwhile householders in areas likely to be affected were getting worried and making their voices heard, particularly in Oldfield Park.

The council was about evenly split on the proposals; the Labour opposition opposed, and several councillors came out with their own plans. When the question was debated in principle in July 1971 the scheme was passed by only two votes and it was the same narrow majority which gave the go-ahead in January 1972 when there was uproar in the gallery. In June the council decided to ask Buchanan to have another look, providing Whitehall would pay seventy-five per cent of the cost, but they wouldn't, so he didn't. It was then proposed to hold a public inquiry and by the deadline for written objections the Minister had received over 300. Whether this made Whitehall nervous or not is impossible to say but in June 1973 the Secretary of State for the Environment, Geoffrey Rippon, proposed that instead of a public inquiry there should be consultation between the about-to-be born Avon County, Bath Council, and the Bath Preservation Trust who were to set up a Steering Committee and commission yet another report. For this they brought back Buchanan and Partners and added Nathaniel Lichfield and Associates and Services and Systems Co-Partnership who presented the "Bath Planning Review" in May 1974.

In July 1974 the Secretary of State for the Environment, in letters to Avon County, Bath City Council, and Bath Preservation Trust said that it was unlikely that there would be money for some time for the tunnel scheme, which would now cost some £9 million, and suggested that while the authorities were preparing the new plans, Structure and Local, required by the Town and Country Planning Act of 1968 and the Local Government Act of 1972, they should prepare three special studies (again!)—one on dealing with traffic by management and public transport, a second on a detailed programme for conservation, and the third to look at the consequences of adopting a minimum physical growth policy for the city. The last, again by Nathaniel Lichfield and Partners, was published in December, 1976, and the second came out as a Stage One Report in 1976 and a Final Report, "Saving Bath", in 1978 over the names of the latest (but now gone) City Architect and Planning Officer, Roy Worskett, the Director of Environmental Health, Ronald Redston, and the Director of Estate Management, Hugh Gunton; the preamble stated "The Final Report . . . is now the City Council's approved Policy". Various traffic management palliatives have been tried and there are now plans for improving the approaches along the Lower Bristol Road where a new bridge has been built connecting the Upper and Lower Bristol Roads. In 1979 the Buchanan scheme, which was now far too expensive, was officially dropped.

So the rebels, if perhaps by no more than creating delay, had won. But it was more than just a local matter for the whole tide of opinion about the nature and purpose of planning had changed and it had changed because people got fed up with what they were getting, fed up with having so little say in what affected their lives and of being disregarded by experts who they were coming increasingly to distrust. It is not surprising that with increasing affluence, increasing leisure, better (dare it be said?) education, and the increasing influence of television, which gave a good platform to the conservationist/ecological pressure groups and showed people what was happening *in pictures*, some sections of the community began to demand an active part in planning or in the frustration of planners.

At first the situation had seemed simple. We had, had we not, won the war by doing what we were told, by accepting planning, by accepting rationing and conscription and standing quietly in queues—in that way, then, we could win the peace. All we needed were wise men to tell us what to do. Surely, new was better—new roads, new housing, new amenities—new Jerusalems! It was an attitude which the Georgian developers of Bath would have applauded; after all, if they had not thought in that way we would never have had a Georgian Bath to admire—indeed, if no one had ever thought like that we would presumably still be living in caves. The trouble was that people did not like the New Jerusalem—one suspects that a lot of people won't like heaven when they get there. They didn't like concrete and rectilinearity and rooms and streets in the sky and urban motorways thundering past their windows and having to walk a quarter of a mile to a drying-room or toil up interminable concrete stairs because the lift wasn't working, or having water dripping down the walls because they couldn't afford to keep the heating going, or suddenly finding that the pub round the corner had disappeared overnight, or not being able to sell their house because a new road might or might not be coming through their front garden some time in the future. When Georgian, or even Victorian, or even pre-war buildings are knocked down there are howls of protest but when post-war high rise is blown up a cheer goes up from the nation.

All this is highly simplistic and there is still a good deal to be said on the other side, but the main point is that the ideas filtered through to Government and affected legislation, advice, and grants. CDAs are no longer in favour, nor are urban motorways; tower blocks and insufficiently tested industrial building methods are out, conservation and rehabilitation are in. Public participation is not only encouraged but is required by the 1971 Town and Country Planning Act, following the 1969 Skeffington Report, "People and Planning".

The 1947 Town and Country Planning Act introduced the statutory listing of buildings and gave them some degree of protection; an LBC (Listed Building Consent) is required before demolition or significant change is allowed—and Bath has some five thousand listed buildings, but the result was that there was no provision for the setting and the building often became flanked with new and unneighbourly structures. In 1967 the Civic Amenities Act improved matters by giving grants for work in conservation areas and the 1974 Town and Country Amenities Act extended listed building protection to all buildings in such areas. Bath declared five conservation areas, including a large central one, and then extended them to cover a very large single area nearly two-thirds of the city and covering over 3,000 acres. Within this the 'Save Bath' plan identifies three priority areas—Walcot Street, Monmouth Place, and Widcombe, and gives detailed proposals for their rehabilitation with the minimum of destruction.

Grants to bring old houses up to a minimum standard (putting in baths and so on) were introduced in the Housing Act of 1969 which also gave help to authorities who declared GIAs (General Improvement Areas). The Act of 1974 increased these grants and introduced the use of HAAs (Housing Action Areas) to be rehabilitated within five years. Bath has at present seven GIAs—East Twerton (Nov. '79), Larkhall (May '71), Church Road, Weston (Oct. '73), New King Street (Oct. '73), Dafford Street (Feb. '76), Wellington Buildings (March '77), and Prospect Place, Weston (April '77). Two others, Norfolk Crescent and Beaufort Square, are proposed. Some private work on rehabilitating old property has been done by, for example, the Preservation Trust in Abbey Green and by private developers in Pierrepont Place and Old Orchard Street. The latter scheme cost £106,000 but attracted grants from the council, the Historic Buildings Council, and under the 1969 Housing Act. The council, having knocked down most of the Ballance Street area and replaced it with modern flats, went on to restore the remaining top part of Morford Street and the juxtaposition of the two types of development is an illustration of the change in attitude. On the other hand, rehabilitation can create problems by producing houses which are too expensive for the original inhabitants to rent or buy and this not only has unfortunate results for them but may also result in a change in the socio-economic class of the neighbourhood.

A much more flexible approach to planning came in with the Town and Country Planning Act of 1968, although it also introduced new problems. There are now two types of plan, the Structure Plan, which is Avon's responsibility and is a written statement of general aims for the next twenty years, and Local Plans which are the 'nuts and bolts' details of physical planning at the local level. Only the structure plan requires Government approval but local plans must accord with its objectives. After the Local Government Act of 1972 was implemented in 1974 Bath became a District, although it still has the right to call itself a city and to have a coat of arms and a mayor. It must therefore conform to Avon's structure plan. Moreover, education and highways (except for trunk roads) come under Avon, but neither Avon nor Bath have control over hospitals (run by the Area Health Authority), or water supply and sewerage (under a Water Authority). Bath collects its rubbish but Avon disposes of it (if it can). And lastly, *no* local authority is autonomous for it cannot pay its way without a subsidy from central Government. This gives the latter the whip-hand as can be seen in their present imposition of cuts on local government spending. All of which makes it increasingly difficult for a rebel to know exactly who he is rebelling against.

But let us not forget the Minimum Physical Growth study. One of the virtues of Bath is that it is small—about 85,000 people—and it is, as it always was except for that frenetic outburst of social activity in the eighteenth century, a provincial town, a shopping and service centre with unobtrusive industries, a pleasant, companionable place in which to live and be blessed, thanks to that uncharacteristic century, with an incomparable environment of beautiful building. So why not keep it that way? Not a lotus-land, not lacking endeavour, but not panting after growth or gargantuanism. The conclusion of the MPG report was that it could be done without killing the economic life of the place—indeed, even without conscious planning, it was almost inevitable because there was hardly any room left for expansion. Yet without economic expansion can the expensive business of maintaining the fabric be carried on? The answer is no and the reports on the four historic towns emphasize this, MPG or no MPG.

In May 1973, when the Buchanan battle was at its height, the *Architectural Review* devoted a large part of its current issue to "Bath, City in Extremis" and came up with a plan to set up the nation's first Old Town Corporation with national funds and wide powers to stop demolition. It is a splendid idea—especially for Bath ratepayers—and it might just be possible in times of unparalleled national prosperity but it would hardly be a vote-catcher in regions with problems of their own and with people who have never seen Bath, or indeed heard of it, nor would it appeal to any government intent on cutting public spending.

Well might a Bathonian say, "I will lift up mine eyes to the hills. Whence cometh my help?" Some help must come from the Lord, in the form of Government grants, for Bath is a national treasure, but the rest must derive from the vitality of the city's economy and the rallying cry might well be "Small is beautiful—and efficient—and inventive—and, given the appropriate national economic policy, profitable."

Remember the roof-top—"Ye Must Be Born Again"—but with the same clothes?

2

Central

In the middle of Bath lies the flagged open space of the Abbey Churchyard where a Tudor church looks with Perpendicular face towards a Georgian colonnade and Pump Room, and in the summer season when the café tables are out in the open and the place is thronged with people sitting on benches, walking about, talking, gazing, and photographing with such frequency and in so many directions that it is impossible to move without ruining someone's snapshot, it would seem patently obvious that here is the pulsating heart of the city, the hub of the urban wheel.

This is not quite true, for most of these people, especially the ones with cameras, are tourists. Try the place on a wet Wednesday in February when the only human figures are a few raincoated Bathonians making a short-cut dash from one corner to another and the impression is somewhat different. True, it livens up at Christmas with a Santa Claus and collecting-boxes and electronic carols, and on Armistice Day there is a bright splash of colour from a great cross of poppies, but except for the long season when the churchyard air is filled with foreign accents and the explanatory tones of guides this is a quiet place with only a minor backwash from the main stream of shoppers in the streets outside.

Yet historically this *is* the heart of Bath, for it is beside the great hot-water spring which brought Roman Aquae Sulis into being and was a major focus of activity through medieval, Georgian, and Victorian times. As a result there now stands within a small compass a range of what men have wrought in stone in their response to changing needs and architectural fashions from Roman Classicism through late-medieval Gothic, early Georgian Palladianism and late Georgian Adamesque, to Victorian Baroque and post-war neo-Georgian. It seems logical to start at the beginning with the Roman Baths and Temple and to see these we leave through the colonnade, turn down past the

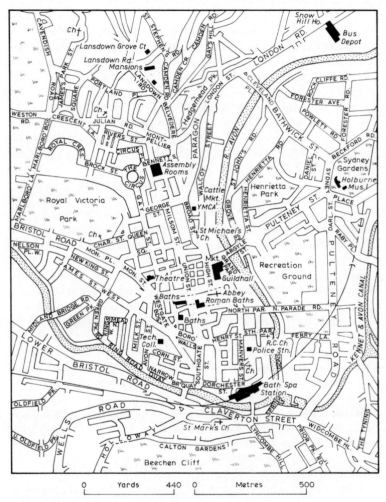

Based with permission on the Ordnance Survey. Crown Copyright.

end of the Pump Room and get our tickets by going through a door in a matching colonnade, which originally masked the front of the New Private Baths of 1788–9.

The tour immediately frustrates our intentions to stick to chronology for it moves straightway into the interior of the splendid Pump Room, built in 1789–99 (following the Improvements Act of 1789) to replace a smaller one of 1704–6. The design with its tall windows and giant attached Corinthian columns was by Thomas Baldwin the City Architect but in 1792 he was sacked when he refused, for some obscure reason, to let the corporation see his account books, and was replaced by John Palmer who was probably responsible for the interior. Both men had been earlier sent to submit the improvements designs to the then MP for Bath, the illustrious William Pitt.

In the apse at one end is a serpentine musicians' gallery but today the Pump Room trio plays not on it but under, behind masses of pot-plants flanked by two ornate sedan-chairs containing wax ladies. In the apse at the opposite end is a statue of Richard 'Beau' Nash, the Master of Ceremonies who imposed on the rackety social life of early eighteenth-century Bath a strict code of public life and manners. The statue was, as Fielding wrote, paid for by "several of the principal inhabitants of this place out of gratitude for his well-known prudent management for about forty years, with regard to the regulations of the diversions, the accommodation of persons resorting hither, and the general good of the city." Nash is dressed in the full-skirted coat of the early Georgian period and his hand rests on a plan of the General Hospital for whose building he was an active fund-raiser. Below him is a long-case clock given in 1709 by the famous London clockmaker Thomas Tompion and which came from the earlier Pump Room, as did the statue and the two brass plates on each side, one of which is dated 1706 and records that "this Building [the earlier one] was erected at the charge of the Chamber of the City".

Of the various portraits round the walls note should be taken of long-nosed, steady-eyed, Ralph Allen, Bath's eighteenth-century plutocrat who made one fortune out of the Post Office by means which he refused to disclose (there is no suggestion that they were improper) and another out of the Bath stone quarries. He contributed time and money to the founding of the General Hospital, was on the council (although he tended to be something of an absentee), served as Mayor for a year, and was instrumental in getting the elder Pitt as MP for the city. An honest, private, and reticent man, Allen was acutely embarrassed by the incident which caused Pitt to refuse to serve further as Bath's representative, writing in 1763 to Allen to say, "I perceive that I am but ill qualified to form pretensions to the future favour of gentlemen, who are come to think differently from me, on matters of the highest importance to the national welfare." The occasion was the Peace of Paris which ended the Seven Years War and which had been vehemently opposed by Pitt. The corporation sent him an address to be presented to George III. This he refused to do, leaving it to Bath's other MP, and he was particularly incensed by the phrase "an adequate and advantageous peace" (which it was not). Allen took full responsibility for including the word "adequate", but Pitt was adamant, sold his house in the Circus, and severed connections with Bath, although he continued as MP until 1766. Allen retired from the council and in the following year, 1764, he died, leaving Pitt £1,000 in his will.

Next to this portrait, and between the two fireplaces, is a nineteenth-century, glass-sided bay inserted to take the drinking fountain and from here we look out over the King's Bath towards the Roman Baths. The King's Bath, originally medieval but much altered since, was built over the Roman reservoir and its arched recesses stood against the outer enclosing walls. The Pump Room itself covers part of the northern half of the reservoir. Set in the present wall is the balustrade, part copy, which Sir Francis Stonor presented in 1618 in gratitude for relief from "gout and aches in the limbs" and in a niche is a statue of Bladud, mythical British founder of Bath. The legend has it that Prince Bladud contracted leprosy, was dismissed from his father's Court, and got a job as a swineherd at Keynsham. The pigs caught the disease but cured themselves by wallowing in the steaming mud on the site of Bath so Bladud followed suit, returned cured to the Court, and after a spell in Greece came back, became King, and established a town at Bath. He died, says the legend, in attempting to fly with home-made wings.

In the 1880s the energetic City Architect, Major Charles Edward Davis excavated the Roman Baths which had lain for centuries below the city and in the course of his work took up the floor of the King's Bath, dug down to the Roman reservoir and sold off its lead lining. He then put a concrete floor to the bath leaving below the muddy unlined walls of the reservoir in which a rather nasty amoeba began to multiply with the result that the water is now dangerous to drink. Because of this, and because settlement had left the floor largely unsupported, it was decided to remove the concrete and clean out the spring, work starting in the autumn of 1979. The resulting archaeological excavation directed by Professor Barry Cunliffe has already greatly increased knowledge of the reservoir although it will be some time before all the finds are fully investigated.

These include some six to eight thousand coins. A few are Celtic but the main time for throwing them in appears to have started with late-Nero (AD 54–69) and reinforces the idea that the baths were started in the last half of the first century AD. Other offerings deposited in the reservoir include numerous curses scratched on sheets of metal, often lead, many of which were rolled up before being thrown in. One, for example, offers a cloak to the goddess if she causes the death of Maximus, who stole it. A previously discovered curse, scratched backwards on lead, is in the Baths Museum. An interesting feature is six masonry pillars which, it is suggested, may have supported statues which would have appeared to be standing on the water and would have been intended to impress onlookers, for the surface of the reservoir was on a view, at first in the open and later through an opening in walls which were subsequently put round, probably in the third century AD, to support a barrel vault; this enclosure was rectangular but the reservoir itself is an irregular polygon. The water was let out through a sluice and there was a lower sluice for draining off the sand thrown up by the spring. Both waste water and sand ran off into a masonry-lined drain high enough for a man to walk in. This can be seen on the left as you enter the bathing establishment and is, Cunliffe claimed in an article in *Popular Archaeology*, May 1980, "the oldest functioning sewer in Britain".

Now out of the Pump Room, through a small ante-room with portraits of 'Beau' Nash and the Italian Rauzzini, Musical Director in Bath from 1780 to 1810, and along a passage to the Baths Museum. On the way it is worth looking through the door to the apse-ended concert room with its highly decorated dome and ceiling and its marble Corinthian columns, all handsome, if a little florid, and all the work of Brydon in 1897 when he was commissioned to build what the newspaper insisted on calling a "kursaal".

The entrance to the underworld (Roman Bath is some three metres below present street level and much of it was discovered by digging about in cellars) is along a dim passage lined with illuminated panels which illustrate the history of Bath backwards and are well worth a study, which is not easy when the crowds are pressing through—the baths are great money-spinners. The museum itself, vastly improved by the reconstruction of 1978, houses a fine collection of carved stonework, inscribed tombs and altars, and various smaller finds which include coins, carved gemstones, pewter moulds and vessels, and leatherwork from a cobbler's shop.

The inscriptions establish that the presiding deity was Sul-Minerva, combining the Celtic local goddess Sul with the Roman goddess of wisdom and healing (although most dedications are simply to Sul) and name a random selection of people who were living or dying in Bath at the time. Here we find, for example, a couple of centurions, one from the Sixth Legion, the Victorious, the other from the Second Augusta; Julius Vitalis, a Belgic tribesman who joined up, became an armourer in the Twentieth Legion, the Valeria Victrix, and had a funeral paid for by his guild; Tancinus, a cavalryman from Spain; and Gaius Jovelinus Saturnalis, standard-bearer of the Second Augusta. Civilians include Priscius, a stonemason from Gaul, and Sulinus, a sculptor (there would have been plenty of work for them in Bath); an eighty-year-old town councillor from Glevum (Gloucester); and seventy-five-year-old Gaius Calpurnius Receptus, priest of the temple of Sul, whose tombstone was set up by his wife. Incidentally, Sulinus dedicated his altar not to Sul but to the Suleviae, Celtic goddesses, and another altar set up by Peregrinus from Trier is dedicated to Mars Loucetius and Nemetona—neither of these was found in the temple area, which is not surprising. Loucetius, 'Lightning' or 'The Shining One', was a Celtic deity often associated with Mars, while Nemetona was 'Goddess of the Sacred Grove'. They are probably the figures to be seen in the museum on a small carving; both carry sceptres and she has her hand on a cylindrical object which may represent a tub of holy water; he wears a short cloak and a horned helmet. Another carving of particular interest was part of a funerary monument, an outsize female head with the hairstyle of the end of the first century, a mass of curls at the front and a bun at the back.

The major structural fragments—a façade of the Four

Seasons, a Luna pediment with a female with a whip and with a crescent encircling her head, remains of pillars and friezes and mouldings, and fragments of a great triangular pediment all relate to the temple of Sul-Minerva and its inner and outer precincts. The front of the temple lay under the corner of the area dug out to make foundations for the Pump Room in 1790 and the excavations turned up important fragments of the pediment. The rest of the temple stretched backwards under the present Stall Street to the far side where the building of the Grand Pump Room Hotel in 1867–9 and its demolition in 1959 to give place to the modern Arlington House offered opportunities for further investigation. Post-war trench-digging amongst the cellars has led to an increase in our knowledge and work started in 1980 to clear out an area under the Pump Room, replacing cellar walls by steel supports, initiate a controlled archaeological disembowelment and extend the museum so that some of the features may be shown *in situ*, particularly the sacrificial altar which stood in the precinct and of which two corners are in the museum. A third corner is built into a wall of the church at Compton Dando, some eight miles away. The statue base which stood in front of the altar, discovered in 1965 and now in the museum, displayed its inscription *"Deae Suli L. Marcius Memor Harusp[ex] D[ono] D[edit]"* (To the Goddess Sul, Lucius Marcius Memor, augurer, gives this gift).

The precinct was the area for public ceremonial and worship, centred round the altar. The temple was for the priests and it was normal for it to contain the cult image of the presiding deity; it is possible, although impossible to prove, that the bronze-gilt head of Minerva, now in the museum, was originally part of such an image. The temple was, unusually for Britain, of Classical pattern, rather like the larger Maison Carrée at Nîmes, with a tetrastyle (four-column) porch whose Corinthian columns supported an entablature and a highly decorated triangular pediment. The whole was raised on a six-foot high concrete podium faced with ashlar, and was approached by steps. According to Cunliffe's reconstruction (*Roman Bath*, 1969) the back, sides, and corner of the temple were decorated with attached columns. The carving of the tympanum, the space inside the pediment, is represented by six blocks discovered in 1790 and now exhibited on a wall of the museum in their conjectural but probably correct relationship. The central feature is a representation of the Gorgon Medusa, who had snakes for hair and whose gaze turned men to stone. She is associated with the Greek goddess Athene, the Roman Minerva, because, according to legend, it was Athene who gave the hero Perseus a polished shield which he used as a mirror, thus avoiding Medusa's direct gaze while he was cutting off her head. Later, Athene set the head in the centre of her shield.

What is remarkable about the Bath Gorgon is that firstly it is male, with beard and moustaches, and secondly that it is a face of great power and suffering—compare it with the soppy Minerva head. This is almost certainly because it is native Celtic craftsmanship and to Celts the head was the seat of the spirit, an object of mystery and power—they were, indeed, head-hunters. The wedge-shaped nose, curling eyebrows, and prominent eyes are typical of Celtic sculpture.

Passing between the main drain and the reservoir overflow we come out from the muted light of the museum to stand blinking by the side of the Roman Great Bath where we can be picked up and taken round by electronically magnified, well-briefed guides. Two facts will help to correct initial impressions; firstly, the Roman bathing establishment had a roof, secondly everything above about shoulder level is late Victorian, including the row of Roman emperors perched on the top of the wall. Before us is the big lead-lined, warm-water swimming-bath and around it the paved walkway and wall with alcoves (*exedrae*) some still with remains of Roman plaster and, near the water, are the bases of stone piers, enlarged when the early wooden roof was changed for a heavier masonry vault. Beyond the modern doors on our left lies the eastern range of baths which was first discovered when the Duke of Kingston's baths were being constructed in 1755 and was further explored and opened up when the Kingston baths were pulled down in 1923. It contains a small swimming-bath and beyond that a set of heated rooms with a rather complicated history of alterations. To our right is the original entrance hall which at a later date was altered to include a large circular cold bath into which today's visitors are successfully encouraged to toss coins (but not curses), and beyond that a further set of heated rooms which display clearly the system of hypocausts by which the floors were heated. These sweat-rooms were the normal kind of Roman bath, the sort you would find in a house, and it was here that you might be lightly coated in sand and oil which would, when you had sweated sufficiently, be scraped off again with a kind of blunt razor called a strigil. It was rather unusual to have two separate sets of such rooms in an establishment and it has been suggested that one might have been for women and the other for men.

The tour ends by the western hypocaust where the guide may invite you to go back and look at anything which has taken your fancy. This is good advice because if you go up the stairs you are in the souvenir shop and you will not be allowed back down unless you need to go to the ladies' lavatories. Going up that short flight of stairs hurls us forward eighteen hundred years, but we may lessen the shock by going back to the churchyard to nearly five hundred years ago when in 1499 Oliver King, Bishop of Bath and Wells, servant and friend of Henry VII, began to build the last great church of the late Gothic, Bath Abbey.

Everyone calls it the abbey and it is perhaps pedantic to point out that it had in fact become a priory in 1088 when John of Tours, one-time physician to William II ('Rufus'), moved his cathedra, or bishop's chair, from Wells to Bath, making the old abbey church his cathedral and demoting the head of the Benedictine monastery to prior. Later bishops, however, preferred to return to Wells and from about 1240 Bath, although still sharing the episcopal title, ceased to be the seat of the bishop. The priors who followed seem on the whole to have been a sorry lot and the great Norman church fell into such a state of disrepair that when Oliver King made a visitation in 1499 he found it "ruined to its foundations".

Turning the problem over in his mind, he is reported to have had a dream in which he saw a ladder to heaven with angels going up and down and heard a voice saying "Let an Olive establish the Crown, and a King restore the Church", which he interpreted as Divine support for what he probably intended to do anyway. This dream is as good a reason as any for the stone ladders and angels on the towers of the west front, although it does not explain why one of the angels is coming down head first (or going up backwards?)—perhaps the sculptor was simply showing off. Oliver's rebus also appears, twice, a mitre above an olive bush encircled by a crown—Bishop Olive(r) King. Indeed, the whole west front is a picture gallery in stone with Christ in Majesty at the top with the Heavenly Host below, the twelve apostles beside the ladders, Saints Peter and Paul on either side of the great door and Henry VII above (although this statue is Victorian), emblems of the Passion in the spandrels of the door frame, one or two indefinable images and bits of lettering, and the Holy Ghost as a dove high up in the great west window. Yet it is not fussy or overcrowded and it serves to enhance rather than confuse the clean vertical emphasis which is the hallmark of the Perpendicular, while the calm symmetry of the front sits well with the Classical proportions of the other buildings in spite of the complete difference in decorative motifs.

It is impressive but not overpowering and fits comfortably into its urban setting, requiring no great grassy Close. Indeed, it is a much smaller church than its Norman predecessor, being built on the site of the former nave. Excavations in 1979, however, suggest that the old church was not as long as previously supposed and stated. When the east end of the Norman church was pulled down the land was used as an open space known as Miter Green. In 1717 trees were planted to form the Grove but this was levelled in 1730 and in 1735 renamed the Orange Grove after the obelisk to the Prince of Orange who had visited the previous year and found some benefit from the waters. Later road developments left a circular garden round the obelisk and this enabled the Bath Archaeological Trust to organize a dig under the direction of Tim O'Leary. Three metres down they came upon a massive foundation raft and trenches with a gravelly infill which marked where the original walls had been robbed of their stone. This is interpreted as the remains of an apsidal chapel at one corner of the east end of the Norman church and places the length of the church as about fourteen metres rather than the previously stated seventeen. Inside the church, at the east end of the south aisle a Norman arch can be seen enclosing a later window and in the cloister, added in 1923 as a war memorial, are exhibited fragments of Saxon and Norman work.

The abbey interior, flooded with light from the great windows which gave it the title of "Lantern of the West", has a grave dignity and a consistency of style which is rather surprising when we consider the building history. Oliver King never saw his church finished and after the surrender of the Benedictine monastery to Henry VIII's commissioners the unfinished building was sold and stripped of its bells, glass, lead, and iron. The shell was later presented to the corporation in 1572 and the slow process of completion and rehabilitation went on until 1616 when James Montague was bishop. He was later translated to Winchester but wished to be buried in Bath and got the biggest tomb in the church, with black Corinthian columns and his effigy in Garter robes. It was commissioned by his brother, Sir Charles Montague, and another brother, Sir Henry, in 1617 presented the great oak west doors decorated in profuse ostentation with their coat of arms.

Much of the uniformity of style dates from the extensive and effective restoration of 1864–74 by Sir George Gilbert Scott, that eminent London Gothicist, compulsive restorer, and designer of the Albert Memorial. In this the choir screen and organ loft were removed to give an uninterrupted view down the nave which was given an excellent fan vault to match the Tudor originals. Restored also was the sadly mutilated little chantry chapel of Prior Birde, who started the rebuilding with Oliver King; it is a splendid little Perpendicular design with miniature fan vaults, wall tracery, Birde's coat of arms under a prior's mitre, and, appropriately, small birds (the bishop wasn't the only one to have his little pun). A new stone reredos (literally 'behind the back') was put up behind the altar and later, in 1873, the great square-headed window above was re-glazed with fifty-one scenes from the life of Christ—damaged in wartime bombing it was restored by M. C. Farrow Bell, the great-grandson of the original designer. Outside, the restorers added pierced battlements and new pinnacles to the turrets.

An earlier restoration of 1824–33 under the City Architect, George Philip Manners, who went on to design St Michael's (1835–7), Broad Street, in an Early English style, had added flying buttresses to the nave, given the tower pinnacles, and changed the eastern turrets from square to octagonal. At the same time the corporation cleared away a clutter of houses, shops, dens, and taverns which had been built against the north wall. Between the two restorations the church ceased, by the Municipal Reform Act of 1835, to belong to the corporation and the advowson (patronage) was sold for £6,330 to the Simeon Trust founded by the Reverend Simeon in 1836 for installing evangelical incumbents. It is still used by the council, however, when it feels a need to acknowledge God, and as well as being a busy centre of parish life it also, as the largest public hall in Bath, is the scene not only of corporate worship but also of entertainment.

The abbey is the only substantial piece left over from medieval Bath. A few gables can be found, in Green Street and Broad Street, for example, and the Abbey Church House in Lower Borough Walls has gables, bays and mullions but this is a reconstruction after wartime bombing. Pre-Georgian Bath is illustrated in little drawings round the edge of Gilmore's map of 1692–4 and is well dealt with in *Bath before Beau Nash* by Meg Hamilton (1978), but what makes Bath famous is its eighteenth-century townscape and inevitably any portrait of the city must take this into account. The Abbey Churchyard is a good place to start such a study and to introduce the background necessary for an understanding of the more extensive and famous developments such as the Circus and crescents.

The early Georgian architectural style is dubbed Palladian because it was strongly influenced by the *Four Books of Architecture* by Andrea Palladio (Palladio was a nickname, his father's name was della Gondola) published in Venice in 1570 when England was ruled by Elizabeth. The first English translation was published in London in 1715. Palladio, himself an architect with a considerable output, was totally convinced that the architects of Classical Rome had all the answers to questions of design and he set himself to study their works and the writings of Vitruvius, an undistinguished Roman architect of the first century BC whose ten books, *De Architectura*, formed the only complete architectural treatise to survive from Classical times.

Palladio expressed his allegiance to antiquity right at the start of his preface,

Guided by a natural inclination, I gave myself up in my most early years to the study of architecture: and as it was always my opinion that the ancient Romans, as in many other ways, so in building well, vastly excelled all those who have been since their time, I proposed to myself Vitruvius for my master and guide, who is the only ancient writer of this art, and set myself to search into the relics of all the ancient edifices, that, in spite of time and the cruelty of the Barbarians, yet remain; and finding much more variety of observation than at first I had imagined, I began very minutely with the utmost diligence to measure every one of their parts; of which I grew at last so felicitous an examiner, not finding anything which was not done with reason and beautiful proportion, that I have not only travelled in Italy, but also out of it, that I might entirely, from this, comprehend what the whole had been, and reduce it into design.

The purpose of writing the book, he said, was to publish the designs and "rules which I observed, and now observe" so that the reader may learn to "lay aside the strange abuses, the barbarous inventions, the superfluous expense, and (what is of greater consequence) avoid the various and continual ruins that have been seen in many fabrics." He concluded the preface by saying that as there were very few whole examples from the ancients he would insert plans and elevations of the "many fabrics" he himself had designed "in the manner Vitruvius shows us they were made".

Proportion, by which he meant the proportions used in ancient Roman buildings, was the essence of beauty. "Beauty", he wrote, "will result from the form and correspondence of the whole, with respect to the several parts, of the parts with regard to each other, and of these again to the whole; that the structure may appear an entire and complete body, wherein each member agrees with the other, and all necessary to complete what you intend to form." For his module he took the diameter of the column near the base, and calculations get quite complicated— "The columns are nine modules high . . . the architrave, frieze, and cornice are a fifth of the altitude of the column, the inter-columnations are two diameters and a quarter; the base must be half a module in thickness and divided into three parts"—and so on. He also lays down mathematical rules for the heights of rooms. Façades, it is evident from his drawings, should be symmetrical.

This, then, is the first characteristic of Georgian Bath—symmetry and standard proportions, an almost obsessive concern for arithmetic. The second is the use of standardized Roman ornament for which Palladio gives very strict instructions. This is based on the Five Orders—Tuscan, Doric, Ionic, Corinthian and Composite. Each Order consists of a column, which Palladio shows both plain and fluted, made up of base, shaft, and capital, and the horizontal members it supports, the entablature, consisting from bottom up of architrave, frieze, and cornice.

The Orders most commonly used in Bath are the Doric, Ionic, and Corinthian and they can be most easily identified from the form of the capital—plain for Doric, curly volutes like rams' horns for Ionic, and acanthus leaves for the Corinthian, the most showy. Ionic and Corinthian have plain friezes, although in the latter there may be swags or other carving between the capitals, but the Doric, as if to make up for the plainness of the capital, has a decorated one. Here are vertical blocks, or triglyphs, with two grooves down the face and half grooves down each edge, with a little row of six wedges or guttae at the bottom. The space, or metope, between the triglyphs may be decorated with further carving, and the top of the cornice is supported on square brackets or modillions. Modillions are also character-istics of the Corinthian Order and Palladio shows their under-side carved as a rose. Below them is a band of moulding and then a series of small blocks, or dentils, which are used in both Ionic and occasionally in Doric cornices.

Columns may be free-standing but, as in the case of Bath, more frequently attached to the face of the wall, forming decor-ative features rather than structural elements. If the attached column is rectangular, projecting slightly from the wall, it is known as a pilaster. When columns or pilasters run up through more than one storey they form a Giant Order.

While Palladio gave a great deal more detail about the Orders the other ornamental details are best obtained from a study of the profuse illustrations to his work and here we see large triangular pediments as central features; small triangular, segmental, and straight pediments over doors and windows; moulded frames (architraves) round windows and doors; balustrading, either open or blind; niches with or without statues; keystones with or without carved heads; window openings both rectangular and round-headed; a liberal sprinkling of large, rather affected-looking statues on the roof line, an example not much followed by English Palladians; and grooving-out between the stones of the ground-floor elevation to create the rugged effect of rustication. On the whole Palladio seems to have been rather more exuberant than his British followers.

What we see little of in Palladio's house or villa designs is the parapet above the cornice which is ubiquitous in Bath, nor does he have that later invention, the double-sloped mansard roof so convenient for giving headroom to the servants' quarters, which is named after the French architect François Mansart (1598–1666) who first used it on a wing he added to the château at Blois. Nor did Palladio know anything of sash windows, which were not invented until the seventeenth century and are reputed to have come to Bath in about 1680 after which they rapidly became standard.

It does not follow that the collection of stonemasons, glaziers, and plumbers who turned architect-developer to cash in on the Bath building boom had actually read Palladio, although it is interesting that one of the subscribers to Isaac Ware's translation of 1738 was a Mr John Wood. What in fact they had available was a host of pattern books with drawings to show them how to design in the new Palladian style. Batty Langley, to take one example only, produced in 1722 some twenty books of this nature, including the 1741 *City and Country Workman's Treasury of Design, or the Art of Drawing and Working the Ornamental Parts of Architecture*. This goes far to explain the degree of standardization although it hardly applies to men of genius such as the Woods.

Classical motifs were being used in England in Tudor and Jacobean times, as witness the columns on the Montagu tomb, but in an arbitrary way mixed in with medieval decoration. It was Inigo Jones (1573–1652), Surveyor of the King's Works to Charles I, who, having travelled in Italy and possessing his own copy of Palladio's book, introduced a pure Italian Classical style to this country. Notable examples are the Queen's House at Greenwich and the Banqueting House in Whitehall which although completely refaced in the nineteenth century in Portland stone has a façade which is an accurate reproduction of the original. His influence was largely confined to Court circles and although many provincial buildings, including the old Guildhall at Bath in the middle of the High Street, have been ascribed to him, this is usually a matter of wishful thinking.

With the Restoration a less restrained, more individual, more highly ornamented Classical style emerged, the English Baroque, exemplified in Vanbrugh's Blenheim Palace and Wren's St Paul's, although it never got as wild as on the Continent. In Bath the only example, and a mild one at that, is Rosewell House built in Kingsmead Square in 1736 and possibly designed by the Bristol architect John Strahan. The exuberance of English Baroque was however repressed by the stern eighteenth-century Palladian revival led by Richard Boyle, Earl of Burlington (1694–1753) and this basically back-to-Inigo attitude was brought in full force to Bath by John Wood the Elder (1704–54), a young man of considerable force of character, not always easy to deal with, who combined an invincible belief in the rightness of his own judgement with a deep scorn for other builders then working in Bath. It is fortunate that he was an architect of genius who set the Roman stamp on the new range of buildings which marched up and down hill and along the slopes with all the firm strength of the legions.

A tentative, pre-Wood, 1720s Palladianism appears in two houses at the north-east corner of the churchyard, next to the abbey, and here we can make an introduction to motif-spotting. The more splendid is the house, now a National Trust shop, which was built for General Wade, patron of Ralph Allen, MP for Bath from 1722–48, and best known for his road-making in the Highlands after the 1715 rebellion.

> If you'd seen these roads before they were made
> You would bless the name of General Wade.

"Made" here meaning surfaced.

The ground floor has a rather nice Regency shop-front which is of course later, but above a Giant Order of fluted Ionic pilasters supports a pediment with architrave, convex-faced (pulvinated) frieze, and modillioned cornice. Above this is an attic storey with shallow pilasters, simple cornice, and shallow parapet with urns. Between the first and second floors are decorative swags, and first- and second-floor window openings are framed in bolection mouldings, in section like a fat S with the fattest part next to the opening, a characteristic of late seventeenth/early eighteenth-century buildings and to be seen, for example, in Westgate Street and Broad Street. The architraves of the top windows are different and seem later in style. The house shows what is possibly the first use of giant orders in Bath, later to become a common feature of the big set pieces, starting with Wood's Queen Square (1728–36) and followed by the triumphant march of columns along the face of his son's Royal Crescent (1767–74).

The neighbouring house on the corner, also with ground-floor shop-windows, has another 'first', the use of superimposed orders, Ionic pilasters below, Corinthian above, the correct Palladian sequence, a theme developed more fully and effectively in Wood the Elder's Circus (1754–8). There are only short sections of entablature, above the pilasters, and these are joined by string courses. Another feature much to be seen in other parts of Bath is the use of pediments, triangular and segmental, over the windows. The top storey of the house is out of scale and probably later.

One noticeable thing is that the houses are designed quite

separately and we have yet to meet the major contribution
which the eighteenth-century builders made to the Bath scene,
the treatment of a street as a whole rather than a collection of
individual houses. This has been hailed as a great advance in
town planning and in some ways it was; on the other hand there
is also a great attraction in a street which displays a variety of
styles and roof lines, providing there is nothing excessively out
of scale, and there may be a suspicion that the repeating
Palladian pattern can be just a bit boring. This is not over-
evident in Bath as the topography and the piecemeal development without an overall master plan produced no excessively
long streets and introduced many elements of surprise, while
further variety was introduced by bending streets into crescents
or circles or opening them out into squares.

This unification of separate units into one composition is to be
found in the churchyard in the range towards the colonnade
which includes the tourist information centre. The centre of this
range is marked by a shallow-triangular pediment and more
elaborate decorations above the windows—a straight pediment
with a swag beneath—but it does not have the decorative band
which runs on either side in the form of a wave, a Vitruvian
scroll. This decoration only appears once in the *Four Books*, in
an illustration of the Temple of Mars, and is not used in the
early Palladian buildings in Bath. It was a favourite device of
Baldwin's and it is probable that he designed this range. It is
evident that the details and ornament are much less heavy than
in the earlier houses and this is even more evident in the front of
Baldwin's Pump Room.

What had happened was that as the century wore on the early
no-nonsense Palladian style, described by Inigo Jones as, "solid,
proportionable according to the rules, masculine and un-
affected", had lost some of its attraction and a lighter, more
ornamented, finer-drawn, more elegant style began to develop
and was given impetus by the work and writings of Robert
Adam (1728–92) who was noted not only for his architecture but
also for his interior design—thus we have Adam ceilings and
fireplaces and furniture. He wrote of the need for "the rise and
fall, advance and recess, and other decorative forms" and of "a
beautiful variety of light mouldings, gracefully formed, deli-
cately enriched, arranged with propriety and skill"; buildings
he said should have "movement". The Augustan Age of Reason
was moving into the Age of Sensibility.

Adam's only work in Bath is the elegant Pulteney Bridge (1769–74) with its little shops domed tollbooths, and delicate central Venetian window in a shallow depressed arch, but the style is handled with assurance by Baldwin, particularly in the interior decoration of the magnificent banqueting room in his Guildhall of 1776. Baldwin also designed the spine of the new development over the river, Great Pulteney Street, which continued the axis of the bridge, but here the light ornamentation is not too well suited to a street of such breadth. It is however perfect for the narrow, quadrant-ended, colonnaded, Bath Street, the one piece of eighteenth-century corporation town-planning in Bath, constructed in conjunction with the Pump Room and New Baths, and paid for partly by slapping on an extra charge at the city's turnpike houses. It leads to Baldwin's rebuilding of the Cross Bath whose serpentine front and delicate enrichment contrast with the younger Wood's four-square, no-nonsense Hot Bath (1776–8) across the road and the elder Wood's rather heavy rebuilding of St John's Hospital behind. Baldwin motifs have been used in the new souvenir shop and spa offices, the only post-war building in Bath of which Bathonians generally approve, which replaced an amazing Jacobethan effort of 1889 by Charles Edward Davis, the City Architect. A sample of the Davis work remains in his bridge across York Street designed to carry pipes across to the laundry, for which he provided a Classical chimney. The York Street end of this building has been converted into a small but interesting toy museum.

The Victorians began to take against the Classical as being unromantic, un-English, and moreover pagan, but although they submerged it in an advancing tide of Gothic and Italianate it surfaced again towards the end of the century as a revival of the English Baroque which numbered amongst its advocates and practitioners a certain John McKean Brydon (1840–1901). Brydon was born in Dumfermline, trained in Liverpool, and practised mainly in London, but some of his most notable work is in Bath where in 1891 he was engaged to add wings to Baldwin's Guildhall and produced fine, strong, compatible compositions with cupola turrets which foreshadowed his more elaborate ones on the Government Buildings in London's Parliament Square (1898–1912). In 1896 he was called in again to design an art gallery in Bridge Street (now the art gallery and public library) and in 1897 he added a concert-hall beside the

Pump Room and a setting for the newly-discovered Roman baths. To make way for the concert room they had to pull down a range of shops and these can be seen in blown-up print in Monk's Café opposite the Pump Room. Brydon's style was quieter than the more exuberant pomposity of much Edwardian Baroque and marries very well with the eighteenth-century townscape.

Palladianism, the Adam style, and Baroque were all rooted in Rome, but by the 1760s new knowledge of Greek architecture was coming through, particularly after the publication in 1762 of Stuart and Revett's *Antiquities of Athens*—and Greece under the heel of the Turk was not only Classical but also mysterious and romantic. The result was a neo-Grecian movement in architecture which was influential from the 1790s to the 1820s. The Greeks had tended to build more simply than the Romans, because their techniques were less advanced (they had not discovered the arch and depended on trabeated, post-and-beam construction), they were poorer, and they lacked the Roman spirit of vulgar ostentation, although they did tend to cram their pediments with painted sculpture in remarkable contrast to the elegant simplicity of the rest of the building. Minor differences are that the Greek Ionic had parallel volutes instead of angled and the Greek Doric did not have a base. Greek Revival reflects the greater simplicity, has a preference for pillared porticos and colonnades, and may have such features as rectangular or low-pitched triangular pediments.

The style is not much in evidence in Bath but an example is to be found in York Street which runs along the south side of the baths and was cut in the late eighteenth century, destroying one of the Assembly Rooms in the process. This, the Friends' Meeting House, was built in 1817–19 as a Freemason's Hall and then passed through several hands—the date on it, 1842, refers to a brief period as the Bethesda Chapel for a Baptist group. The architect was William Wilkins (1778–1839) who travelled in Greece and Asia Minor, wrote *Antiquities of Magnae Graecia*, and is best known for his not altogether successful National Gallery in London. Examples further afield are the reference library which was inserted into Queen Square in 1830 and designed by a local architect, John Pinch the Younger (died 1849); Doric House, up at Sion Hill, of 1810 by Joseph Michael Gandy; the tollhouses on Cleveland Bridge (1827) by another Bath architect, Henry Edmund Goodridge (died 1863) who also built Beckford's Tower on Lansdown and crowned it with a version of the Athenian Choragic Monument of Lysicrates, Partis College at Newbridge Hill (1825–7); a group of large buildings designed by a London architect Flood Page as housing for Anglican "decayed gentlewomen" and, opposite the railway station, a couple of corner hotels.

Although in the Victorian battle between Greeks and Goths the Goths won, Bath architects were sensitive to the Georgian Classicism of the city and apart from very few exceptions it is to the suburbs we must look for Gothic Revival. It is true that Brunel's Great Western Railway came in from Bristol in 1840 over castellated Gothic arches to a Jacobean railway station but this was then open ground. Less happy was the rebuilding of the Blue Coat Charity School in Upper Borough Walls by the local firm of Manners and Gill in 1860. It is in a rather crowded Jacobean style with a curly gable and strap-work. Even more noticeable is Davis's Empire Hotel of 1899–1901 which bulks obtrusively beyond Orange Grove. It is mainly Jacobean but goes crazy round the tops with gables and corner turret. As it has so often been anathematized it is with some diffidence that I admit to a certain fondness for it and tentatively suggest that it is sufficiently far from the abbey not to be overwhelming. It was taken over by the Admiralty during the war and its future seems uncertain.

When it came to churches there was, of course, no argument, and central Bath got a couple of steepled Goths, St Michael's (1835–7), rebuilt by Manners in rather stringy Early English, and St John's Roman Catholic (1861–2) in a satisfyingly showy Decorated by Charles Hansom, a considerable local architect who in Bristol designed the Gothic Clifton College (1860–6) and University College (1880–3) in University Road. His elder brother was Joseph Hansom who amongst other things designed Birmingham Town Hall as a Roman temple and invented the hansom cab, which one imagines could cause some embarrassment. "And this, my dear, is Mr Hansom"—"Why Mr Hansom, only the other day I was riding in one of your. . . ."— "No Madam, it was my brother who. . . ." In Manvers Street, a bit further down from St John's is a pleasant little neo-Gothic Baptist chapel with a rather jolly turret.

What these bits and pieces demonstrate is that architectural styles can be neighbourly and compatible without being identical and that in order to fit into the Bath scene it is not absolutely necessary to ape the Georgians or even to use blocks of imitation oolite. Not that compatibility is easy to obtain, and two examples from the central area where it hasn't worked out may be seen. At the top end of Stall Street two opposing corners were redesigned in the late nineteenth century—one carries the date 1895. They are not Palladian, or Adamesque, perhaps they are faintly Baroque, and they are a bit out of scale, but they fit. One other corner, however, is a clumsy neo-Georgian Boots, which in spite of its excellent intentions fails to convince. The second example is a post-war insertion into the top of the High Street of the so-called 'Harvey' block. Here, it was claimed, the architect had used modern methods and a modern idiom to produce a building which was not only fitted to modern use but also by its proportions, fenestration, and so-called mansard roof (in effect an extra storey) would avoid visual intrusion. In fact, it sticks out like a sore thumb.

However—back to the Gothic for a moment. By the mid-eighteenth century architects' patrons were getting interested in more exotic forms—Chinese, Indian, and Gothic, the mystic East and the romantic Middle Ages—and the pattern books began to include Gothick designs for summer houses, grottoes, and other bits of garden fancy-work. This early Gothick was a fun style which was later to become serious when it got allied to nationalism and Christianity, but in its early stages it had little impact on firmly Classical Bath. There are two minor examples. In York Street we can find the ornate Classical front which Wood the Elder added in 1727 to Ralph Allen's town house and up on the hillside over the river is the little castellated Sham Castle designed by Sanderson Miller and built to add a touch of romance to the view; it is floodlit at night. The name is appropriate for there is no back, just a face with a gateway and two end towers.

The other example is a little later, 1765, and is the house and chapel in the Vineyards, on the London Road, which was built for Selina, Countess of Huntingdon, and her 'Connexion', her own aristocratic version of Methodism. Bayed and battlemented, with pointed windows, the composition is a pleasant little essay in romantic Gothic although the interior of the chapel has still, in spite of the pointed windows, a Classical flavour and lacks the elaborate 'medieval' plasterwork of Horace Walpole's Strawberry Hill house at Twickenham which was well under way when Selina's chapel was being built. Walpole himself visited the place to hear Wesley preach and he

found it "very neat, with true Gothic windows", which was quite
a compliment as he disliked Methodism, the Countess, and Bath
itself. He also disliked Bristol, which he called "the dirtiest
great shop I ever saw". One other minor Gothic example is the
porch to No. 16 Brock Street which in its skimpy details could be
of the 1760s although there is no other evidence to support the
date and it may well have been a later addition.

For a genuine medieval arch we can go behind the Empire
Hotel to find down a steep incline the unimpressive and gloomy
little East Gate of the city. The other gates were grander but
were pulled down in the eighteenth century with the usual
Georgian contempt for conservation, but their names are commemorated in streets. So in part is the medieval wall and from
the top of the High Street Upper Borough Walls leads westward
between the side of the Harvey block and earlier buildings
which are at the moment being torn down because they are the
back of New Bond Street which is being redeveloped after years
of argument and indecision.

Off to the left, heading from Upper Borough Walls towards
Cheap Street and the Abbey Churchyard, is narrow Union
Passage which perpetuates the line of the medieval Lock's Lane,
known vulgarly, said Wood, as Cock's Lane. It is not at all grand
and the architecture is undistinguished, but with its shops and
the feeling of containment which it generates it has a special
atmosphere of its own; moreover it has going off it Northumberland Place, short, full of little shops, and in summer ablaze with
flowers, a little jewel of a place, and further down, the Corridor,
a cool little covered street with a musicians' gallery holding two
lonely statues, and a row of gilt lions' heads and garlands,
designed by Henry Edmund Goodridge in 1825. It was at No. 7
that William Frieze-Green had his photographic studio as
advertised in 1874—

> Is she dark or is she fair,
> Auburn locks or golden hair;
> Hazel eyes or sweetest blue;
> Laughing eyes or grave and true?
>
> If you would see her beauty rare,
> To Seven, the Corridor, repair;
> For there her Photo may be seen,
> Charmingly taken by Mr. Frieze-Green.

In 1889 he filed a patent for an early form of cine-camera to take

"rapid action photographs" on "perforated strips of paper or
other material". He was not successful in marketing his ideas
and when he went to London and founded a company he ran
badly into debt. His end was both sad and romantic for he
collapsed and died while making an impassioned appeal for
unity at a meeting of the Cinematographic Exhibitors Association in 1921. More details are given in *Bath: Some Encounters
with Science* by Williams and Stoddard, 1978. A little further
along Upper Borough Walls we meet the end of Union Street
which was cut through the yard of the Bear Inn in the early
nineteenth century and it is here that we cross the shopping
spine of Bath which runs from Milsom Street on our right down
through Union Street and Stall Street to the post-war shopping
precinct in Southgate Street.

In the *Bath Chronicle* of 14th June 1762 appeared a notice
which advised its readers that there was "To be lett on a Building
Lease for 99 years (absolute), granted by the Corporation of
Bath and Mr Charles Milsom, of the same City, (in order to
Build a Street 53 feet wide, from House to House), a piece of
Ground, lately known by the Name of Milsom's Ground, situate
in the parish of St. Michael's, in the City of Bath. The terms are
four Shillings for every foot in Front, with good outlets." As
indicated, this was meant to be a street of houses, and they were
built to a standard pattern (the architect is uncertain) with
first-floor windows in threes, the centre one with triangular
pediment, and with the usual parapet and cornice.

It was, however, in a prime commercial situation, handy for
the new upper town and the city centre, so it was not long before
retailing crept in and the ground floors developed a frill of
bow-fronted shop-windows. By the time of Jane Austen it was
the major shopping street in Bath, although it was still quite a
good address for lodgings—she put General Tilney there in
Northanger Abbey. It was in Milsom Street that Isabella Thorpe
in the same book saw "the prettiest little hat you can imagine in
a shop window". The transformation of ground floors continued
unabated during the nineteenth century and the bows gave way
to large expanses of plate glass set in new surrounds, as in the
new shop-front which Jolly's put in in 1879 and which is still
there with its date. James Jolly had originally owned a woollen
merchant's house in London which traded under the happy
name of Nice and Jolly. In 1830 he opened a branch in Bath in
Old Bond Street and the next year moved to Milsom Street

where he opened the Bath Emporium selling linen drapery, silk mercery, hosiery, haberdashery, shawls, merinos, lace nets, etc., and "almost all the multifareous articles usually kept in Bazaars", including "Fancy China, Italian Alabaster Vases and Figures, British and Foreign Cabinet Goods, Jewellery, Perfumery, Stationary [*sic*], Combs, Brushes, Cutlery, and a great variety of Toys" (i.e. knick-knacks). Prices were fixed (no haggling) and sales were for cash only. Today it is still a variety store but belongs to Dingle's and you can use credit cards!

There was a gap in the street where the old poorhouse stood and in 1782 it was filled by a large and showy composition, Somersetshire Buildings, by Baldwin with end pavilions whose modillioned pediments are supported by attached Corinthian columns which also appear on the centre feature, which is a bow. Above the modillioned cornice is a balustraded parapet. The ground floor was originally all rusticated, with round-headed doorways and windows, and fronted by iron railings, but it has been considerably modified as later commercial occupants endeavoured to establish their individual identities. The centre house was soon converted to the Somersetshire Bank, now the National Westminster, which still has a fine original plaster ceiling. The Somersetshire, which later became Stuckey's, was one of some twenty private banks in Bath at the end of the eighteenth century.

A little lower is the entrance added in 1905 to the Octagon which started life in 1767 as a proprietary chapel designed by Thomas Lightholer and run as a business venture by The Revd Dr Dechair and a banker called Street. The octagonal form, with galleries supported on Ionic pillars and with a central dome, is set in a square and the corners formed alcoves in which there were fireplaces. It was luxuriously furnished and very popular. Mrs Piozzi described one service in lively terms—"You will rejoice to hear", she wrote, "that I came out alive from the Octagon Chapel, where Ryder, Bishop Gloucester, preached on behalf of the missionaries to a crowd such as in my long life I never witnessed: we were packed like seeds in a sunflower." By the end of the nineteenth century it had ceased to be a chapel and was converted to a furniture warehouse and showrooms, from which time dates the showy front. Today it is an exhibition room for the Royal Photographic Society.

Meehan, writing in 1901, said that going up Milsom Street the right hand was "the shilling side" and the left "the half-

crown", a distinction which does not seem to have been per-
petuated. Already by the end of the nineteenth century there
had been a further invasion of banks with two big, ostentatious
buildings at the top and another at the bottom. Somersetshire
Buildings is now all banks and offices and other offices have
taken over from previous shops, but Milsom Street still carries
the image of being primarily an up-market shopping thoroughfare. It has not quite lost its residents—there are a few flats.

From the bottom of Milsom Street, after it has split into Old
Bond Street and Burton Street, Upper Borough Walls continues
past the eighteenth-century Royal Mineral Water Hospital for
Rheumatic Diseases. Originally called the General Hospital its
name was changed to the Mineral Water Hospital and it got its
Royal from Queen Victoria in 1887. In 1935 George V gave
permission for the name to be changed to the Royal National
Hospital for Rheumatic Diseases. The hospital resulted from
the combined efforts of Nash, Allen, Wood, and Dr Oliver,
inventor of the Bath Oliver biscuit (which is now made not in
Bath but in Reading), and was for sick, impoverished visitors,
provided they brought a certificate of recommendation from
their parish and three pounds caution money to pay for their
return, if cured, or their burial, if not. Allen, Wood and Oliver
were among the thirty-two committee members and Nash and
Oliver, with the Hon. Benjamin Bathurst, were treasurers.

According to Wood the hospital was first proposed in 1716 by
Lady Elizabeth Hastings and Henry Hoare, Esq., and the first
subscription was opened in 1723, raising £273.12s.1d.
Humphrey Thayer was put in charge of the money and in 1726
he instructed the twenty-two-year-old Wood to draw up plans.
Wood then got Gay to give a plot of land but the deal fell through
and eventually the trustees bought the old theatre of 1705
together with adjoining houses and stables. "So," wrote Wood,
"after some eleven years spent in fruitless attempts, the Work
was put upon such a Footing as to be carried on without the least
Impediment", and on 6th July 1738 the first stone was laid by
William Pulteney who later became Earl of Bath. Subscriptions
had now reached £4,268.6s.6½d. and by 1742, when the
hospital opened, stood at £8,643.10s.9d. "in Money, besides
considerable Gifts in Stone, Lime, Timber, etc."

The fine Palladian building with its central Ionic columns
supporting an entablature and pediment is as Wood designed it,
although the royal arms in the tympanum date from the late

nineteenth century and the proportions were spoilt by the addition of an extra storey by Palmer in 1793. Incidentally, the plans which Wood had printed for publicity and negotiation were not quite the ones he intended to carry out and the real ones were not produced until April 1738 when they were approved by the trustees, who presumably had known what was going on. In May 1739 they got an Act of Parliament making them a charity and Wood noted, a little sourly, that the governors named in the Act included several people who had never subscribed. After repair of wartime damage costing £300,000, it was reopened by Princess Marina in 1965.

Next to Wood's hospital is the second of the three medieval ways, Vicarage Lane, now called Parsonage Lane, and beyond that a second block of the hospital designed in 1859 by Manners and Gill and opened in 1861. It is a fitting companion to its older neighbour and has a representation of the story of the Good Samaritan in its tympanum, a theme which Wood had originally intended for his own building. Opposite is a short section of the old city wall with battlements added by the Victorians to make it look more medieval, and below is a small courtyard which was once the burial-ground for the hospital.

Beyond the courtyard and running parallel to Upper Borough Walls is Trim Street, begun in 1707 according to Wood, and thus the first eighteenth-century development beyond the walls. It was named after George Trim, who owned the land, and contains an early Palladian house in which lived General Wolfe, who died in 1759 above the Heights of Abraham in the conquest of Quebec. Small, chinless, sandy-haired, not strong (he was in Bath for his health), and reputedly a manic-depressive, Wolfe was a fine strategist and leader of men. His victories are celebrated by a profusion of martial motifs above the doors but these are a later addition. Close to the house is an archway which is often called Trim Bridge but more properly St John's Gate for Trim Bridge lies underfoot and was a crossing of the city ditch.

Mr Trim's street was originally residential but later developed industrially and became very run-down in appearance. One side is being reconstructed and the other has been rebuilt as Trimbridge House, one of the more successful attempts to integrate a modern building into the Bath scene. At the end is the now secularized Unitarian chapel of 1795 with an apse added in 1860.

Opposite the end of Trim Street is the entrance to Beaufort Square, built about 1727 to designs by John Strahan, a modest little composition with segmental door pediments, on brackets, and a Doric frieze below a cornice and parapet. The east side has been rebuilt with a facsimile façade but with a modern backside to Barton Street which offended the conservationists. The south side of the square is the original front of the Theatre Royal (1804–5) with pilasters, swags, heavy cornice, and shallow parapet which supports a large royal coat of arms and a number of mouldering lyres. The houses in the square are at the moment having their faces washed.

The earlier new theatre of 1749, where Sarah Siddons established her reputation and which saw many of the great performers of the eighteenth century, was in Orchard Street and in 1767 it became the first provincial theatre to get a royal licence. From 1779 to 1817 the company, some twenty to thirty strong, worked both Bath and Bristol and it is said that it was their use of a special "social conveyance" which gave John Palmer (1742–1818 and not to be confused with the architect) his idea for the national mail-coach system which he pioneered. Palmer's father, a local brewer, had established his theatre and the young Palmer took it over, got the royal licence, disastrously reconstructed the interior which had to be re-done in 1775, and master-minded the move to Beaufort Square. In 1786, with the support of Pitt, he became Surveyor and Comptroller-General to the Post Office. After a monumental row with the Postmaster General he was suspended in 1792 but after badgering Parliament came out of the affair with considerable financial advantage. The story is dealt with in detail in *John Palmer* by C. R. Clear, 1955.

The new theatre was burnt out in 1862 on Good Friday, cause unknown, and a new entrance was built at the side. Single-storeyed, with round arches, it was tacked on to, and spoils, the house of about 1720, now the Garrick's Head, in which 'Beau' Nash first lived before moving round the corner where his home is today a restaurant bearing a commemorative plaque. The first house is impressive—Wood complained that it was "so profuse in ornmanets that none but a mason to shew his art could have gone to the expense of these Inrichments"—the second is much plainer but has a fine doorway with Corinthian pillars and two big stone eagles. Both houses were part of St John's Court, so called because the land had been acquired by St

John's Hospital, and are attributed to Thomas Greenway who was a mason and sculptor.

The present theatre entrance faces on to the Sawclose, once a timber-yard, then a cattle market, and now a car-park backed by the old Blue Coat School, worth looking into for its laudatory wall tablets to a headmaster and his wife. Behind the old school is another of the old medieval street lines. Originally this was Spurriers Lane, the place of the harness-makers, but when a prison, or bridewell, was built there (now gone), it became Bridewell Lane. The school was started in 1711 by the efforts of Thomas Nelson and got a building on the present site in 1722. When the new building was opened in 1866 each boy was given an oak box and each girl an oak pin-cushion made from the timbers of the previous establishment. It was a charity school for a hundred C. of E. boys and girls who at fourteen were put out to apprenticeship or employment. Of the girls who left in 1864, four went to be servants, five dressmakers, one waistcoat maker, one mantle maker and one laundress, while of the boys two were to be cabinet-makers, two carvers (of wood), two brightsmiths, one coachmaker, one plumber, one carpenter, one philosophical instrument maker (!), and one gardener. The school had a good reputation but in the late nineteenth century it staggered from one financial crisis to another and eventually closed in 1920. The building is now used as local government offices.

Below the Sawclose the Victorian Regency Variety Theatre, square-towered, rubble-faced above and plastered below with Corinthian pilasters, now advertises its bars, cinema, and bingo, and faces across the road the low-slung slab of Tiffany's ballroom built on a bomb-site and singularly lacking in external grace or any other character, its flat roof lying lifeless except for a brief period when it became a skateboard arena. One thing in its favour is that it has opened up a view of St John's Court and the neighbouring neo-Jacobean St Paul's Church House and Parish Hall of 1869, now secularized into a double cinema. The Regency opened in 1886 as the Pavilion with Rowland's "New York Circus", later it was partially reconstructed and became the Lyric, which in 1898 presented Charles Chaplin "the celebrated London comedian". In 1903 it became the Palace and its shows between the wars included one of the earliest stage appearances of Gracie Fields.

The wall turned south at Sawclose and ran down to where

once stood the West Gate with its lodgings at the end of Westgate Street which is now a mixture of early Georgian, Victorian,
and recent buildings, including a Hollywood-Classical cinema.
The line is continued by Cheap Street and provides a distant
view of tree-clad slopes. Outside the gate lay the great Kings
Mead, once land on which the citizens put out their cattle. Here
in the eighteenth century was laid out Kingsmead Square with
Avon Street running from it down to the riverside Narrow
Quay. Lower Avon Street deteriorated badly, both physically
and socially, in the nineteenth century when it became a
byword, sufficiently if not entirely deserved, for vice and crime,
and its Georgian houses were demolished after the Second
World War. The end by Kingsmead Square was rebuilt in neo-
Georgian following the Bath Act of 1925 and further reconstruction in an uninteresting rectilinear form took place in the 1960s.
The square itself also deteriorated but has been improved by the
cleaning and repair of the south side and of Rosewell House,
with its little badge of a rose and well above a date, 1736. The
space around the magnificent central plane tree has been
cobbled and set with benches and although Kingsmead lacks a
proper sense of enclosure and is invaded by traffic it is a pleasant
place to sit on a fine day.

The wall went on along Westgate Buildings where the inter-
war, neo-Georgian corner is followed by a building of 1968
which replaced a fine Victorian chapel of 1866. Then comes an
inter-war neo-Georgian Co-op. with giant Ionic fluted pilasters
and a pediment, but with metal-framed windows. The opposite
side of the street is a medley, starting with inter-war neo-
Georgian and continuing with a 1975 addition to St John's
Hospital, called Rosenberg House after William Rosenberg
whose will provided much of the money for its building. This is
not the only modern extension, and if we walk down past it we
can see high up on the opposite wall two dates in a cartouche,
one of which, 1956, is the year in which this new wing was built.
Then we can continue along behind the Cross Bath and through
the gateway of Wood's rebuilding of 1727 with its paired Doric
columns, into one of the pleasant small places of Bath, a little
courtyard with a chapel of 1767 by William Killigrew, who also
designed the first Blue Coat School and whom Wood described
contemptuously as "a Joiner, who laid his Apron aside about the
year 1719", and next to it a rebuilding of 1969 in a basically
Classical style but with gables and a wooden oriel. On the right

The Pump Room, 1789–99 by Thomas Baldwin, then City Architect before he was sacked.

Bath Abbey. Strictly the abbey was a priory and this is the priory church, for a time a cathedral. Begun in 1499 by Bishop Oliver King, it was restored in 1824–33 by Manners and in 1864–74 by Scott. The west front was again restored in 1895–1901 by Sir T. G. Jackson.

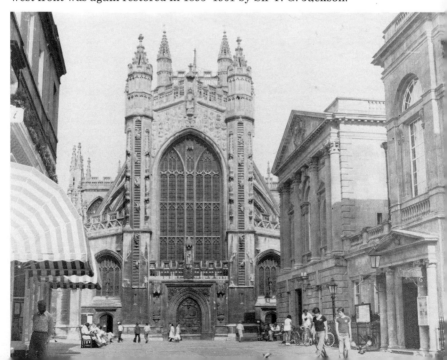

Argyle Street, looking towards Pulteney Bridge (note small dome on original toll-house) and library and art gallery by Brydon. Argyle Street has shops, restaurants, and a chapel.

Pulteney Bridge and weir. The bridge is of 1769–74 by Robert Adam and ruined the builder, Reed. The western (left-hand) mid-stream pier began to subside and was rebuilt in 1804.

Guildhall. The centre section with attached columns and pediment is of 1766–75 by Thomas Baldwin; the extensions of 1891, including the corner cupola, are by Brydon.

(Below left) Empire Hotel. Built in 1899–1901 to designs by Charles Edward Davis, City Architect. His initials are worked into the ironwork of the porch. *(Below right)* St Michael's Church, 1835–7 by George Philip Manners. To the left is the post office, an inter-war neo-Georgian building.

Front of the Theatre Royal. This is the old front of the theatre of 1805. After a fire in 1862 they built a new front round the corner.

Royal Mineral Water Hospital, by John Wood the Elder, 1738. A top storey was added by John Palmer in 1793, destroying the proportions.

Abbey Church House. Although rebuilt after the war, this building gives a good idea of what much of Bath looked like before the Georgians got to work.

Abbey Green, viewed through St Michael's Arch, a new structure.

North side of Queen Square. A terrace turned into a palace front; by John Wood the Elder in 1728–36.

Telephone exchange. One of the earlier post-war buildings which sit uneasily in the Bath scene.

Countess of Huntingdon's
Chapel—a neo-Gothic
structure of 1765.

'The carved house' in Gay
Street—once the home of
Mrs Piozzi and now
offices.

The Circus. Designed by John Wood and started in 1754 the year Wood died, it was finished by his son.

The Circus—detail of the superimposed Orders.

is part of the 1956 building and next to it an eighteenth-century range with a plaque which tells us that Horace Walpole stayed there in 1766.

Passing out of the quiet of Chapel Court through a dog-leg passage takes us back into the street with Wood's Chandos House on our right and left past a pleasant little grassy garden with good ironwork around to the Abbey Church House. This Elizabethan mansion (with alterations) was first built for Edward Clarke in 1570 on the site of a little leper hospital of 1138 but was soon taken over as a town house for the Hungerfords of Farleigh Castle and was renamed Hungerford House. Later it was called Lexington House (Lord Lexington married a Hungerford), then Savill's Lodgings, then in about 1714, when a Mrs Savill married Mr Skrine, a Bath apothecary, it became Skrine's Lower House and was so known in the time of Wood who called it "the second Best House in the City". Later in the eighteenth century it was acquired by William Hetling, a wealthy local tradesman, and became Hetling House. In 1776 Mr Hetling paid the high rate of £1.4s.9d. for his house, about the same as was paid by the Orchard Street Playhouse and about one and a half times that for a house in the Circus. For a time it was the headquarters of the Bath Society for the Encouragement of Agriculture, Arts, Manufactures, and Commerce, later known as the Bath and West. Later the society combined its annual meeting with an agricultural show and in 1852 the location was changed annually until 1974 when the society acquired a permanent site at Shepton Mallet. The centenary show of 1877 was held on the hills above the south of Bath and the nearest approach from the GWR station was over the river by a foot-bridge at the back of the station, the Widcombe Bridge. This was a tollbridge opened in 1863 and the tolls were taken on the far side so that when travellers on an excursion train from Weymouth arrived they so crowded the bridge that it collapsed into the river twenty-six feet below, killing ten people and injuring over fifty. The bridge was rebuilt in iron and now stands toll-free. Details of the history of the society can be found in Kenneth Hudson's *The Bath and West*, 1976.

After the society left Hetling House it was used for a variety of purposes until in 1888 it was bought by the rector and churchwardens of the abbey and the place was repaired and renamed the Abbey Church House. Extensively damaged in the 1942 air raids, it has been restored with great care to its original appearance and, although it is in one sense a fake, it gives a very good impression of the building style in Bath before the Georgians laid their improving hands on it. At the rear of the house was built a pump room designed by Palmer in 1792 with a large pillared portico and on one wall can still be seen "Hetling House" in faded letters. It was there that Jane Austen's brother Edward went for treatment in 1799. "He drinks at the Hetling Pump," she wrote from 13 Queen Square to her sister Cassandra, "is to bathe tomorrow, and try Electricity on Tuesday; he proposed the latter himself to Dr. Fellowes, who made no objection to it, but I fancy we are all unanimous in expecting no advantage from it." In fact Jane did not think much of Dr Fellowes and would have preferred a Dr Mapleton— "there is not a physician in Bath who writes so many Prescriptions as he does." Edward got worse and consulted an apothecary, "a sensible, intelligent Man", who put it down to his having "ate something unsuited to his Stomach". Edward lived to be eighty-four, so Jane was right in her conclusion that although the waters may not have done him any good they had not done him any actual harm.

Past the Church House the wall bends round and its line is followed appropriately by Lower Borough Walls in which the largest building is the bulky neo-Classical technical college which has spawned a couple of large flat-faced offspring over the road, functionally more suitable but disliked by some—Sir John Betjeman called it "the terrible Tech. with a pointed behind". The building was originally for the Royal United Hospital, formed by amalgamating the Bath City Infirmary (1747) and the Bath Casualty Hospital (1786) and was built in 1824–6 to designs by John Pinch the Elder. A top storey and the Albert Wing on which faded letters are just discernible as commemorating "Albert The Good" were added in 1850–60 by Manners and Gill. In 1932 the hospital was moved to Combe Park which had been developed as a wartime hospital and the technical college took over, its principal doubling as Director of Education for Bath. There are more unfortunate and unnecessary changes of street names around here—Nowhere Lane has become Hot Bath Street and Bell Tree Lane is now Beau Street. It is difficult to see what advantage there is in abandoning historic names, so three cheers for the inhabitants of Horse Street who in 1825 successfully petitioned to revive the ancient name of Southgate.

Running at an angle to Lower Borough Walls and finishing up

at the bottom of Southgate Street is St James's Parade, once a cul-de-sac, with its impressive run of first-floor Venetian windows under heavy eyebrows and its pillared and pedimented doorways, and between the two streets is a little green park with trees and multitudinous daisies. Beside the park is the neo-Gothic St James's Hall, now a centre for youth activities, particularly drama, a necessary, successful, and under-financed undertaking, and facing it across the green, hidden by trees, is another neo-Gothic effort, a chapel turned printing works.

Running from north to south between Lower Borough Walls and St James's Parade is Southgate Street, which led *from* the south gate, and eastward of it lay the big open meadow of the Ham which was not developed until the railway came, with its main thoroughfare, Manvers Street, built by the GWR as part of a deal with Earl Manvers who owned the land. This street, which runs parallel to Southgate, has a High Victorian, bay-windowed terrace on the west and an assortment on the east which includes a rather nice Arts and Crafts building which houses a printer's, the Baptist church already mentioned, a horridly utilitarian police station, and down by the river a sorting-office in 1930s GPO Georgian.

The area between Manvers and Southgate Streets, which bombing had obligingly opened up for a post-war bus station, was hardly stuffed full of architectural gems, nor indeed was Southgate street itself of considerable note, but it had been there for some time, it was familiar, it was part of Bath, and when the machines moved in and started swinging iron balls at the buildings many people felt personally affronted. Nor did they like what they got in its place. The west side of Southgate had already been refaced in a kind of 'stripped Georgian' and now the east side got a low block with a shopping corridor running through, metal boxes on the roof for air-conditioning plant, and a heavy-looking, curved canopy. Behind was a concrete ramp so that the shops could be serviced from the roof, a multi-storey car-park, public lavatories (Bath is a bit short of these) and some shops. It was all very blank and impersonal and utilitarian and seemed to have more to do with profit than people, an agglomeration which could be regarded with neither pride nor affection. However, no vehicles were allowed in and now that the street is well provided with trees and large tubs of shrubs the buildings are not obtrusive and the street environment is quite pleasant.

Southgate is the southern end of a shopping spine which runs up through Stall Street, named after the long-gone church to St Mary de Stalls (which probably meant Mary of the Manger), Union Street, Old Bond Street, and Milsom Street which started life in the 1760s as residential but by the end of the century was changing over to shops, got the big insertion of Somersetshire Buildings by Baldwin in 1782 and some Victorian shop-fronts, notably Jolly's of 1879. Shopping is also important in the area around the abbey, where it was mainly centred in the eighteenth century, and in streets at right angles to the main spine, as for example in Quiet Street, Green Street (built on an old bowling-green), New Bond Street (1806 on the site of Frog Lane, and now being demolished), Westgate Street, and Cheap (i.e. market) Street which saw considerable rebuilding in the 1890s.

Georgian antiques or umpteenth-hand Victorian grot, caviare or crisps, jewellery or junk, leather-bound books or paperbacks, jeans or jodhpurs, pizzas or steaks, plastic macs or Burberries, Instamatics or Leicas, plonk or château-bottled, electric guitars or grand pianos, Victorian potties or "low-level suites", Jaguars or bicycles, you can get them all in Bath. Georgian stonework, Victorian grates, health foods, prams, toys, stomach powders, wallpapers, garden plants and tubs and gnomes—department stores and tiny shops, national chains and local enterprise, a Victorian market hall—there is not much you want which you cannot get in Bath and there is the added advantage that everything is within reasonable walking distance of everything else and most of it is in a unique and pleasurable urban setting, which is why Bath continues to be an important regional shopping centre in spite of its proximity to the much larger Bristol.

At the bottom end of Stall Street stands a neo-Georgian Woolworth's built after the war on the site of St James's Church which was gutted by fire during an air raid but whose walls and fine Italianate tower of 1848 by Manners still stood until demolished in 1957. Behind it, and also now gone, were the Weymouth House Schools founded in 1817 by the National Society for the Education of the Poor according to the Principles of the Church of England which was so much of a mouthful that it soon became the National Society. This originally had a remarkable circular building with a covered play space and warm-air stove on the ground floor, a boys' schoolroom for 700 pupils on the first floor, and a girls' room for 300 above that. Warm air circulated from the stove up through the two school-rooms but the system was not efficient, the girls' room was very cold, and the school was rebuilt in 1896.

The wall continued down the south side of St James's and behind the present Orchard Street, and a few courses of it form the base of the wall to a service area behind Marks and Spencer's where it is commemorated by a plaque. Orchard Street itself which has seen rehabilitation of its buildings, leads through St James's portico with its massive Tuscan columns out into Pierrepont Street, facing the end of the block which forms Wood's North and South Parades of 1740–3 where terrible things have been done to the door and window openings. Wood intended the South Parade to be one side of a Royal Forum, or Grand Place of Assembly, but the scheme came to nothing and the area is now occupied by a car-park.

The Halls, wealthy clothiers of Bradford-on-Avon, bought the land at the dissolution of the monastery and it passed by marriage to Evelyn Pierrepont, Duke of Kingston, who on his death at Bath in 1770 left it to his Duchess on condition that she remained a widow. This was unfortunate because in 1743 she had also been the wife of Captain Hervey, the future Earl of Bristol. Although an ecclesiastical court had failed to prove the earlier marriage and had in fact declared her a spinster before she married the Duke, the Duke's nephew, Sir Charles Meadows, contested the will and indicted the Duchess for bigamy. The trial was held before the House of Lords in 1776 but although she was found guilty she escaped the punishment of being branded on the hand as she claimed that as a peeress she could not be subjected to corporal punishment. She also kept her inheritance and it did not pass to Meadows until her death in Paris in 1788. Meadows took the name of Pierrepont and in 1806 was created Earl Manvers, which is why Bath has Pierrepont and Manvers Streets and Kingston Buildings. It also had a Newark Street for Meadows married Frances, only daughter of Viscount Newark. None of the property is now with the family as it was sold late in the nineteenth century.

The Duchess, originally the beautiful Miss Elizabeth Chudleigh, was left with her mother in straitened circum-stances by the death of her father and owed the start of her advance in society to another Bath character, William Pulteney, who later became Lord Bath. He obtained her a place at Court as a lady-in-waiting to Augusta, Princess of Wales, where she attracted the attention of George II who gave her presents and made her mother housekeeper at Windsor. Everyone believed that she was the King's mistress, but this is not certain. By the time of her trial she had, if we are to believe Hannah More, lost most of her looks. "She is large and ill-shaped," wrote Hannah, "and has small remain of that beauty of which kings and princes were once so enamoured." After the trial she left for the Continent, never to return, and lived in various countries, including Russia where she struck up a friendship with Catherine the Great and bought a large estate near St Petersburg (Leningrad).

After which bit of gossip, we might go back to Abbey Gate Street which runs along the side of Marks and Spencer's and leads us to Evans's Fish Restaurant, popularly known as "Fishy Evans" on whose wall can be seen a remaining hinge from the Abbey Gate, and here pass under St Michael's Arch built in 1973 and named after the patron saint of Marks and Spencer's into delightful Abbey Green with its plane tree, pleasant pub, and buildings of varied dates and styles. Numbers 2 and 2A which were derelict have been restored by the Bath Preservation Trust and turned into shops and leading off beside them is old Lilliput Alley, grossly renamed North Parade Passage, with Sally Lunn's gabled house, basically medieval and one of the oldest in Bath although altered. Sally Lunn sold cakes in the seventeenth century and may have given her name to the Sally Lunn teacake although some people have the nerve to maintain that it derives from *"sol et lune"*. Across from Sally Lunn's, appropriately now a tea-shop, is an eighteenth-century precinct which has also suffered a name-change, from Gallaway's Buildings to North Parade Buildings. Gallaway was an apothecary who started developing his garden in about 1740, mainly as lodging-houses. These sturdy Palladian buildings have been well restored and form a quiet backwater. A plaque on a blocked-in doorway at one end records that it was the home of John Palmer, whom we have already met.

Lilliput Alley comes out into an open space which was created in 1933–4 by the demolition of the big building which was the home of the Bath Royal Literary and Scientific Institution. Originally built in 1708 as Bath's first assembly rooms, known as Harrison's, with a ballroom by William Killigrew added in 1720 it was enlarged in 1749–50 and an impressive Greek portico by Wilkins was attached in 1806. After suffering a disastrous fire in 1820 which, however, spared the portico, it was rebuilt and taken over by the institution in 1825, a trust deed and lease of the premises having been granted by the landlord, Earl Manvers, and in about 1860, by the generosity of the Bath MP, William Tite, they were able to buy the premises outright. The opening in 1825 was attended by over 300 and was followed by a dinner for 100 at York House, the Marquis of Lansdown presiding. In 1899 it amalgamated with the Bath Athenaeum which in spite of its pompous name was really a working men's club which had developed out of the ill-fated Mechanics Institute which started in 20 Westgate Street in 1825. In its new home the society continued to lecture to itself about literature, astronomy, archaeology, geology and anything else which caught its fancy, and developed a library and a very considerable geological museum, including the remarkable Moore Collection which it housed in the 1850s and which was purchased for the city on Moore's death in 1881. So large was it that an extra gallery had to be put in, paid for by Handel Cossham, the Bristol coal-owner who was then MP for Bath. Charles Moore, an eminent amateur geologist, was elected a Fellow of the Geological Society of London in 1853, and was the first to discover and identify Rhaetic beds, a division of the Trias, in Britain. The institute also housed the Roman remains then available, and other exhibits included coins, over a thousand cases of birds and other local fauna, and a collection of minerals. In 1854 they set up a small weather station in the institution gardens.

In 1932 the corporation acquired the institute building and proceeded to knock it down to murmurs of approval from the *Bath Chronicle*, "a very striking improvement", and cries of "Vandalism" from some citizens. Their purpose was to improve the road system and to provide underground public lavatories and baths ("useful for motorists") which the corporation anticipated would be a source of revenue—it is ironic that they have recently been closed because of the expense of upkeep and have now been reconstituted as a club. The presence of the lavatories led to the irreverent name of "Bog Island" being attached to the area. Incidentally, 1932 was also the year when the Royal United Hospital was moved to Combe Park with the assistance of ambulances from Weston-super-Mare and Bridgwater—the *Chronicle* noted that Frome did not oblige. The first to be moved was a baby who went the day before and for a night was the sole patient in the new hospital. The well-organized move made, the *Chronicle* said, "a great day for Bath and Humanity".

The institute moved to Queen Square, taking their collections and a set of pictures which had come from Fonthill and are now on the ceiling of the reference library, but affairs got into a bad state between the wars and when in 1958 it finally folded, its property passed to the corporation. The building became the reference library and a minor part of the Moore Collection is now exhibited on the second floor, together with a small tribute to William Smith (1769–1839) who also gets a show-case on the ground floor. Smith, "The Father of British Geology", or "Fossil Smith" as he was known to his contemporaries, was Surveyor to the Somerset Coalfield in 1792 and from 1795 to 1799 was Surveyor to the Somerset Coal Canal which was being cut along the valley of the Midford and Cam brooks to the south of Bath.

His great contributions to geology were his method of identifying strata by their characteristic fossils and the making of the first geological maps. In 1799 a list of strata with their type fossils was written at his dictation by The Revd Benjamin Richardson at 29 Pulteney Street, the house of a mutual friend The Revd Joseph Townsend, Rector of Pewsey in Wilts.— Reverend gentlemen seem to have had more spare time then than they have now. In the same year he produced a "Fossilogical" map of the Bath district, in 1815 "A Delineation of the Strata of England and Wales, with part of Scotland", the first large-scale geological map of any country, and from 1819 to 1824 was engaged in producing a "New Geological Atlas of England and Wales" for which he managed to survey twenty-one English counties. In 1831 he was awarded a medal by the Geological Society and was granted a Government pension of £100 a year, and in 1836 he received an honorary Doctor of Laws degree from Trinity College, Dublin. Although something of a rough diamond, Smith was a man of towering genius, mercifully spared a formal education, who combined a capacity for acute and accurate observation with a creative imagination.

In 1795 he moved to Bath, first to Cottage Crescent (now Bloomfield Crescent), then to No. 27 Pulteney Street. In 1799 he bought Tucking Mill, now called Tucking Mill House, near his canal, where an unsuccessful venture into stone quarrying lost him his money so that in 1819 he had to sell his house, his library, and most of his geological collection. In 1802 he set up as a land surveyor, working from a rented house, No. 3 (now No. 2) Trim Bridge in whose front window he exhibited some of his fossils. After 1819 he left Bath for Yorkshire.

Coincidentally, the year Smith came to Bath another assembly rooms disappeared. This was Dame Lindsey's, later Wiltshire's, and was designed by Wood and opened with a public breakfast on 6th April 1730. This and the extensions to Ralph Allen's house in 1727 had taken much of the old bowling-green and so, according to Wood, put an end to the old Bath pastimes of "Smock Racing and Pig Racing, playing at Foot-Ball and running with the Feet in Bags". Wood also recorded that in digging the foundations "the Workmen met with a vast number of bodies which had been buried" and that one of the labourers "more arch than the rest" did so well out of displaying the teeth and bones of horses as "those of Men of Gigantick Size" that "he soon appeared in fine Linen and the best broad Cloth Garments". The assembly rooms were taken down to make way for York Street which was opened by the Duchess of York in January 1796, after she had opened the new pump room in December 1795, and made a hole in Terrace Walk which Wood had built at the same time as the assembly rooms. Of particular interest in the walk are No. 1 which has a fine eighteenth-century shop-front and No. 2 which was long famous as the Parade Coffee House. Terrace Walk was originally housing but was later converted to shops and when we go round the corner into the Orange Grove we find an even more remarkable change to the return front, for every first-floor window was given a shell hood in 1897 (dated drain head), the roof-line was gabled and barge-boarded, and a corner turret was added. It all looks rather splendid.

The line of the city wall ran parallel with Terrace Walk and then turned northward to the east of the circular garden (which was once square) named after Bath's twin town of Alkmaar in the Netherlands, and passed through the site of the Empire Hotel. Next to the hotel is the new nineteenth-century police station (now vacated) for which older houses were demolished, including the impressive Nassau House, three-storey with a Doric doorway with entablature, giant Corinthian attached pillars and pilasters, and a roof line decorated with urns. According to Peach (1883), who is not always reliable, it was designed in about 1730 by Lord Burlington. In his photograph, which shows the house disfigured by a large board labelled "The

Dye Works", it looks rather too baroque for the grimly Palladian Earl. The columns and frieze above the door were transferred to the riverside colonnade in the Parade Gardens where they can still be seen.

This was all part of the improvements approved by the council in 1898 which cleared out a motley collection of market buildings overlooking the river in New Market Row, extended the roadway on a colonnade over the gardens below, which were leased from Earl Manvers, and created the present Grand Parade. Buildings removed included not only Nassau House but also the Athenaeum, the Grove Tavern, the Sun Tavern, and Winchester House. The Empire Hotel, which was approved by council, resulted from an arrangement between the City Architect, Davis, who designed it, and a Mr Alfred Holland who wrote, "I am taking it for granted there are no restrictions as to its height." The improvements opened up a fine view of Pulteney Bridge and the weir from the Grand Parade and today we can not only see this but also the award-winning new weir and automatic sluice which were installed in 1972 as part of the flood alleviation scheme. The sluice is adjusted automatically by a float chamber which is fed by water from upstream so that it anticipates changes in river level. Originally there was to be a café on top but this part of the scheme never materialized.

From the Grand Parade we can either cut through the covered market of 1895, its central rotunda supported on iron pillars with their flower capitals in gaudy colour, or go round the corner into Bridge Street for which the corporation gave land in exchange for a site for a new prison on the other side of the river when William Pulteney wanted an approach to his proposed bridge. One side of Bridge Street is converted to shops but the other, including the White Lion on the corner of High Street, was destroyed to make way for Brydon's technical schools and art gallery. The schools marked the council's move into the field of secondary education. In 1891 they set up a committee to consider the implications of the 1889 Technical Institutions Act which authorized local authorities to set up schools for technical and manual instruction and the 1890 Taxation Act which allocated "whisky money" from Customs and Excise to support such ventures. In the following year they set up the Bath City Science, Art and Technical School which in 1896 moved into its new premises which were opened by the Mayor who was congratulated by the council on "the admirable manner in which he sustained the dignity of his office" and was thanked for the "distinguished generosity" of the reception he provided. Classes were held in drawing, painting, design, modelling, geometry, engineering, building, carpentry and joinery, cabinet-making, plumbing, house decoration, electricity and magnetism, chemistry, botany, mathematics, cookery, laundry-work, dress-making, needlework, and manual instruction, and examin-ations were set by the Government Science and Arts Depart-ment and by the City and Guilds of London. In 1894–5 they had a total of 196 passes. Initially the school was for part-time instruction, mainly to young people in work but by 1915, when it had changed its title to the Bath Secondary Day School for Boys and Girls it was giving full-time instruction from twelve to seventeen, had broadened its syllabus, and was entering pupils for the Oxford Local Examination. Religious instruction was "Biblical and non-sectarian" and there was also a full range of extra-curricular activities which included games, music, and a cadet corps. The building proved too small and branches were established as technical institutes in Long Acre (on the London Road) and Twerton. In 1918 a domestic science centre was established at 23 High Street and then in 1934 moved to Brougham Hayes as a domestic science training college. After the Second World War it moved to new buildings at Sion Hill and in 1975 amalgamated with the post-war Newton Park College to form the Bath College of Higher Education. After 1918 the technical college hived off its secondary school element to form the City of Bath Boys' School (now Beechen Cliff Comprehensive, in conjunction with Oldfield Boys' School) and the City of Bath Girls' School (now part of Hayesfield Compre-hensive). The technical element moved, as we have seen, in 1935 to the old Royal United Hospital.

The Victoria Library and Art Gallery with its fine dome and regal statue of the Queen under the royal coat of arms, flanked by Britannia and India staring stonily at each other, owed its inception to Victorian civic pride backed by a legacy from Mrs Arabella Roxburgh and a thousand pounds from Henry Overton Wills, the Bristol tobacco manufacturer. It was opened in 1900, the foundation stone having been laid by HRH The Duke of Cambridge in 1897, the year of Victoria's Diamond Jubilee.

It was a long time since October 1830 when Victoria herself visited Bath as a pop-eyed little Princess of eleven who got headaches when she travelled, and was being carted round by her mother and Major Conroy on a publicity tour. It was by no means certain at that stage that Victoria would become Queen and in reply to Bath's loyal address her German mother, the Duchess of Kent, after remarking on the people's "attachment" to her daughter said that she fondly hoped to train the Princess to "repay it by that line of conduct which is suitable to the station that Providence *may* destine her to fill . . . in this great, free, and enlightened country". Leopold of Saxe-Coburg, later King of the Belgians, had visited Bath the previous month and told them how sorry he was not to be the future King of England—which he would have been if his wife Charlotte, daughter of George IV, had not died in childbirth in 1817.

Victoria and her entourage had been at Bristol and arrived at York House on the Thursday afternoon where they were greeted by the town notables and refused to go to the Guildhall for what the papers called a "superb dejeuné" laid on at great expense and provided by Mr Reilly who did the corporation catering and also ran York House. However, they went to the Guildhall in the morning and followed with a tour of the Assembly Rooms, Pump Room, Milsom Street, and the Royal Crescent; in the afternoon they visited the institution and the abbey and bought some jewellery at Messrs Payne. Saturday morning they visited the Improvements which the Princess "graciously condescended" to permit to be called the Royal Victoria Park, and they left Bath at 2 o'clock. A few days later the Mayor received a letter—"Sir, I have the honour to receive the Duchess of Kent's command to require you will be good enough as to apply for Her Royal Highness the accompanying check in the following manner—To the General Hospital £25. To the United Hospital £25. To the Bath Park Improvements £25. I have the honour to be, Sir, your most obedient humble servant, John Conroy."

Victoria never came again, but in 1843 the corporation managed to catch Albert and present him with a civic address when his train stopped at the station on its way to carrying him to the launching of Brunel's *Great Britain* in Bristol.

The other grand openings of the nineteenth century were of the Pump Room Annexe and Roman Promenade by the Duke of Connaught in 1887, which we have noted, and of the New Baths by Princess Helen Frederica Augusta, Duchess of Albany, in June 1889. This last set the council in a tizzy as they had asked for Princess Louise who at the last moment was too ill to come and later annoyed Bath by going to a German spa for her cure.

Discussions in council showed that committees haven't altered much. The Town Clerk thought they should meet the Princess at Sydney Gardens, Mr Jolly thought they should meet her at the station, Mr Oliver thought it was a pity that she couldn't see Pulteney Bridge, Mr Quin objected to the idea of her using "the wretched railway station" (cries of "hear, hear"), and Mr George, the station-master, said Paddington hadn't told him what train she was coming on. Mr Chaffin recalled that when the Duke of Connaught came they used North Parade Bridge, but nobody paid any attention to him and finally it was agreed to greet her at Sydney Gardens. The line went through the gardens in a cutting and there was no station but the Great Western Railway obliged by erecting a temporary halt although in the event the train missed it, went on to Bath Station and then backed back.

There was further dispute about decorations. One councillor objected to covering up Bath's architecture with greenery, another thought decorations were vulgar anyway. The Floral Fête Committee proposed an evening show of fireworks and illuminations in the gardens, entry to be a nominal sum. "What would you make it free for?" asked Mr Rodney. "Eighty pounds," said Mr Dawson, to which Mr Rodney replied, "Then make it free." Local jollifications in the evening were to be a Mayor's At Home in the Pump Room, a Tea for the Aged Poor in the Drill Hall, which was attended by 1,200 people and ended with the Doxology, and a Mayor's Conversazione in the Assembly Rooms.

Later they changed the start and had two receptions at Sydney Gardens, one at 12.45 for distinguished visitors who were taken off to the Guildhall for lunch from which the civic dignitaries dashed back to meet the Princess at 2 o'clock, she having had lunch on the train.

One of the most noticeable things in photographs of these Victorian and Edwardian junketings is a passion for bunting and dead greenery. This has become rather old hat, but what we have now, and very pleasant too, is an annual flourish of flowers throughout the centre of the city as window-boxes and hanging baskets and flower troughs on the ground and up in the air provide an instant spring, a mass of bloom which by care and contrivance is maintained through until the autumn: Bath won the Britain in Bloom competition in 1964, the year it was started, and by 1980 had won it five times, while in 1975 and

1978 it won the international Entente Floriale. This is a separate adjudication for shop displays which Bath has won six times and much of the success of the project results from the co-operation between the city council, the city traders, and the local community.

3

Eighteenth-Century Bath and 'The Season'

The international reputation of Bath rests on its Georgian townscape which we shall be considering in the next section, and the root cause of this expansion of building in the eighteenth century was a unique period in the history of the city when for a time it became the focus of social life outside London—the Bath Season. It all started with a gambling craze at the beginning of the century which set people looking for somewhere outside London where, as Goldsmith said, they could win each other's money. They picked on Bath presumably because it was already known to many of the nobility and gentry who had gone there for "the cure", and Queen Anne had visited it in 1702. For a time Bath became a sort of eighteenth-century British Las Vegas and the consequences might have been disastrous as the little city was totally unprepared for the invasion, and totally lacking in suitable facilities whether for public assembly or private lodging. In a rapid space of time it became a riotous, brawling place and would probably never have attained its attraction for Society if the Welshman Richard 'Beau' Nash had not become Master of Ceremonies in 1705 and by the sheer force of his personality imposed order and a civilized public life upon the visitors. The other important factor was that sharp-eyed developers, notably John Wood, Senior, saw that there was likely to be a building boom and moved in with borrowed money to cash in on the anticipated, and realized, demand. It was fortunate that these speculators and their clients were agreed on a single style for Bath—neo-Classicism, starting as Palladian and moving into Adamesque—and that they used a common facing material—the local Bath stone. Inside the walls they transformed the face of the city, not without some opposition from the council, and outside they covered the green fields with new streets, squares, and crescents.

As far as the city's economy was concerned it became as closely geared to holiday traffic as any modern package-deal

tourist trap mushrooming on the Costa Brava. Daily the
coaches rumbled in, disgorging their passengers and luggage
for the self-catering lodgings where instead of being serenaded
by canned music they were subjected to a hearty performance by
the city band, and were pressurized to take tickets, not for
barbecues and jolly coach tours, but for the weekly balls, the
baths, the pump rooms, the gardens, and the proprietary
chapels. Equivalent to modern car-hire firms were the livery
stables where you could get a carriage for five shillings (25p) for
a ten-mile trip, or a horse for two shillings (10p) a day or twelve
shillings a week. The streets were thronged with visitors walking up and down and gazing at each other and at the increasing
number of shops, dropping into coffee-houses or tea-rooms or
inns, browsing among the latest novels and newspapers in the
booksellers, gorging themselves on cakes and sweetmeats at the
confectioners, and getting local colour and cheap vegetables at
the markets. No cameras were clicking but sketching was
beginning to be fashionable, there were plenty of prints to be
had in the shops, and you might get your portrait painted by one
of the several artists in Bath—perhaps the young Mr Gainsborough who started by charging five guineas and later could
command a hundred, or Thomas Lawrence who only charged
half a guinea before, like Gainsborough, he went off to London.
There was gambling, if you were that way inclined (cards, not
bingo), and for the young there was Romance. Instead of discos
and flamenco dancing there were the second parts of the
assembly balls where the graver minuet gave place to energetic
country dances for which ladies were requested to take off their
hoops in private, which suggests that they were doing it
publicly. There were even swimming pools and although these
had a serious purpose they also afforded opportunities for a good
deal of mild sportiveness between the sexes and in any case, like
the swimming pools of today, were attended as much, if not
more, by spectators than bathers. One difference was that while
the chance of meeting a pop star or a film star on a package
holiday is somewhat remote the equivalent eighteenth-century
thrill of meeting a member of the aristocracy was readily available at Bath, a feature which attracted middle-class snobs and
nouveaux riches

men of low birth, and no breeding, having found themselves
suddenly translated into a state of affluence, unknown to former

ages; and no wonder that their brains should be intoxicated with
pride, vanity and presumption ... and all of them hurry to Bath,
because here, without any further qualification, they can mingle
with the princes and nobles of the land. Even the wives and
daughters of low tradesmen, who, like shovel-nosed sharks, prey
upon the blubber of those uncouth whales of fortune, are infected
with the same rage of displaying their importance; and the slightest
indisposition serves them for a pretext to insist upon being conveyed
to Bath, where they may hobble country dances and cotillons among
lordlings, 'squires, counsellors and clergy.

Or so said Matthew Bramble in Smollett's *Humphrey Clinker*
published in 1771. Bath, said Bramble, was "a stew pan of
idleness and insignificance", but his niece Lydia had very
different sentiments. "Bath", wrote Lydia, "is to me a new
world: all is gaiety, good humours and diversion: the eye is
continually entertained with the splendour of dress and equip-
ages, and the ear with the sounds of coaches, chairs, and other
carriages. The merry bells ring round from morning till night.
Then we are welcomed by the city waits in our lodgings." The
city waits, or town band, had previously been mentioned by
Christopher Anstey in his immensely popular *New Bath Guide*
of 1766, a mildly satirical work of fiction written as letters from
a young man visiting Bath, a work whose form and some of
whose substance Smollett had shamelessly cribbed for his own
more considerable book. Anstey wrote in verse and his report
runs—

> If a banker or statesman, a gamester, or peer,
> A nat'ralis'd Jew, or a bishop comes here,
> Or an eminent trader in cheese should retire,
> ....
> With horns and with trumpets, with fiddles and drums,
> They'll strive to divert him as soon as he comes.

Greeting by "merry bells", about which resident invalids complained frequently and without success, cost the visitor a guinea
or half a guinea, according to rank, and the serenade from the
waits half a guinea or five shillings. Unsolicited music in his
lodgings had cost Samuel Pepys five shillings in 1668 so apparently the price had not gone up much. Music was also played for
private parties and for dancing lessons, sometimes to the
annoyance of neighbours.

Lydia's reference to "coaches, chairs, and other carriages" is in keeping with the very considerable increase in road traffic through the eighteenth century and although visitors moved about the city on foot or in sedan-chairs there were constant arrivals and departures and many visitors and residents had their own vehicles. Jane Austen noted in *Northanger Abbey* that "Everyone acquainted with Bath may remember the difficulty of crossing Cheap Street . . . it is indeed a street of so impertinent a nature, so unfortunately connected with the great London and Oxford roads, and the principal inn of the city, that a day never passes in which parties of ladies . . . are not detained on one side or the other by carriages, horsemen, or carts."

Most of the transport in town was by sedan-chair, more usually called a glass chair or a Bath chair although it had not originated in Bath. In 1660 Celia Fiennes wrote that in Bath "there are chairs as in London to carry the better sort of people" and added that "no control is exercised over them; they [the chairmen] impose what fares they choose and when these were disputed would not let their customers go. If it was raining they would open the top and let him or her, often an invalid, be exposed to the wet until in despair their charges were met." Nash had all this altered and by his influence a system of fixed fares and licensing of chairmen was introduced and disputes were settled at a special Mayor's Court held on Mondays where not only could a customer bring a chairman for over-charging or abuse (or both) but a chairman could bring a passenger for damaging the chair. The fares were sixpence (2½p) inside the city and another sixpence for up to 200 yards outside and then a shilling a mile. Lodgings in the North Parade were advertised with the inducement of being within walking distance of all the main attractions so that visitors could save on transport. Chairs could be hired at ranks in the street or ordered, in which case they might come to the door of your room and Anstey describes how his hero hears a noise in the maid Tabitha's bedroom—

> And would you believe it, I went in and found her,
> In a Blanket, with two lusty Fellows around her,
> Who both seem'd a-going to carry her off in
> A little black box just the size of a coffin.

Apparently Tabitha had ordered transport to the baths and then changed her mind, much to the disgust of the chairman, who says—

Why Master, 'tis hard to be bilk'd of our Fare,
And so we are thrusting her into a Chair'.

Towards the end of the century, chairs with wheels were introduced and can be seen in the Rowlandson cartoons of 1798. At first they were heavy and clumsy but in the nineteenth century developed into light, convenient, pull-along carriages.

"At eight in the morning", wrote Lydia, "we go in *déshabillé* to the Pump-room which is crowded like a Welsh fair; and where you see the highest quality and the lowest trade folk jostling each other, without ceremony, hail-fellow well-met." The Pump Room was open for social purposes from eight to ten in the morning, while the band played, but drinking the waters, a recommended three pints a day in contrast to the heroic ten pints or so at the beginning of the century, began at six o'clock in summer and seven in winter. "Right under the Pump-room window", continued Lydia, "is the King's Bath; a huge cistern [Anstey called it a "great smoking Kettle"] where you see the patients up to their necks in hot water. The ladies wear jackets and petticoats of brown linen, with chip hats, in which they fix their handkerchiefs to wipe the sweat from their faces."

Entrance to the baths was free but there was a fixed scale of charges for attendance which in 1773 was 3d. to the Sergeant of the Baths, 1s. to the Guide (whose main job was to see you didn't fall over), and 3d. to the Cloth Woman, although people in "low circumstances" were required to pay only a single charge of 6d. to the Guide. Bathing costumes could be hired for 6d. a time. Next door were the Kingston or Abbey Baths of 1766 with an entrance charge of 5s. a time. They were, wrote Philip Thicknesse, in 1778, "now the only place where Persons of Condition, or Delicacy, can bathe decently". Incidentally, the baths and pump room Lydia visited were the old ones before the great rebuilding of the 1790s.

"Hard by the Pump-room", she continues, "is a coffee-house for the ladies, but my aunt says young girls are not admitted, inasmuch as the conversation turns upon politics, scandal, philosophy, and other subjects above our capacity. . . ." This coffee-house, which was also a lodgings, was kept by a Mr Immins and is mentioned in Cruttwell's *Stranger's Assistant and Bath Guide* of 1771 as being in the Abbey Churchyard. The three main coffee-houses (men only) were at that time in the Orange Grove, the North Parade, both of which were near the Pump Room, and the New Assembly Rooms, higher up in the town. They were, as Lydia indicates, great talking-shops and in addition to gossip and politics and philosophy the subject under discussion was often a matter of business. Their rivals in gossip were the booksellers—and Lydia was allowed to accompany the older ladies to these "charming places of resort; where we may read novels, plays, pamphlets, and newspapers for so small a subscription as a crown and a quarter; and in these offices of intelligence (as my brother calls them) all the reports of the day, and all the private transactions at Bath, are first entered and discussed."

The bookseller's was as much a reading-room and library as a shop, and had something in kin with the small circulating libraries to be found in sweetshops between the wars where for threepence you could borrow well-thumbed novels by Ursula Bloom or Agatha Christie. Faded letters on No. 43 Milsom Street still proclaim it as a "Circulating Library and Reading Room, Bookseller, Binder and Stationer, and State Lottery Office". These places would also sell you notepaper and lend you a quill pen to write your letters. You could read the London newspapers, but in addition from 1744 there was a local paper, the *Bath Journal*, from 1755 the *Bath Advertiser* (continued after 1760 as the *Chronicle*, which is still published), and from 1792 the *Bath Herald*. These local papers carried mainly national and international news; local information consisted mainly of advertisements, lists of visitors (a practice continued up to the Second World War), and details of Bristol shipping.

There were also poems, book reviews, and puzzles—the *Journal*, for example, had mathematical teasers such as "In an Oblique-angled Triangle there is given the Base = 2.5 chains, with the Angle opposite thereto = 112 Deg. 37 Min. Required the other Parts of the Triangle, by a simple Equation." Mathematical friends tell me it can't be done!

Most of the advertisements were for patent medicines which the eighteenth- (and nineteenth-) century visitors seemed to have demanded in spite of the plethora of doctors and apothecaries in the place. Some went into great detail. Dr Boerhaave's Aurea Medicana or Scots Pill Improved would, it was claimed, "work with ease on the Blood and Juices of the

Body, discharging at the same time all foreign and vitiated
Particles thereof, promote Perspiration, purge Choler,
Melancholy, Phlegm, and Waterish Matter, cleanse the Body of
all putrid, gross and thick Humour, open Obstructions [eight-
eenth-century people seem to have suffered a great deal from
obstructions], restore lost Appetite, release the Spirits, comfort
the Nerves, and exceedingly strengthen the Stomach and Intes-
tines." It was taken with wonderful success, the advertisement
said, for "all Pains and Diseases of the Head, Stomach, and
Bowels of Men and Women, but especially for the Head-ache,
Giddiness, Vapours, Phrenzy, weak and sore Eyes, Deafness,
Palsy, Loss of Appetite, Melancholy, Choler, Phlegm, Worms,
Ulcers, Rheumatism, Gout, Gravel, Scurvy, Dropsy, Chilick or
Gripes, and [inevitably] all Obstructions whatever, either in
Men, Women, or Children."

Local news included some reports on marriages—brief, and
showing a keen interest in the monetary value of the bride—
"Miss Snell, the only daughter of Sir Thomas Snell, an agreeable young lady of very great Fortune"—"Miss Biggs, Niece of
the late Sir Fisher Tench Bart., a young lady of great Beauty
and fine Accomplishments, with a Fortune of £10,000"—"Miss
Fanny Maria Cooksey, a beautiful young lady, and an Heiress of
£15,000 Fortune". There were also lists of bankruptcies and
occasional denials of financial responsibility—as in the warning
that "Whereas Anne, the wife of Thomas Gibbs, of Batheaston,
hath eloped from her said husband, and run him into Debt. This
is to caution all Persons not to trust the said Anne Gibbs, for her
Husband will not pay any Debts she may contract from the Date
hereof." *That* must have added interest to the chat at the bookseller's.

"From the bookseller", wrote Lydia, "we make a tour through
the milliners and toy-men; and commonly stop at Mr. Gill's, the
pastry-cook, to take a jelly, a tart, or a small bason of
vermicelli." Most of these shops were concentrated in a small
area around the heart of the city—in the Abbey Churchyard, the
Grove, Parades, Cheap Street, and Stall Street. Southgate
Street, now a major shopping area, was then lined mainly with
workshops, warehouses, breweries, wine vaults, and poor
housing; retailing there developed with proximity to the
railway station, built in 1840. Milsom Street to the north of the
centre was beginning its rapid change from residence to
shopping. None of these shops was purpose-built and many had

to be considerably remodelled in Victorian times. Some sold a wide variety of goods as shown in an advertisement by Francis Bennet whose shop in Abbey Churchyard sold "all sorts of Linnen-Drapery, Woollen Draper, Mercery and Haberdashery Goods; all sorts of Blanketting, Flannels, Swan-skin and Shag; all sorts of Teas, Coffees, Chocolate and Sugar; with all sorts of Snuffs and Cards; All of which are sold as cheap as in London for Ready Money." He added an NB that he also furnished "Funerals with a new Pall and Cloak; and all necessaries, as decent and cheap as in London." This claim of cheapness was very common and Bath indeed gained a reputation for inexpensive shopping, particularly for food, and at the end of the eighteenth and into the nineteenth century this was one of the attractions which caused people to take up residence there.

Most of the shopping for meat, fish, fruit, and vegetables took place in the markets and was made a good deal more comfortable when a new, covered market was built in the 1770s on the site of the old flesh (meat) market in the High Street. The eighteenth-century entrances remain but the interior was made smaller and remodelled when the Guildhall extensions were built in the 1890s. The fish market was down by the river beyond the East Gate. In addition, streets, particularly High Street, Cheap Street, and Upper Borough Walls were lined with temporary stalls on market-days, as they continued to be until suppressed by an Act of 1851. There was no pre-packaging and this helped the cheats. Mrs Smith in her *Compleat Housewife* of 1729 had a section on "chusing" foodstuffs and warned that "When you buy butter taste it yourself at a venture, and do not trust the taste they give you, lest you be deceived by a well tasted and scented piece artfully placed in the lump . . . if it is a cask it may be purposely packed, therefore trust not the top alone, but unhoop it to the middle, thrusting your knife between the staves of the cask, and then you cannot be deceived." If Mrs Smith's advice on "chusing" was followed the market would be full of shoppers sampling, pinching flesh, squeezing fat, sticking knives into bacon, butter, and cheese, feeling the feet of rabbits, and smelling the fish. Hence the cry, "If you don't want the goods, don't handle them!"

The corporation continued to do what it could to regulate the markets. It had its market officers, its own weigh-bridge in the Sawclose, its standard weights, and it held a weekly Court of

Conscience for the recovery of small debts. In the 1770s Philip Thicknesse was sued by his butcher before this court for the recovery of 3s.2d. (about 17p) but the court ruled that the butcher had overcharged "by a trifling difference between his weights and those of the Public Market". Thicknesse also warned visitors not to leave "calling in their bills" to the last moment as they would then have no opportunity of checking them. Some allowance must be made for the fact that Thicknesse was suspicious and contentious almost to the point of paranoia, but there is no doubt that shoppers had to keep their wits about them. Another complaint that he made was that the town butchers used to smuggle out their waste at night and dump it in the river, a practice which received further condemnation in the nineteenth century.

From her shopping Lydia moved on to "another place of entertainment on the other side of the river, opposite to the Grove; it is called Spring Garden; a sweet retreat, laid out in walks and ponds, and parterres of flowers; and there is a long room for breakfasting and dancing." Here was another aspect of eighteenth-century social life, the considerable extent to which it was carried on out of doors. A good deal of time was spent in simply strolling about (Wood called it "the Rotations of Walking") for which the new wide pavements were well-suited and for which the Grand Parade was well-named, and the Bath novels of Jane Austen, *Northanger Abbey* and *Persuasion*, are full of perambulations and chance and not-so-chance meetings in the street. The first gardens, where now lie the Parade Gardens, were laid out in 1708 by the proprietor of the Lower Assembly Rooms and were known as Harrison's Walks—Wood wrote that after a visitor had subscribed to the Baths, Pump Room Music etc., "his next subscription is a crown, half a guinea, or a guinea, according to the Rank and Quality, for the Liberty of Walking in the Private Walks belonging to Harrison's Assembly House". The walks were superseded by Spring Gardens over the river and they in turn gave way to Sydney Gardens Vauxhall. The breakfasting which Lydia mentions was satirized by Anstey—

> The Company made a most brilliant appearance,
> And ate bread and butter with great perseverance;
> All the chocolate, too, that my host set before 'em,
> The ladies despatch'd with the utmost decorum.

The chocolate may well have been brought from Bristol where

in 1765 a young Quaker, Joseph Fry, had bought Mr Churchman's patent machinery for its manufacture. The chocolate of those days was a thick concoction drunk from chocolate pots with a hole in the lid through which the drink could be stirred.

Returning to indoor entertainment Lydia wrote,

> The great scenes in Bath are the two public rooms; where the company meet alternately every evening. They are spacious, lofty, and when lighted up appear very striking. They are generally crowded with well-dressed people, who drink tea in separate parties, play at cards, walk or sit and chat together, just as they are disposed. Twice a week there is a ball; the expense of which is defrayed by a voluntary subscription amongst the gentlemen; and every subscriber has three tickets. I was there Friday last with my aunt. . . . The place was so hot . . . that I was quite feverish when I went away.

The two rooms were the Upper, or New, opened in 1771, and the Lower, then also known as Gyde's. The lower were the old Harrison's Rooms, opened in 1708, with a ballroom added in 1750. Lindsey's (later Wiltshire's) Rooms, which opened in 1730 opposite Harrison's, were superseded by the New and became a warehouse until their demolition late in the eighteenth century to make way for York Street. Both rooms had a ballroom, a card-room, and a tea-room but those at the New were larger—its ballroom, for example, was 105 foot by 42, as against the 90 by 36 at the Lower. The New also saved floor space by putting its musicians in a gallery, or "orchestra", and had the added advantage of a colonnade for chairmen while at the Lower Rooms the chairs were in a rank in the Grove and only four at a time were allowed at the entrance. The *Bath Guide* of 1778 described the Lower Rooms as being "much inferior in point of magnificence".

Until 1769 there was one post as Master of Ceremonies, or "King of Bath", and it was under the long rule of Nash from 1705 to 1761 that the pattern of social life in the city was established. The Welshman, Nash, was succeeded by a Frenchman, Collette, and he in his turn in 1763 by a diminutive Irishman, Samuel Derrick, a scribbler of verses and a man of little authority. Lydia thought him "a pretty little gentleman, so sweet, so fine, so civil and polite . . ." but it took more than sweetness to keep order in Bath. When Derrick died in 1769 a fearful row broke out between contenders for his job and there was fighting in the

Lower Rooms. The matter was settled by the appointment of Captain Wade, a nephew of the Marshal, who managed to retrieve the situation but was forced to 'abdicate' in 1777 when he seduced a lady and had to pay damages to her husband. After that there were two separate MCs one for each room, but Wade's portrait by Gainsborough continued to look down on the card-room of the Upper Rooms until it was sold in the nineteenth century.

At a ball the evening was divided into two parts. Beginning at 6 o'clock were the formal minuets, elaborate dances performed by couples in strict order of social rank. Then there was a break for tea and after that the more informal country dances which were danced in long lines. Although freer and more energetic and sweaty these were still a long way from the simple folk-dancing which the name suggests, but even so they were unsuitable for the big hooped skirts of the more formal dress and the majority of people seem to have arrived after the tea-break, often from private parties, and suitably attired.

The theatre, the Assembly Rooms, the Pump Room, the gardens, the outdoor parades, were all necessary to the open, public society which Nash had imposed on Bath but in the second half of the century they became increasingly adjuncts, although still important, to a social life which centred on what Jane Austen called "the elegant stupidity of private parties". They were not always particularly elegant and those of us today who have suffered from the booming of record players, the slamming of car doors and loud voices in the small hours will sympathize with Philip Thicknesse when he wrote—

> These private parties are announced from one end of the Street, Square, Circus, or where ever they are, by Oaths, quarrelling, and indecent language, to the great Annoyance of all sober people, and the great entertainment of the Young Ladies and the Chamber-maids at the Nursery Windows, who cannot sleep on their Mama's Rout-Night, and therefore may as well sit at the window with BETTY and MOLLY, to hear all the obscene and balderdash Conversation which passes between the most abandoned set of Men in the Universe.

Some, perhaps most, of the parties were quiet gatherings of a few friends, but other were bigger affairs whose main ingredients were gossip, flirtation, seduction, matchmaking, social-climbing, and opportunism. In a full-scale rout there was hardly room to move, certainly not to sit, most of the furniture would

have been packed away into one room, and throughout the
evening there would be constant coming and going of guests and
gatecrashers, but for the smaller parties there might well be
"carpet dancing" and, nearly always, cards. The early explosion
of social life in eighteenth-century Bath had been based, as we
have seen, on public gaming but in the forties new laws drove
the activity into private and the rules said that "no hazard, or
unlawful games, will be allowed in the Rooms, on any account
whatsoever". The craze did not abate and there was no lack of
professionals to take full advantage and insinuate their way
into the lives of visitors. Daniel Clarke in his *Tour through the
South of England* in about 1790 may have overstated the case
but there was a good deal of foundation for his claim that "There
is perhaps no part of the world, setting aside the infernal
purlieus of St. James's, where gaming is carried to a pitch as at
Bath," and that "This is owing, in great measure, to that swarm
of demons who under the general name of black-legs, or
sharpers, infest all places of public amusement. In Bath one is
never secure from the insidious designs of these indefatigable
harpies. They infest the rooms, the promenades, nay, incon-
sistent as it may seem, the very churches. . . ."

The lodgings which visitors hired at about 10s. (50p) per room
per week improved considerably in quality and comfort during
the century, and in 1740 Wood wrote that "to make a just
Comparison between the publick Accomodation at Bath at this
time, and one and twenty years back, the best Chambers for
Gentlemen were then just what the Garrets for Servants now
are." Bare floors whose boards, according to Wood, had been
made brown with soot and small beer "to hide Dirt as well as
their own Imperfections" became covered with carpet, walls
were wainscotted with painted panelling, oak furniture gave
way to fashionable walnut and then to mahogany, looking-
glasses increased in size, quantity and quality, and the materials for bed hangings, coverlets, table-cloths, and curtains
greatly improved from the early "Kidderminster stuff" and
"fustian". Brass took over from iron as the material for locks and
latches and for fire-irons. Wallpaper was originally very expensive and mostly imported from China but became cheaper and
more common about the middle of the century, although it is
interesting to note that in 1803 Mrs Powys noted in her diary
that a gentleman who had a house in St James's Square had
visited Paris and "finding that paper-hangings were there call'd

vulgar" returned to Bath and "immediately took all down and hung all with satin".

Rooms and their furniture became increasingly specialized. There is a good deal of variety behind the uniform façades of Bath buildings, depending largely on the position chosen for the staircase, but basically the arrangement was a basement kitchen; a reception room, small hall, and one or two other rooms, one of which would be the dining-room, on the ground floor; a large (with) drawing-room or salon and one or two smaller rooms on the first floor; bedrooms above, and in the roof the garret bedrooms for the servants. Stairs may be at the side or at the back in which case they are often accommodated in a curved projection. In the first half of the century the stairs were usually of wood, with wooden balustrades, but later they were mostly of stone and often with ironwork supporting a mahogany rail.

Dining-room furniture developed considerably in quantity and form during the century—indeed it is wrong to think that there was a single Georgian style. At first the gate-leg table was popular but by the 1740s the drop-leaf tended to predominate, only to be superseded in the sixties by either a pedestal type or else a single table with the addition at each end, when needed, of separate small tables, often semicircular. There would be side-tables against the wall, or else mounted on wall brackets or consoles, often elaborately carved. In the sixties serving tables with urns at each end were introduced and in the eighties had been developed into sideboards with drawers. One of the urns held iced water and the other hot water which might be used to wash the silver knives and forks between courses. The pedestal of the hot urn might be used as a plate warmer and that under the cold as a wine-cooler. Another common feature was the dumb-waiter, two or three circular trays on a central column supported by a tripod which towards the end of the century was fitted with castors.

One of the social graces was carving the meat, for a guest might well be asked to perform this task. Lord Chesterfield in one of his letters to his son in 1748 enquired, "Do you use yourself to carve adroitly and genteely, without hacking half an hour across the bone, without bespattering the company with the sauce, and without overturning the glasses into your neigh-bour's pockets?"

The use of china increased considerably during the eighteenth century, particularly after the discovery of kaolin (china clay) in Cornwall in 1755 and the founding of the Wedgwood company in 1760. Another innovation, probably of the 1730s was the production of "services", a set of china for a meal, all carrying the same design. Wedgwood himself in 1762 presented Queen Charlotte, wife of George III, with a breakfast service. The eighteenth-century rings with the names of famous porcelain factories—Chelsea, Derby, Bow, Worcester, Coalport—as it does with furniture-makers—Chippendale, Hepplewhite, and Sheraton being the best known today.

The increased use of china led to a demand for glass-fronted china cabinets in which the best pieces could be displayed and glass doors were also fitted to bookcases, many houses now having a room designated as a library and fitted out with a library chair with a candle-holder on one arm, a library table, often of the drum-top variety, and perhaps a reading-desk with an inclined book-rest. Drawing-room furniture would probably include a sofa (an eighteenth-century word), and very possibly a harpsichord or, later, a pianoforte. There were several teachers of the harpsichord in Bath including in 1778 the daughter of Mr Guest "a sensible, honest Tailor", who had a studio opposite the Pump Room. Shops sold sheet music and you could, for example, in 1770 get a set of "Elegies for three Voices accompanied by Harpsichord and Violoncello" for 10s. 6d. (52½p) by Thomas Linley. In musical households, or those with pretensions to music, there would be other instruments such as harp, viol, cello, and flute. For more serious pastimes there were baize-covered card tables, often of quite elaborate construction.

In the bedrooms the four-poster bed with hangings was still normal but there was an increase in other furniture. Wardrobes for hanging clothes did not come into use until the end of the century but the word was used for tall chests on short legs, the front opening with full-length doors on to shelves and drawers. Another feature was the tallboy, a chest on a chest, both with drawers, and chests of drawers with looking-glasses on top which developed into dressing-tables. A wig stand would be on a table handy for the bed. A new development from about 1760 was the wash-stand, a bowl on a tripod, with drawers underneath for soap and other toilet articles, and a shelf for the water jug. As men were generally clean-shaven a shaving mirror was normally provided and this was often equipped with a magnifying glass to show the stubble in all its horror.

An indispensable feature, especially after a heavy night's drinking, was the night-commode containing the chamber-pot. There were two main kinds; one a chair with a pot concealed below a hinged seat, the other disguised as a chest (hence the name commode) with a pot in a drawer which was pulled out and supported on legs. It was important to make the affair airtight and commodes are often fine examples of cabinet-making. The use of chamber-pots, upstairs and downstairs, was common-place as the "necessary house" was usually out at the back, perched over a cesspit. There were water-closets, but they were not common and lacked a water trap, or U-bend, which was not invented until the nineteenth century, so they were liable to be noisome. The great architect of Bath, John Wood the Elder, seems to have been particularly inept at the details of plumbing and there were rows between him and Chandos over the instal-lation of WCs. They smelt, and the Duke wrote crossly that this was "a sure sign of your ignorance and that had they [the WCs] been connected with cesspools just above the drain (which is the manner of building them everywhere else) they would not have been subject to this inconvenience which is so great I must be forced to have them stopt up." The result, complained the land-lady, was that there was "not one W.C. in the whole house" and that this was very inconvenient for any lodgers who were "out of order". In addition to the primitive sanitation there were rarely any bathrooms and in any case the hot water had to be carried toilsomely up from the basement by servants.

They also had to carry coal, for heating was by open fires which created such draughts that many rooms were equipped with portable screens. The coals were burn either in a hob grate fixed into the opening or else in a free-standing basket grate, while the surround, often in marble, was one of the finest features of the room. Down in the kitchen, cooking was still carried on over an open fire with the help of a variety of devices for turning the meat on spits and often with a kind of iron crane with which kettles and pans could be swung over the heat. At the end of the century cooking stoves were beginning to make an appearance but they were not common. There was a not incon-siderable fire-risk and some houses in Bath still carry the badges or "fire-marks" of insurance companies. The corporation itself bought a fire-engine which was used in 1746 to put out a fire in Queen Square.

So far we have been considering the life-style of the well-to-do visitor to eighteenth-century Bath but this did not constitute the whole life of the city for these people created a demand which produced a host of jobs for other people from the more prosperous tradesmen to the poorest beggar, not to mention the work-force of the booming building industry. Many of these people were respectable tradesfolk who lived a comfortable life in which housing, furniture, and clothing were subdued versions of those of the fashionable and who also required, in a lesser degree perhaps, services from other people. It was these people, with social aspirations, particularly the wives, who were laying the foundations for the emergence of a prosperous middle class or bourgeoisie which was to be a predominant feature of the Victorian age.

Of the poorer people the "upper" house servants formed a favoured class for although their wages were low they had free board and lodging and uniform, and associated with the social round of their employers. Within their own ranks there was a strict hierarchy and the possibility of promotion up the ladder, and in general they considered themselves by their association with the upper classes as superior to the "workers".

At the bottom of the social pile were the really poor, crowded into subdivided, once fashionable houses down in the lower quarters of the town, where rates in 1766 were about 1s. 3d. as compared with 15s. in the Circus and Queen Square, or in mean streets across the bridge, or round the backs of the architectural show-pieces, or in infamous doss-houses, or sleeping rough under area steps or on the streets, or, as a last resort, in the parish poorhouses. Dressed in the cast-offs of more fortunate people, begged, stolen, or bought off a barrow, or attired in cobbled-up imitations, and often fuddled by cheap rot-gun gin until the heavy taxes of the fifties put it beyond their meagre purses, these people maintained themselves on odd jobs, thieving, begging, and the cheapest forms of prostitution. This is not to say that there were not some amongst them who still strived desperately to maintain some form of respectability.

The multitude of beggars is something which cannot be realized by looking at the prints of the time where street scenes are gracefully embellished with fashionably dressed figures, a chair or two, and the occasional carriage. In fact Bath was a kind of Mecca for mendicants who crowded its streets and whose importunity was a source of annoyance to many of its citizens. Nothing, however, was done about it until 1805 when there was set up a "Society for the Suppression of Common Vagrants and Impostors" (later called the Monmouth Street Society) whose manifesto stated that "Beggars are (probably without exception) systematic impostors." They were proved wrong; out of the 400 cases they investigated in their first year only 25 were rejected.

There is not a great deal of information about Bath's eighteenth-century poor—the nineteenth century is much better documented in this respect for the Victorians had, in general, much more of a social conscience than had the Georgians whose upper and educated classes, with some outstanding exceptions, took a very complacent view of their social system. We do, however, have quite a lot of information about the visitors although a complete list would be uninteresting—after all anybody who *was* anybody visited Bath at some time—except reigning monarchs.

Not that Bath was short of royal visitors—the somewhat hoydenish Princess Amelia, second daughter of George II, came seven times between 1729 and 1776 in spite of one or two little arguments with Nash; Frederick, Prince of Wales, and Princess Augusta came in 1728 and 1750 and Nash had a commemorative obelisk erected in Queen Square; William, Prince of Orange, came in 1734 and another obelisk went up in the renamed Orange Grove; the Duke of Cumberland, 'Butcher Cumberland' of Culloden, came twice, and the next Duke of Cumberland, his nephew, came no less than eight times; George IV when he was Prince of Wales visited in 1790, '97, and '99, and on the last occasion was with his brother, the King of Hanover. There were visits from Princess Caroline, third daughter of George II, the Duke of York (three times) and the Duke of Gloucester, brother of George III.

An early visitor was the redoubtable Sarah Churchill, Duchess of Marlborough, a keen gamester, who disliked the place and Nash's open society but was prepared to stay as long as she thought the waters were doing the Duke some good. She made something of a friend of Nash, however, and consulted him over her plans for the building of Blenheim Palace. Nelson too, visited Bath for his health after his tour of duty in the West Indies, staying in Pierrepont Street, and liked the place. His wife also spent some time in Bath while her husband was away, and after his death, Emma, Lady Hamilton, had a short stay in Pulteney Street. General Wolfe lived in Trim Street before going off to lose his life fighting against the French at Quebec and securing Lower Canada for his country, and Marshal Wade, victor against the Young Pretender in the 1715 Jacobite Rebellion, had close connections with the city and a house in Abbey Churchyard. In 1794, '95 and '98, Admiral Earl Howe, whom Nelson judged to be "the first and greatest sea officer the world has produced" was living at No. 71 Great Pulteney Street. Admiral Arthur Phillip, whose convict settlement at Sydney was to develop into New South Wales, retired to Bennett Street, where he died in 1814. He was buried at Bathampton where the church now has an Australian chapel.

Bath, as a social centre where many contacts could be made, also attracted statesmen, artists, and writers. Pitt was MP for Bath for a time and had a house in the Circus (Nos. 7 and 8), and the younger Pitt stayed for a time in Johnstone Street, off Laura Place. Lord Chesterfield stayed in Bath but found it boring and did not take to Nash. On one occasion he referred to the over-dressed Master of Ceremonies as "a gilded garland" and on another, when Nash was complaining about how much he had lost at cards, remarked that he was not so much astonished at how much Nash had lost as at how he got the money in the first place. Alexander Pope, top poet of the age, was a frequent visitor at Ralph Allen's Prior Park, and Henry Fielding was befriended by Allen, dined frequently at the great house, and wrote *Tom Jones* while living at Twerton, then a village outside Bath.

Artists connected with Bath included Gainsborough who came, under the patronage of Philip Thicknesse, in 1759 and left after the inevitable quarrel in 1774; he also acquired a house in the Circus. Thomas Lawrence, later Sir Thomas and President of the Royal Academy, and one of the most fashionable portrait painters of the day, started his career in Bath in 1780–1 before going to London. Another painter, William Hoare, who did portraits of Ralph Allen, Anstey, Pitt, Nash, Samuel Richardson (author of *Clarissa*), John Palmer, and himself, all of which are in the Guildhall, reversed the process as he started in London and then came to Bath for the rest of his life.

Richard Brinsley Sheridan joined his father in Bath in 1771, fell in love with Elizabeth Linley, carried her off to the continent, came back and fought two duels, married her, and left for a successful career as a playwright in London. The Bath stage was notable for the enormous success of Sarah Siddons from

1778 to 1782, and of John Henderson who went on to become a leading London actor. Also resident in Bath was the retired actor James Quin, a very fat man, a great eater and drinker, and another frequent visitor to Prior Park.

The great Doctor Johnson himself visited Bath to see his friend Mrs Thrale who as the widowed Mrs Piozzi was to live in Gay Street and become the leader of the "bluestocking" tribe of literary ladies in Bath. Another of her visitors was her old friend Madame d'Arblay, better known as Fanny Burney the novelist, whose *Evelina* portrays life at the Bristol spa of Hotwells. The name most usually associated with Bath, however, is that of Jane Austen, which is a little strange as she hated the place. Another Bath authoress, whose *Mysteries of Udolpho* (1794) helped to set the fashion for the Gothic novel which Jane Austen satirized in *Northanger Abbey*, was Mrs Ann Radcliffe, and another 'Gothic' writer was Horace Walpole with his *Castle of Otranto* (1764). Walpole visited Bath but disliked the society and the steep slopes. The local poet/satirist was Christopher Anstey who lived at No. 5 The Royal Crescent and whose *New Bath Guide* we have already quoted from. Walpole thought it terrific—"it will make you bepiss your cheeks with laughing. . . . So much wit, so much humour, fun and poetry, so much originality, never met together before". As we can see it was lightweight stuff but it secured Anstey a place in Poets' Corner, Westminster Abbey.

In an early meeting of the Bath Literary Club, founded in 1852, a paper was read on "Literature and Literati of Bath" which listed some thirty authors who had been at Bath in the eighteenth century, although few had written anything about the place. Names included Southey and Scott (who were there as children), Goldsmith (who wrote a somewhat unreliable life of Nash), Burke (the statesman who produced *Reflections on the French Revolution* in 1790), Gibbon (*Decline and Fall of the Roman Empire*, published 1776–88, to whom George III said "Hey, what, Mr Gibbon, scribble, scribble, scribble!"), Wordsworth (at 9 North Parade), Landor (whom we will deal with later), and Thomas Malthus (*Essay on Population*, 1798) to whom there is a memorial just inside the north door of the west front of the abbey. It was in Bath that Southey introduced Coleridge to the Fricker sisters whom they married—Southey happily, Coleridge less so.

Few of these people had much effect on the development of

eighteenth-century Bath apart from the fact that they visited, required accommodation, spent their money, engaged in the social round, and maintained the reputation of the place as a major social centre.

4

Georgian Suburbs— West and North

In no way could updating the old city provide sufficient accommodation for the annual eighteenth-century invasion of visitors and so from about 1720 onwards a tide of building burst out from the city walls, soon to be demolished, and settled on the fields around as streets, squares, crescents, and a Circus arose clothed in gleaming new ashlar in speculative response to market forces. It was, apart from a new Upper Assembly Rooms, all housing, as services and entertainment continued to be concentrated in the old city and it was then suburban for the present city fringes are the result of nineteenth- and twentieth-century additions—in the eighteenth century the population rose from about 3,000 to 30,000 but since then it has risen to 85,000, partly by boundary extensions.

The first phase of building, about 1725–50, started with Bristol's John Strahan (Avon Street, Beaufort Square, Kingsmead Square, Monmouth Street, all in the 1730s) and Bath's Thomas Greenway (St John's Court, 1720) but was soon dominated by the elder John Wood (Queen Square, 1728–36; North and South Parades, 1740–3). The second phase, about 1750–5, saw some westward extension south of the Lower Bristol Road (New King Street, 1764–71) but was mainly occupied with Walcot New Town to the north, stretching from the Royal Crescent (1767–74) to Lansdown Road where cellars are above ground behind a high pavement, and was mainly by the younger John Wood, although other builders such as Thomas Warr Atwood and Thomas Jelly were also cashing in on the building boom.

The last quarter of the eighteenth century extended Walcot New Town northward, put new building along the London Road, filled in some open space in the south-west down by the river (e.g. Milk Street, Green Park Buildings), while beyond Adam's Pulteney Bridge (1774) the core of Bathwick New Town arose. The dominant architects of this Adamesque age were Thomas

Baldwin (Pulteney Street, 1788); John Eveleigh (Camden Crescent, 1788; the Grosvenor, 1791; Somerset Place c. 1790); Thomas Palmer (Lansdown Crescent, 1789; St James's Square, 1790s).

The south-west quarter down towards the river has suffered the most. From the post-war packing-case architecture of shops and offices stretching back a short distance from the end of Southgate Street to the one remaining limb of Green Park is an area which deteriorated socially and physically as Bath developed to the north and east. Invaded by industry in the nineteenth century, including Bowler's establishment, part bottling and part metal-working, whose contents have been removed to the excellent Camden Works Museum established in the old Real Tennis court up in Morford Street, bombed during the war, and lying outside the Bath Conservation Area designated in 1973, it forms a chaotic wasteland of which the chief features are a car-park, some starkly functional technical college buildings, and the Kingsmead Flats of 1932 built round three sides of a court as a slum-clearance venture and character-ized by a multiplicity of balconies, where today the tenants' washing contributes a welcome note of colour to an otherwise drab scene.

Here, surely, was an opportunity for post-war comprehensive redevelopment which, given good design, could have created a modern townscape of quality, but although it was designated in 1953 as a Comprehensive Development Area (CDA) nothing coherent came out of it. It is true that we now have a useful road and that the riverside has been opened up with a grassy space and a pathway although the view of the nineteenth-century buildings on the opposite bank is not particularly inspiring; which is perhaps why the benches provided have their backs to it and face the car-park instead!

At the western end is the not unattractive post-war Green Park House, flatlets for the elderly, which runs its own shop, and beyond is another post-war building, the Salvation Army Citadel which shows an appreciation of practicalities in having a door in the foyer which is labelled "Infants Cry Room". It was at this end, over the road, that the LMS intruded in 1869 its Green Park Station (at first confusingly named Queen Square) with a fine Classical front and a *porte-cochère* in ornamental ironwork. The line closed in 1966 and the corporation bought the station in 1972, leaving it subject to deterioration and vandalism for eight years while it tried to think what to do with it. In 1980 they decided to let Sainsbury's have it for a super-market after having conducted an expensive shopping survey to see if it was needed.

North of the station lies a small area built mainly in the late eighteenth and early nineteenth centuries with the three parallel roads of James Street West, New King Street, and Monmouth Place, and having at its western end Norfolk Crescent which was started in 1800 although building was held up by financial troubles during the Napoleonic Wars and did not get going again until 1810. Ison suggests that the first design was by Palmer and that the work was concluded by Pinch.

This little area also became rather run-down and was invaded by workshops but it is in the conservation area and is one of the priority areas designated by the council. So mixed is it in quality of architecture, state of fabric, and variety of usage that proposals for dealing with it, including the possibility of making New King Street traffic-free, are complicated. Some work has already started on rehabilitation, largely due to pressure brought by the Residents' Association, and it is to be hoped that New King Street, which is of some merit, will again present a brave face to the world, although James Street West has had so much intrusion and demolition that it is beyond recall except for workshop development.

At the east end of New King Street is the Percy Boys' Club, built in 1961 on the site of a Methodist chapel whose foundation stone was laid by John Wesley himself in 1777, but which in 1847 was replaced by a large Gothic job by the local architect James Wilson and which was bombed in 1942. Nearby is a Christadelphian Hall bearing the date 1880. On No. 8 on the opposite side of the road a plaque commemorates the fact that here lived Thomas Sheridan and his son Richard Brinsley Sheridan; they later moved to the Royal Crescent where another plaque may be seen.

Another inhabitant of the street was William Herschel at No. 19 where in 1781 he may possibly have made his discovery of the planet Uranus, although this has not been established without question. Earlier, in 1770, he had rented No. 7 New King Street for thirty guineas a year, but he also lived at other places in Bath. The original No. 7 had been demolished and the façade replicated with flats behind. In 1981 No. 19 was turned into a Herschel museum. Herschel was a German musician who became organist in 1766 to the Octagon, a proprietary chapel in Milsom Street and now the home of the Royal Photographic Society; he was replaced ten years later but was kept busy with musical appointments in Bath and Bristol and succeeded Linley in 1776 as Director of Music at the Upper Rooms. He was a very competent musician but his international fame came from his work as an amateur astronomer, contributing substantially to the charting of the heavens with telescopes he made for himself with the help of his sister Caroline, herself a proficient observer who in 1828 was awarded a gold medal by the Royal Astronomical Society. His first report of a new heavenly body, which at first he thought was a comet, was made to the Bath Philosophical Society, founded in 1779, of which he was an active member. By 1782 it had been established that the new body was a planet. Herschel wanted to call it Georgium sidus (George's Star) after George III, others had suggested calling it Herschel, but eventually it was called Uranus, following the established practice of naming planets after Classical gods. "Herschel," wrote Fanny Burney in 1791, "you know, and everybody knows, is one of the most pleasing and well-bred natural characters of the present age, as well as the greatest astronomer." He was also the discoverer of infra-red heat rays. As a result of his discovery Herschel was made astronomer to George III and in 1782 left Bath to be nearer the Court. His work is dealt with in detail in *Bath: Some Encounters with Science* by Williams and Stoddart. In 1816 Herschel was knighted.

Norfolk Crescent, with its rusticated ground floor, Ionic giant pilasters, shallow central pediment, and row of balconies, is pleasant without being remarkable (Bryan Little thought it ugly, Ison noble) and has the advantage of a large triangular grassland in front on one corner of which stands what looks like an oversize stone pillar-box and was, in fact, a watchman's hut. Under the Bath Plan of 1952 Norfolk Crescent would have contained a county college but like so many of these colleges envisaged in the 1945 Education Act it never materialized and the crescent has been subdivided into flats, a conversion of the north end gaining a Civic Trust Award in 1963 for a design which preserved the façade but developed a rather graceless back. The crescent is named after Nelson's home county and buildings on the north of the green which echo features of the crescent are called Nelson Place with next to it the modern Nelson Flats and beyond Nelson Villas, a little Victorian row with ground-floor bays. And if we continue past the villas we come out on the riverside path in sight of Mr Dredge's patent Victoria suspension bridge of 1836 with iron strap-work instead of chains and cables, the straps arranged in increasingly acute angles as the centre of the bridge is approached.

In much better condition, a good deal of it recently cleaned, and much better known because more visited and photographed, are the first and second phase Georgian developments west and north of the old city which start with Queen Square and go steeply up to a natural shelf on which are perched the Circus, Royal Crescent, Assembly Rooms, and surrounding streets. The approach from the bottom of Milsom Street, with its banks and posh shops is along Quiet Street, so called said Wood because the foreman had what was considered a remarkable phenomenon, a silent wife, and with Wood Street is architecturally interesting as it exhibits styles from four periods in a small space.

The north side of Quiet Street has a Victorian façade of 1871–2 provided by the City Architect, Charles Edward Davis, but opposite is the Auction Mart and Bazaar of 1824 which is being turned into a bank after having passed through several uses. More graceful than Davis's work opposite, it has highly stylized piers on the ground floor and framing the big three-light, first-floor window with an arched and traceried window above, flanked by wreaths. On either side of the main window are niches with statues of "Commerce" and "Genius"—Genius has wings and appears to be scratching her stomach—and perched on the roof-line appears another statue representing goodness-knows-what.

The north side of Wood Street, however, is a very plain no-nonsense early Palladian composition except for the later shop-fronts and contrasts with Northumberland Buildings opposite, an Adamesque work of 1778 by Baldwin, seven houses forming a single composition with the two ends set slightly forward and crowned with shallow pediments. Along the front runs the inevitable Vitruvian scroll with oval paterae above. The change in the basically Classical style, which had taken place in fifty years is remarkable and shows how misleading it is to lump together all eighteenth-century architecture and call it "Georgian".

Like many bits of Bath, Queen Square comes as a surprise as you cannot see it until you arrive—although even then it is masked in summer by the trees in the centre. Originally it had a formal garden in the middle and some people would like to see this restored so that the square can be appreciated as a whole. On the other hand the foliage and the rounded forms of the trees make a happy contrast with the straight lines and somewhat rigid forms of the buildings and the garden is a pleasant place to sit or lie in and eat sandwiches or read books or embrace (some people seem to manage all these at once) so there is quite a lot to be said for keeping it as it is. In any case the square is not a single composition and each side is different. The north is formed into a magnificent palace front with a giant Corinthian Order, rusticated ground floor, first-floor windows with alternating triangular and segmental pediments, and a great central pediment with stone vases, while the south side is a much plainer version with rustication and giant Order only in the central part.

The east side is a plain street of stepped houses—the common pattern of doorways with triangular pediment, first-floor windows with straight pediments, and a roof-line with cornice and parapet, but the west side got an entirely different treatment. Originally there were two double houses, each treated as a single composition, one at the top and one at the bottom, with a third one set back between them. The middle space was however filled in by two houses, again treated as one but this time in a neo-Grecian style by John Pinch in 1830; this, as we have seen, was taken over by the institution in 1932 and is now the reference library. The corner houses are quite elaborate with centre features of Ionic pilasters and a large pediment which, as the bottom house shows, was originally decorated with vases.

In the middle of the garden is an obelisk, now without its extremely tapered top which Wood claimed to prove was the proper shape for all obelisks. It was erected in 1738 for 'Beau' Nash in honour of the visit of Frederick, Prince of Wales, a man who was detested by his father, George II, and his mother, Queen Caroline, who said, "My dear first-born is the greatest ass and the greatest liar and the greatest *canaille* and the greatest beast in the whole world, and I heartily wish he were out of it." He in his turn opposed his father politically, socially and artistically, but died before him and it was his son who became George III. Some people liked 'Poor Fred' and he gave Nash a snuff-box, hence the monument. Nash pestered Alexander Pope to write an inscription until the poet, who did not want to do it at all, produced one so flat-footed that it was almost insulting. A copy can be seen on a plaque in the corner of the garden and reads—"In Memory of Honours conferr'd and in Gratitude for benefits bestow'd in this City by His Royal Highness Frederick Prince of Wales and his Royal Consort in the Year MDCCXXXVIII this obelisk is erected by Richard Nash, Esq."

Queen Square is a delightful spot and would be even more so if it could be freed of the traffic which introduces noise and fumes and makes access difficult to the garden, which is treated as a roundabout. It was a financial success for Wood, who lived in one of the houses—not, according to Ison's researches, on the north side, which bears a plaque, but at No. 9 on the south from which he could contemplate his masterpiece. He also built round the corner, in Chapel Row, a proprietary chapel, St Mary's, after some opposition from St Michael's in whose parish it lay. Such proprietary chapels were not uncommon (we have already mentioned the Octagon), and were in many ways business ventures, backed by private money and selling tickets, but Wood's main object was to provide a place of worship convenient for the inhabitants of the square. The chapel, a handsome Classical building, bought by the LMS Railway in 1871, was destroyed in about 1875 for road widening to give better access to the station but the site is now marked by a small structure found in the back garden of one of the houses.

In 1839 a further change was made by cutting a new road, Charlotte Street (named after Lady Rivers, wife of the Lord of the Manor, The Revd Sir Henry Rivers Bt), to the north-west corner of the square and at the top of this is an interesting trio of buildings near the entrance to a large car-park. These are a savings bank (1841, now a Register Office) in Italian Renaissance style, a Greek Revival Moravian (now Christian Science) church, and an extraordinary large Italian-style chapel of 1854, arcaded and with an octagonal lantern. Of less distinction but considerable utility are the public lavatories opposite by the entrance to a car-park.

Queen Square was built for houses and lodgings and it was in No. 13 at the west end of the south range, that Jane Austen with her mother, her sister Elizabeth, and brother Edward lodged in 1779 with a Mrs Bromley, "a fat woman in mourning". They liked it and when they were house-hunting in Bath in 1801 Jane wrote, "My Mother hankers after the Square dreadfully" although in fact they settled at No. 4 Sydney Place opposite the Sydney Gardens. Indeed as the tide of building swept northward the square became rather old-fashioned, which is why in *Persuasion*, written in 1816, Jane causes Miss Musgrove to remark, "Remember, Papa, if we do go [to Bath] we must be in a good situation—none of your Queen Squares for us!" Today it is occupied almost entirely by offices in addition to the library and much of the south range is a hotel but residence is coming back with the conversion of Nos 21 and 22 into "Prestigious Flats". The east end of the Frances Hotel was damaged in the air raids and was refaced after the war in facsimile—anything else would have been disastrous; compare it for instance with the most recent addition round the corner which, while not unpleasant in itself, sits very uneasily with its surroundings.

The east side of the square continues up the hill in Gay Street, named after Robert Gay a London surgeon who owned the land above, and it starts with the remarkable, bow-cornered house where the younger Wood is reputed to have lived although Ison has shown that there is no evidence for this. This bow is one end of a diagonal room which runs through the house with a bow at each end.

This elaborate and striking composition by the elder Wood has a curved Venetian window and the first-floor windows have Gibbs surrounds, heavy blocks threaded, as it were, on columns, in this case Ionic, and named after the architect James Gibbs (1682–1754) whose style was basically English Baroque. The doorway on to Gay Street carries a grotesque mask or satyr head, and the whole design shows that Wood was not so firmly wedded to Palladianism that he could not occasionally indulge in a *jeu d'esprit*.

A little further up on the left is a road leading to Queen's Parade on one side (mostly flats) and the Royal Victoria Park on the other; this entrance was widened in the mid-nineteenth century to improve access to the park and two houses in Gay Street were knocked down so that the monumental return façade with its pediment dates from the later period. The main road then curves round to the right into George Street but Gay Street continues up the hill, entering the second phase of building. George Street was built in the 1760s and although its south side up to Milsom Street received a good deal of alteration in the nineteenth century, mainly to accommodate shops, the north side, set up on a broad, high platform is a good example of the style of the period, particularly in Edgar Buildings whose central pedimented feature forms a satisfactory eye-stopper to Milsom Street. Alongside Edgar Buildings narrow, steep Bartlett Street leads up past more shops and an antique market to Alfred Street and the Assembly Rooms, while opposite, beyond the two big late-Victorian banks which guard the top of Milsom Street is the old post office conveniently sited by one of Bath's major coaching inns, York House.

At York House (now the Royal York Hotel) we come to the traffic lights which control the meeting of George Street with three other roads. Straight ahead runs the main London Road with Bladud Buildings (shops) and the long sweep of the slightly later Paragon (Atwood, 1768), its backside propped up by a masonry cliff. On the opposite side of the street to the Paragon, in what is called the Vineyards, is the chapel and manse built in 1765 in the Gothick style for the Countess of Huntingdon's Connection. It later became a Presbyterian chapel until the Presbyterians and Congregationalists combined to become the United Reformed Church. A little further along and up some steps is the previous Catholic Apostolic church built in a Norman style in 1840 and now serving as Kingdom Hall for the Jehovah's Witnesses. Beyond that rears up the dominating bulk of the nineteenth century one-time Walcot Schools.

To the left at the traffic lights the road leads up to Lansdown Road via the Belvedere, with shops and pubs tailing off into residential buildings, and to the right Broad Street drops steeply down past the Victorian YMCA (1860 with a modern extension at the back), past the fine front of King Edward's Grammar School (Jelly, 1752) which is now the junior school as the rest moved to new premises in North Road after the war, and a miscellaneous collection of shops housed in early eighteenth-century buildings, to take one down to the High Street. Broad Street is not very wide and may possibly have got its name from the making of broadcloth, woollen manufacturing being the mainstay of Bath's late medieval economy. Inside a shop at the bottom, No. 7, is a bit of an Elizabethan house with stone-mullioned window and a date MB 1640 referring to a lease of the premises to one Mary Barber. It was near here, at No. 4, that Mr James Heath had his Bath Chair Works in the nineteenth century (Dallimore, *Exploring Bath*).

Back in Gay Street, which is now mostly offices, and toiling upwards, we find a piebald effect as at one time the door surrounds were painted black, the stone itself has blackened, and the houses are being cleaned individually so that cleaned and uncleaned are in juxtaposition. The frontages are standard with some individuality being shown in doorway treatment, but No. 8 is sufficiently showy to have been nicknamed 'the carved house'. It has swags and Corinthian pilasters and a window pediment and blind balustrading, and it was the home of Mrs Piozzi who in her days as Mrs Thrale was Dr Johnson's dearest friend, to the annoyance of Boswell. Indeed, when Mr Thrale died in 1781 the gossip was that his widow would marry Johnson, but she confounded rumour by marrying Gabriele Piozzi the Italian Roman Catholic musician introduced to her by her friend Fanny Burney and engaged by Mrs Thrale to teach singing to her daughter Queenie.

When the possibility of the marriage was in the air Johnson wrote to her imploring her to give up this "ignominious marriage" and saying that she was "the first of human kind". When she did not he would have nothing further to do with her and burnt her letters—she, on her part, published his! She married Piozzi in 1784—twice—first in a Roman Catholic cere- mony in London and then at St James's, Bath.

Mrs Thrale had visited Bath in 1776 with Queenie, Dr Johnson, and Boswell; the Thrales and Fanny Burney were there again in 1780; Mrs Thrale and Queenie visited once more in 1783, and the next year the widow was "awaiting Piozzi at Bath". The Piozzis lived mainly at Brynbella the house they built in North Wales, spending most winters at Bath, and it appears that she did not take the house in Gay Street until 1816, some years after Piozzi's death in 1809, and after she had raised some money by selling the contents of Thrale's house at Stretham Park. She lived there until her death at Clifton in 1822 at the age of eighty, always lively and a leader of society. On her eightieth birthday she gave a ball at the Assembly Rooms for six to seven hundred guests and led off the dancing with her adopted son, Sir John Salusbury, Piozzi's nephew, and continued to dance "with astonishing elasticity" until early in the morning.

Gay Street appears to be heading for a group of trees, of which more later, and in no way prepares you for the sudden surprise of breasting the hill and finding yourself in Bath's most remark- able architectural composition the Circus (1754–8), a unique design which the irascible Matthew Bramble in Smollett's

Humphrey Clinker (1771) called "a pretty bauble, contrived for
shew, and looks like Vespasian's amphitheatre turned outside
in". He didn't like it—"If we consider it from the point of view of
magnificence, the great number of small doors, the inconsiderable height of the different orders, the affected ornaments of the
architrave, which are both childish and misplaced, and the
areas projecting into the street surrounded by iron railings,
destroy a good part of the effect upon the eye"—and he would
have preferred the areas to be covered with an arcade which
would have kept the sedan-chairs and chairmen out of the rain
"which was almost continual" and would have made the place
"more magnificent and striking".

He also pointed out that it was inconveniently distant from
"all the markets, baths, and places of entertainment" (the
Upper Rooms had not then been built) and that the entrance
from Gay Street was slippery and dangerous. It was all, he said,
part of the "rage for building" which had "laid hold on such a
number of adventurers that one sees new houses starting up in
every out-let and every corner of Bath; contrived without judgement, and stuck together with so little regard for plan and
propriety, that the different lines of the new rows and buildings
interfere with, and intersect one another in different angles of
conjunction. They look like the wreck of streets and squares
disjointed by an earthquake."

Strong words, and with some basis of fact, as witness the
number of summer visitors poring in puzzlement over street
maps, but it is this haphazardness which gives Bath much of its
charm by introducing elements of contrast and surprise.
Smollett realized that there could be other points of view and
in the same novel Lydia Melford writes to a friend (the whole
novel is in letters)—"The Squares, the Circus, and the Parades,
put you in mind of the sumptuous palaces represented in prints
and pictures; and the new buildings such as Princes-row,
Harlequin's row [now the Vineyards], Bladud's-row, and twenty
other rows, look like so many enchanted castles raised on
hanging terraces"—although this view seems to be coloured
more by the early Gothic novel than by any appreciation of
Palladianism. The Classicism of Bath was also not to be taste
of the Picturesque school of the end of the century and
Catherine Morland in Jane Austen's *Northanger Abbey* (1801)
was so well instructed in this by her friends the Tilneys that
"when they got to the top of Beechen Cliff she voluntarily

rejected the whole city of Bath as unworthy to make part of a landscape".

Smollett's reference to "Vespasian's amphitheatre" was a shrewd one, for Wood had indeed taken the superimposed Orders of the outside of the Colosseum and used them on the inside of the Circus—which is, of course, very much smaller, and round instead of oval. The decorative enrichment of the surface which Bramble thought "affected" and which is particularly evident on the ground floor, gives something of interest to be seen close to, while the repeating pattern of double attached columns and the continuous bands of entablatures and cornice create a satisfying and complete composition when viewed from further away—a design with a dual purpose which is lacking in so many modern buildings which may be impressive at a distance (if such a distance exists) but at close quarters present nothing more interesting to the eye than a blank sheet of glass or slab of unadorned concrete. The ground-floor Order is Doric and its frieze is not only decorated with triglyphs but in the spaces, or metopes, between these, are carved over three hundred emblems of industry, science and the arts—few of them repeated. The second, Ionic, storey has a plain frieze, as has the third, the Corinthian, although here the capitals are linked by garlands to blank-eyed female heads. The parapet is crowned with stone acorns, the food of swine, put there by Wood to commemorate the legend of Bladud in which he firmly believed.

The three entrances to the Circus are spaced equally so that on coming in you are faced with a segment of building and the sense of enclosure is immediate. In fact if the original scheme had been carried out the eye would first have been attracted to a statue of George II in the centre of the Circus, and, as it was actually built, to the three lampholders round a central covered reservoir which supplied water to the houses. Today the eye is immediately attracted to a group of huge and magnificent plane trees rising out of a grassy disc. Some people would like to get rid of these trees on the grounds that they were not originally intended, that they are out of scale with the buildings, and that they obstruct the view of the architecture. Some, more extreme, argue that Town is Town, Country is Country, and that there should be no mixing of organic and inorganic forms—which would seem to argue for the removal of people as well. Unfortunately for the purists the trees are greatly admired, even loved, and provide a much more pleasant outlook from the houses than would be given by an expanse of paving which, anyway, would probably end up as a car-park!

Changes which can be seen in many other parts of Georgian Bath have taken place in the windows, most of which have had their glazing bars replaced by big blank sheets of plate glass and on the first floor have been lengthened downwards. More striking, though less obvious, are the changes in function for these were originally family houses leased sometimes on a long term but more frequently for the season, some once occupied by famous people—Nos 7 and 8, William Pitt, Earl of Chatham; 13, now a dental practice, where Dr Livingstone stayed in 1864; 14, Clive of India; 17, Thomas Gainsborough, and 22, Major André, who negotiated with the American traitor Benedict Arnold and was caught and hanged as a spy by the Americans in 1789. Today, however, most of the houses are divided into flats, many of them occupied by young people. In fact we have now entered what might be called Flatlandia for most of the tall houses of this Walcot New Town area have been subdivided, sometimes in a rather bizarre fashion, and by the doorways will be found rows of bellpushes, and even this is not the whole story for numbers of flats are shared by groups of young people—one bellpush, not in the Circus, had six names opposite it.

Conversion is not easy and some of these flats are not particularly convenient, although others are rather splendid. After all, these houses were built without electricity or gas, upstairs piped water, bathrooms, or, in many cases WCs, and they were heated by coal fires, so that to provide separate entrances, kitchens, lavatories, and bathrooms on each floor calls for a good deal of ingenuity, although more recent conversion to what the selling agents like to call "prestigious apartments" is made easier by gutting the building and rebuilding behind the original façade. Moreover, subdivision of Georgian rooms destroys their proportions and creates units which tend to be too high for their width. On the other hand, if a room is left as originally built it is expensive to heat. There are, however, environmental compensations in living in a Georgian street and it is possible to develop a positive affection for eccentricities of layout. In the newer conversions or in updated ones the inhabitants can telecommunicate with visitors, who may be seen shouting into a metal box, but in most they cannot and top-dwellers face weary journeys down flights of stairs to make contact, journeys which are also required for collecting post and milk. Some of the inhabitants, particular of the roomier flats, have been there for a long time but a large number are transients—students, new arrivals, young families waiting until they can get a house, and so on. Most of the alterations are internal but one external change which was common in the past was cutting out parts of the parapet to let light, air, and a view through to the attic-dwellers and more recent conservation-minded repairs to these have given the inhabitants a rather blank outlook.

The Circus had been designed by the elder John Wood but he died shortly after it was started and it was finished by his son. The father had intended to build a couple of short streets off it terminated by "a fine building" but his son saw the possibilities of a larger development. Leading westward he built Brock Street (1767), a rather varied composition due to later alterations and additions but with some pleasant Venetian windows and a good rehabilitation and flat conversion at the corner of Upper Church Street of the house where once lived, according to a plaque, John Christopher Smith, "Handel's friend and secretary". Smith was the son of an old university friend of Handel's, Johann Christopher Schmidt, and was five years old when Handel in one of his German tours found the father in reduced circumstances and brought the family to England, making Schmidt his assistant. The boy was brought up by Handel, studied music, and, with his name Anglicized, succeeded his father as Handel's secretary, copyist, and, after Handel started to go blind in 1751, his amanuensis.

On the north side of Brock Street is Margaret's Buildings, short and broad and for walking only. Set with flower tubs and a seat, flanked by buildings of varying heights, including some post-war reconstruction, this very pleasant backwater has a grace and humanity about it, a fine urban feel, and provides much of what you need if you live in a local flat—wine bar, laundrette, provision shops, bookshop, newsagent's and tobacconist, restaurant, and so on. It leads through to Catherine Place (*c.* 1780), an oblong which runs uphill for we are now off the shelf, and with another of these central gardens with trees and shrubs. It is in the usual Bath style of the period but the central building on the north side, which is actually in Rivers Street, is marked by Venetian windows and a triangular pediment. It all has a pleasant atmosphere of intimacy and seclusion and is, of course, mostly inhabited by flat-dwellers.

Royal Crescent. A general view from Victoria Park of the crescent designed by John Wood the Younger in 1767–74.

Royal Crescent. Detail of the centre to show the giant Ionic order and plain face of the building.

Margaret's Buildings, which takes its name from an adjacent chapel called after Mrs Margaret Garrard, Lady of the Manor.

Upper Assembly Rooms (the New Rooms), 1769–71 by the younger Wood after Adam's plans had been rejected. This is the tea-room.

Lampard's Buildings—
post-war flats replacing
Georgian streets.

Somerset Place, *c.* 1790 by
John Eveleigh; with the
only big segmental
pediment in Bath.

Lansdown Crescent, 1789–92 by Palmer.

(Below left) Lansdown Crescent. Detail, showing ground-floor
rustication and fine ironwork. *(Below right)* Beckford's Bridge. An
addition by William Beckford to connect his two houses in
Lansdown Crescent, it is topped by metal palms in urns.

Camden Crescent, *c.* 1788 by John Eveleigh. This was the centre feature but is actually off-centre as one end of the crescent was never built.

Camden Crescent. Doorway showing the Camden badge, an elephant.

(Above left) St Stephen's Church, 1840–5 by James Wilson. *(Above right)* Kingswood School, neo-Gothic of 1852 by James Wilson.

Kingswood School. General view of the front.

Beckford's Tower, 1825–6
by Henry Edmund
Goodridge.

Beckford's tombstone,
near his tower.

Victoria Obelisk, Royal Victoria Park, 1837, by George Philip Manners.

Locksbrook Cemetery Chapel. The chapel, rising out of a forest of tombstones, is of 1861–2 by Charles Edward Davis.

Brock Street appears to be heading for a range of houses called Marlborough Buildings but these were not erected until some time later and originally it would have appeared to be going nowhere. In fact it takes us to one of those Bath surprises, probably the greatest, for as we come to the apparent end and turn the corner, there suddenly bursts on the eye the magnificent sweep of the Royal Crescent which the younger Wood built between 1767 and 1774. Cobbled roadway, broad flagged promenade of Pennant sandstone, a massive march of a hundred and fourteen giant Ionic attached columns with plain frieze, modillioned cornice and balustraded parapet. Open areas, some made bright with flowers in summer, and good ironwork. The only things which mark the centre which is now a hotel are a doubling of columns and the use of a round-headed window and this lack of strong emphasis is proper as the optical centre depends on where you are standing. Below is a big open grassy space and beyond that a row of trees along Victoria Park cuts off a sight of the city. Once again the glazing bars have gone, which is a pity, and first-floor windows have been lengthened. To see what it was originally like look at No. 1 which has been restored by the Bath Preservation Trust and pay to go inside to see what one of the houses would have been like for the rooms have been furnished with furniture and decorations of the eighteenth century.

No. 1 was started in 1767 and leased in 1764 to Thomas Brock, Wood's father-in-law who partnered him in the venture, but the first occupier noted in the rate books was a Mr Henry Sandford in 1778. In 1796 the local paper reported that the Duke of York, second of the thirteen children of George III, had "engaged the first house in the Crescent, late Mr. Sandford's", but from 1796 to 1800 the ratepayer was Henry Milsom and the Duke was at No. 16. In later years the place became a rather run-down lodging-house and in 1967 it was bought by Mr Bernard Cayzer and presented with an endowment to the Preservation Trust. This information is in a well-illustrated booklet which can be bought at the door and also gives details of the rooms and their contents.

In No. 17 lived, in his later years, Sir Isaac Pitman who came to Bath as a penurious young teacher and in 1844 published his little grey fourpenny book on Stenographic Sound-Hand explaining the system of shorthand which was to bring him fame and fortune. He was knighted in 1894 and died at No. 17 in

1896. His house is now five flats. No. 11 bears a plaque recording that this was the house from which Elizabeth Linley eloped with the young Richard Brinsley Sheridan. It is a tangled tale and the truth of it uncertain. Elizabeth, a beautiful girl of seventeen and a charming singer, loved and admired by all, was the daughter of Thomas Linley, himself a fine musician as well as an able organizer and director of music at the Assembly Rooms. For some time they lived at 1 Pierrepont Place which is now called Linley House and is the headquarters of the Bath Festival. Undoubtedly he exploited his young daughter, but what shocked society was his choice of a wealthy old man of sixty called Long to be her husband. Elizabeth at first obeyed her father but eventually could bear the prospect no longer and asked Long to release her from the engagement, which, to his great credit, he did. In 1771 Sheridan came to Bath to join his father and in the following year eloped with Elizabeth, took her to the Continent, possibly went through a form of marriage which would have been invalid as they were both under age, and lodged her with nuns at Lille, claiming that he had done so to rescue her from the unwelcome attentions of a married man, Captain Matthews.

Matthews denied the charge—there is no clear evidence that it was true—and in a notice inserted in the *Bath Chronicle* called Sheridan "a liar and treacherous scoundrel". Linley brought Elizabeth back and Sheridan returned to fight one duel with Matthews in London and a second near Bath, winning the first, which gained him an apology, and losing the second which ended with Sheridan on the ground and Matthews stabbing at him with a broken sword. The following year Sheridan married Elizabeth.

The marriage was a happy one and he was grief-stricken at her death in 1792 at Hotwells, Bristol, yet in 1795 he was remarried to the daughter of the Dean of Winchester who had the remarkably theatrical name of Esther Ogle. His London career as a playwright, manager of Drury Lane, politician, and confidential adviser to the Prince of Wales who, in true Hanoverian fashion, was at odds with his father, was brilliant, but in his last years a disastrous fire at Drury Lane, the loss of his seat in Parliament, the illness of his second wife, financial difficulties, and hard drinking affected his health and he died in 1816. Horrifying tales were told of his final poverty but there were strenuous denials from friends and family and it is difficult to decide the truth. He was given a magnificent funeral in Westminster Abbey. Although his time at Bath was brief he has left us what is perhaps the best-known of descriptions of social life in the city in *The Rivals* (1775) which was initially a flop and only succeeded after revision and re-casting.

The other road out of the Circus is Bennett Street which leads past the Upper Assembly Rooms. Robert Adam produced plans for assembly rooms on this site but they would have been too costly to build and a less ambitious scheme by the younger Wood was accepted in their place. Money was raised by a tontine subscription, that is one in which as the subscribers die their shares are distributed amongst the survivors, and in 1769 the foundation stone was laid. In 1771 the rooms were opened with a "Grand Ridotto". Twelve hundred tickets were sold at a guinea each which gave entrance for one gentleman and two ladies and there were half-guinea tickets for unaccompanied gentlemen. Linley directed the music and Elizabeth sang. Sheridan had a half-guinea ticket and published a poem about the occasion in the local paper—

> Two rooms were first opened—the long and the round one
> (These Hogstyegon names only serve to confound one)
> Both splendidly lit with the new chandeliers
> With drops hanging down like the bobs at Peg's ears

"The long" (over 100 feet) was the ballroom, resplendent with Corinthian pillars and pilasters, plasterwork, chandeliers, orchestra gallery, and seven marble chimney-pieces. With the fires going and hundreds of sweating bodies dancing the atmosphere must have been shattering—no wonder Matthew Bramble fainted and Philip Thicknesse wrote in his *New Prose Bath Guide* (1778), "We really think that the Wit of Man could not contrive a more certain Method to defeat the Efficacy of all Medicine, or endanger the Lives of those who come to Bath for their Health, than attending a Dress Ball in full season." "The round" was in fact an octagon ("Hogstyegon"?) which formed the card room and which linked the ballroom to a parallel tea-room, sixty feet long, also splendidly decorated and chandeliered. A later addition at the back, in 1777, was another card-room, this time rectangular. From the beginning there were separate ladies' and gentlemen's water-closets, and along the Bennett Street side of the ballroom was a long arcade, later glassed in, as a shelter for chairs and chairmen.

There were two separate MCs for Upper and Lower Rooms, the first for the Upper being Captain Wade, a nephew of the Field Marshal, but programmes were arranged so that major events did not clash. The Upper Rooms, however, developed as the venue for musical events and under Linley, Herschel, and his successor the Italian Rauzzini, Director of Public Concerts from 1780 to 1810, these became an outstanding feature of Bath social life. This was important for the rooms as public balls became less well attended towards the end of the century, their place being taken by private parties, or "routs", although people might go on to the rooms for the second, informal part of the evening. In 1801 Jane Austen wrote that "After tea we cheered up; the breaking up of private parties sent some scores more to the Ball, and tho' it was shockingly and inhumanly thin for this place, there were people enough I suppose to have made five or six very pretty Basingstoke assemblies." The dances started at 6 o'clock and "tea" was halfway through the evening. The formal minuets were danced in hooped skirts which were not suitable for the more energetic "country dances" and Wade's Rules of 1771 required that "Ladies who choose to pull their hoops off will be assisted by proper servants in an apartment for that purpose", but by the nineties hoops were going out of fashion.

In the nineteenth century the rooms continued to be an important part of Bath's social and artistic life and saw such eminent performers as Johann Strauss, Liszt, Madame Patti, Rubinstein, and Charles Dickens (who disliked Bath audiences), but after the First World War they lost their eminence and became a cinema and warehouse. In 1926 the "cinema that is different" was showing such films as *The Only Way* with Sir John Martin Harvey and *The Tower of Lies* with Norma Shearer and Lon Chaney, and was experimenting with a Popular Dance each Saturday from 8–11.30 at a cost of 2s. (10p), "Right of admission strictly reserved"; they also staged the touring version of the Wembley Empire Exhibition. In 1925 the Alliance of Honour showed a film on sex—for women only. There were various proposed projects for their use but eventually in 1931 they were restored by the National Trust and reopened in 1938 by the Duchess of Kent. The rooms were back in glory and it was a bitter blow when incendiary bombs gutted their interior in the 1942 air raids. For fifteen years they lay forlorn until in 1957 the National Trust was able to set in motion another restoration by Sir Albert Richardson with a new décor by Oliver Messel. The magnificent glass chandeliers are the originals, having been stored in a local stone quarry during the war. Reopened in 1963, one of its new features was a museum of costume of international importance. A great attraction for visitors it is also a centre of research and now has a Costume and Fashion Research Centre at No. 4 the Circus where the reference library and collection is available for use by members of the public.

The interior of the rooms was, and is, magnificent, but the outside is almost severe with plain walls, first-floor windows with architraves and triangular pediments, roof-line with modillioned cornice and balustrading, and rectangular chimney-stacks. The best front is towards Alfred Street on the south side, with projecting porches at each end of the tea-room, a view of the apse formed by the back of the old card room, and the pedimented new card room. Against the end of the tea-room is a pleasant arcaded passageway.

The opposite side of Alfred Street is in two blocks. One got the 'palace' treatment and the other is a straightforward Georgian range, altered at one end for shop-fronts, including a restaurant with anachronistically-styled leaded lights, and ending with the elaborate doorway of No. 14 which has a head of King Alfred flanked by Classical vases above a highly decorated architrave.

This house has a variety of fine ironwork with a lampholder, windlass, and link extinguishers. Links were torches of pitch and tow carried by link-boys to light people through the streets at night and the sight of sedan-chairs and groups on foot streaming away from the rooms after a ball, each preceded by the fiery glow of a link, must have been remarkable. It also gave employment, if poorly paid, to a lot of youngsters, and it reminds us that Bath society in the eighteenth century generated a great deal of work for household and inn servants, chairmen, coachmen, ostlers, baths and Pump Room and Assembly Room attendants, coachbuilders, furniture-makers and repairers, tailors and dressmakers, shopkeepers, hairdressers and wig-makers, gardeners, printers and bookbinders, pastrycooks, builders, glaziers, plumbers, carpenters, stonemasons, and the like, as well as hordes of beggars, prostitutes ("the nymphs of Avon Street") and card-sharpers. There was also plenty of work for doctors, surgeons, nurses, and apothecaries, as well as quacks. A great deal of what was required was made in Bath itself which in addition was a major market for local farm produce. John

Wood in his advertising map of 1735 was careful to point out that "It is supply'd with best Provisions of all kinds, and that in great Plenty; and on terms more easy than perhaps in most places in the Kingdom."

Alfred Street comes out into Oxford Row where early Palladian houses step upwards to Lansdown, all very solid and agreeable, with one exception—the serpentine porch added to the side of No. 1 Belmont which in its plasticity and delicate ornament illustrates once more, and with great clarity, the difference between mid- and late-eighteenth-century style. At this point we can turn uphill past the end of Bennett Street and turn back round an awkward corner for vehicles into the end of Julian Road which is here called Montpellier, a short Georgian range with Venetian windows—made into flats, of course. And then Christchurch, a boxy building in the Gothic style of 1798 by John Palmer with an apse (which Pevsner for reasons of his own calls "awful") added in 1886; interesting to see that Palmer, like so many of the later generation of architects was prepared to design in both Classical and Gothic styles—although his Gothic is not very correct. The church had no pew rents, being intended for the poor, and the land was given by Lord Rivers. Nearby is Rivers Street, going off at a sharp angle and marking the limit of the first phase of building. It is tall and black (with an occasional face-wash) with pedimented and pillared doorways, mostly painted black. No. 18 has a more elaborate doorway decorated with a head—all Georgian street details are not identical and it is rather fun to spot the oddities (even Queen Square has some Baroque doorways). It goes without saying that most of the houses have been turned into flats!

South off Rivers Street and focussing on the rooms is Russell Street, built in 1773, stepped ranks in the usual pattern of the period and again mostly flats. Between it and the Circus there curves round Circus Place which contained the stables, or mews—a strange word which originally meant places for keeping hawks, mew coming from the Latin *mutare*, to change, referring to moulting, and it was only after the Royal Mews in London were turned into stables that the name became generally applied to places where horses and carriages were kept. Appropriately, part of the old stabling has been adapted to house an excellent carriage museum whose proprietors, in summer, also run a horse and open carriage in which visitors can go cloppity-rumble round the upper town.

Back at Montpellier and moving into Julian Road two streets, Morford Street and Ballance Street, rise steeply uphill through an area which became very run-down in the nineteenth century, got a small council housing development in 1902, and was scheduled as a Comprehensive Development Area in the 1953 Plan so that in due time the old walls came down and the new ones went up to create large-scale (some say out-of-scale) apartment blocks—Ballance Street flats and Lampard's Buildings, of which the latter is perhaps more human in its proportions. There is also a quite nice little secluded private development including and extending an old chapel. In later years planning attitudes changed, Government grants became available and more liberal, and one side of the top of Morford Street was spared and rehabilitated to make an interesting contrast. Down on the opposite side of Julian Road is a collection of shops in Victorian buildings erected on the ends of the back gardens of the Rivers Street houses—a tobacconist and newsagent, grocer's, hardware stores, shoe repairers, electrical shop, baker—convenience goods for all the people living around.

In the midst of all this busy redevelopment there sat a rather plain looking stone building whose future aroused a great deal of controversy. This was because it had been built in 1777 as a Real (Royal) Tennis court although it had been much altered in 1825 when it became a barley store for a brewery. On the other hand no one had played any Real Tennis there for a long time and if it was restored to its original use it was unlikely that many people would avail themselves of its facilities—preferring as we do to play squash or badminton or lawn tennis, or watch other people doing it on the television. However, a group of enthusiasts had in 1969 acquired the contents of Mr Bowler's defunct bottling plant and metalwork shop in the lower town and were looking for somewhere suitable to exhibit it, with the result that the tennis court is now the Camden Works Museum, and very good it is too, although it won't tell you much about Real Tennis. In 1981 it very properly got a Special Award for Enterprise in the Museum of the Year awards.

A little further west Burlington Street, stepped and flatted, leads up to a tiny triangle of green and the imposing façade of Portland Place set on a high platform, started about 1786 (Ison) and very plain except for the centre feature, now a private school, which has rusticated quoins, rusticated blocks round the doorway, and a large triangular pediment breaking the roof line. Up against the west end is Portland Lodge in Victorian Gothic and here we enter into a region where there is a good deal of Victorian and inter-war building. Near the bottom of Burlington Street is the Roman Catholic Church of Our Lady, opened by Cardinal Manning in 1881, Victorian Gothic by Dunn and Hansom, but without the intended extension to provide a tower and spire, and a bit further west the 1962–4 new building with a school behind, replacing the bombed St Andrew's designed by Sir Gilbert Scott and opened in 1873 when it took over from Margaret's Chapel. In the wall by the front, carved lettering records that this was the site of the Countess of Huntingdon's cemetery of 1765. We have now arrived at a green triangle where River Street also comes in and here, risen from the wartime ashes, is Phoenix House, a not unpleasant, if unremarkable, block of flats.

Along the north side of the green we find Northampton Street going up the hill with Pennant paving not improved by light-coloured pointing, round-headed doorways, houses of brick faced with Bath stone, and some pleasant refurbishment taking us up into nineteenth-century Italianate. A little further west, however, returns us to Georgian, for here is St James's Street with shops and a post office leading us into St James's Square designed in the 1790s by Palmer, with a central garden now dominated by trees, and the houses on each side ranged up the hill like dominoes, the centre ones crowned with triangular pediments. The top and bottom ranges have bows at each end flanked by Corinthian pilasters and with first-floor Venetian windows and a centre feature with four similar pilasters and a triangular pediment. It is all very agreeable, although opinions can differ—Bryan Little thought it "a work of the utmost breeding and charm", Peter Smithson said it was "dull".

The nicest bit, however, is one of those little tucked-away Bath backwater surprises. In the St James Street entrance is an opening with a big triangular pediment filled with ironwork tracery painted white—a nineteenth-century feature but still very attractive—and this leads through into a short dog-legged, glass-roofed, flagged corridor with some nice woodwork. At the time of writing it has a laundrette and an architect's office. This is not the end, however, for it leads into a pleasant open paved space with the backs of houses on one side and a complete house, No. 6 St James's Place, at the end. Nothing remarkable in the way of architecture, but a thoroughly pleasant, quiet little spot.

Then out under a simple wooden arch with keystone and on our left is No. 35 to which Walter Savage Landor moved in 1846 after a row with his landlady at No. 42. After another row he moved to 3 River Street in 1849.

Landor lived under four monarchs from George III to Victoria for he was born in 1775 and died in 1864 at the age of 89. He had something of a literary reputation for prose and poetry during his lifetime, although in a rather limited circle, but his work is little known today and perhaps the best-known lines are in the little poem written when he was leaving Bath and called, quite simply, "Finis".

> I strove with none, for none was worth my strife.
> Nature I loved and, after Nature, Art:
> I warm'd my hands before the fire of life;
> It sinks, and I am ready to depart.

The first line must have caused some wry smiles for he was quarrelsome, opinionated and given to brief rages, and although he could be charming and created lifelong friendships he also made many enemies. He professed republicanism and was rusticated from Oxford for firing a gun at the windows, fortunately shuttered, of a Tory student; in 1808 he joined a volunteer force in Spain fighting, rather inefficiently, against the French in the Peninsular War, but quarrelled with the Spanish; in the 1820s he was expelled from Florence for his attitude to the authorities. He first met his wife at a ball in Bath in 1811 when he characteristically remarked, "That's the nicest girl in the room and I'll marry her"—which he did the same year. He was not an easy man to live with and in 1835, when he was sixty, he quarrelled with his wife at their villa in Fiesole outside Florence and left her, settling by himself in Bath, in 1838. And there he might have ended his days but for the curious episode involving two ladies. For some reason he had given one of them £100 and she had given half to the other who, however, made some unpleasant remarks about the reasons for the original gift. Landor published a bit of satirical poetry about this and had to apologize but went on to publish another which involved him in a libel suit which cost him £1,000 and as he had settled most of the income from his Welsh estate on his wife and children he was now financially dependent on his family and left Bath for the Florence villa in 1859. Here, to the annoyance of his family, he kept wandering off into Florence where in 1864 he died in a room which friends had obtained for him. In the last years his mind was going but people who visited him still found him impressive and charming.

Landor was one of the few literary figures who actually loved Bath—Jane Austen, who is most often associated with the city, disliked it, Smollett hated it, Sheridan ridiculed it, Dickens thought it sad, Walpole was only too glad to get away from it—but Landor also loved Florence and did something of a disservice to the English city by calling it England's Florence. It is not, it is unique, it is Bath—as the *Bath Chronicle* indignantly declared when on a visit in 1830 Leopold, later King of the Belgians, complimented it on being like an Italian city. Swinburne, who was given to gestures, once literally knelt at Landor's feet and he took up the Florence theme in a gooey poem which seems to suggest that Bath is dead and embalmed.

> Like a queen enchanted who may not laugh or weep,
> Glad at heart and guarded from change and care like ours,
> Girt about by beauty by days and nights that creep
> Soft as breathless ripples that softly shoreward sweep,
> Lies the lovely city whose grace no grief deflowers.
> Age and grey forgetfulness, time that shifts and veers,
> Touch not thee, our fairest, whose charm no rival nears,
> Hailed as England's Florence of one whose praise gives grace,
> Landor, once thy lover, a name that love reveres:
> Dawn and noon and sunset are one before they face.

The exits from the square are at the corners and all angled and the top ones lead us into Park Street Mews and the bottom of Park Street, another of those steep, tall-sided, late Georgian thoroughfares with standard elevations and subsequent subdivision into flats. Here the 1790s development took a leap up the steepening slope to string a couple of crescents along the contour line—Somerset Place (1790 by Eveleigh) and Lansdown Crescent (1789–92 by Palmer). To get to it, however, you go up Cavendish Road, with High Common, now a golf course, on your left and on your right a group of later buildings—Cavendish Place (1808–18) and Cavendish Crescent (*c.* 1817) both designed by John Pinch (1770–1827) who started as a builder, went bankrupt soon after 1800, and then built up a very successful business as architect and surveyor. Like many of the new men he was prepared to design in Classical or Gothic according to his client's wishes and was responsible for the very satisfactory Perpendicular of St Mary's, Bathwick (1814–20).

Cavendish Place introduces a new and attractive feature found elsewhere in Pinch's work and in one or two other ranges of the period, the linking of cornices by swept curves so that the moulding is continuous instead of discrete as in the earlier uphill terraces. This is also here applied to the band of Vitruvian scroll above the first-floor windows, although it breaks down round the corner in Park Street. Another notable new feature is the line of first-floor balconies and verandas (balconies on the earlier buildings are usually later additions). The ground floor is rusticated and the doorways are round-headed, another feature of the period. The corner is satisfyingly bowed and the whole composition is attractive, particularly when viewed in the light of a westering sun. Cavendish Crescent is simpler, although window details are similar, and being tucked away behind trees and a pleasant little garden makes less impact.

Just beyond the crescent Pinch designed a double villa, Winifred's Dale, with a pair of round-headed doorways under a bow-fronted canopy supported by Doric pillars and a frieze with triglyphs, and on each side a bow up the full height of the house—an early nineteenth-century (1817) semi on a grand scale. Pinch's other piece of work in the area, Sion Hill Place (c. 1818–20) is tucked away in a pleasantly secluded spot to the north-west. Rusticated ground floor and round-headed door-ways again, with Vitruvian scroll and more balconies, and bows like half-drums at each end of the range. Tacked on one end, with its richly decorated front facing west, is a house, reputedly by the elder Wood, which was moved in the 1940s from Chippenham High Street, and is now used as a boarding-house for Kingswood School.

Of a striking if rather grim Grecian design is Doric House at the top of Cavendish Road, designed in 1810 by J. M. Gandy (1771–1843), a pupil of the great Soane. It was a house and picture gallery for the artist Thomas Barker, a Welsh boy from Pontypool who came to Bath when he was thirteen and bene-fited from the patronage of Charles Spackman, a prosperous coach-builder, who sent him to study in Rome. Barker was popular in his time and his most celebrated painting, *The Woodman* sold for the then large sum of 500 guineas. His brother Benjamin and his brother's son, Thomas Jones Barker, were also successful artists in their day. The house frontage on to the road has a blank wall with a row of massive giant Greek

Doric columns before it and a top storey with windows flanked by slender columns, again Doric. Between is a modillioned cornice and above a plain one. A low parapet is decorated with antifixae, ornamental blocks which in Greek buildings served to conceal the ends of tiles.

Neither of the top crescents has the stunning effect of the Royal. Pleasant they are, but the lighter modelling is not really suited to a broad sweep of building facing open space and Somerset Place is the more successful mainly because it is shorter and has a much stronger central feature which, with its open-topped curved pediment, decorated with carved drapery and modillions, and topped with a stone urn, is unique in Bath. Below it the first-floor windows flank a niche below garlands and a slightly awkward broken pediment (broken in the sense that the bottom line has a gap in the middle). The paired central doorways have, like all the others, a Gibbs surround with a flat pediment on consoles but here the keystones are carved in icicle form to make shadowy faces while the rest are leafy. The wall surface is all smooth and windows away from the centre are without architraves. The crescent falls away at both ends and the continuous cornice and plat-band, a broad projecting plain band above the ground floor, rise gently upwards and then down while the tops and bottoms of window and door openings remain horizontal, which gives a slightly peculiar, though not un-pleasing, effect. The windows are stepped in groups of three. Somerset Place suffered badly during the wartime bombing but was splendidly restored when it was taken over for student accommodation by the domestic science college (now part of Bath College of Higher Education) which was also given a new adjacent building, harmlessly cuboid and largely masked by trees which decorate its pleasant grounds. It was opened by the Queen Mother in 1960. Except for the western end the views from Somerset Place are limited by an abundance of trees.

Lansdown Crescent has been praised for its double curves—a crescent centre with swept-back wings—but it is not a contin-uous composition as the ends are separated from the centre by narrow roads and have differences in detail, while the crescent itself is clearly marked off by a parapet-top urn at each end. The western break is arched over by a bridge but this dates from the time when William Beckford, of whom more later, occupied the houses on either side in 1822–44. The top of the bridge is decor-ated with stone vases from which spring metal palm trees, and his house is being turned into "Luxury Flats". Most of the houses are flats, anyway, except for the far end of the crescent which is the Bath High School for Girls which started in Portland Place in 1876. The road under the arch leads round the back of the crescent in Upper Lansdown Mews where there are some nice conversions of old coach-houses and some modern building. It lacks the unity of the crescent and its views but is none the less pleasant and has a happy air of privacy. Here in 1850 they pulled down a substantial stone building, a kind of early sports centre, for archery, rackets, bowls, foils and quoits, standing in its "National Gardens".

The crescent proper has a rusticated ground floor with rectangular door openings, there is a continuous band of guilloche moulding above the second floor, and at roof level is a modillioned cornice with balustrade above. The two end houses, which have doors at the side, are set forward and have bows all the way up, while the centre ones are also set forward, slightly, and have their doors paired with a niche between and above this four rather skimpy Ionic pilasters supporting a plain entablature and modillioned triangular pediment. Between the middle pilasters two first-floor windows flank a round-headed niche over which the guilloche moulding forms an arc. One of the best features of the crescent is its ironwork with lampholders on arches, or overthrows. In its early days at dusk when the oil lamps created soft pools of light before the shadowy buildings the effect must have been magical. Trees block the view of the city but you can see the hills beyond and, as with the other northern crescent, the sweep of buildings seems separate, private, not part of a town at all.

The development of Lansdown Crescent was largely due to the efforts of Charles Spackman, whom we have already met as Barker's patron, and he was also responsible for getting Palmer to build a chapel for the inhabitants for which Barker designed and painted the windows. The chapel, All Saints, which was a Gothick composition approached by a path from the west end of the crescent, became disused in 1937, was then bombed and has since been cleared away, gone to join the roll of honour of Bath chapels which are no more, either because they have been demolished or have changed their use—St Mary's, Queen Square, sacrificed to road widening; Laura Chapel, demolished; Margaret Chapel, Brock Street, bombed and gone; Octagon Chapel, Milsom Street, now the headquarters of the Royal

Photographic Society; Kensington Chapel, London Road, now a business premises; the Methodist church, King Street, bombed and gone. It implies a comment on social habits if not necessarily on religion.

There is one more major northern crescent and to find this we go down Lansdown Road past Lansdown Grove, a large late eighteenth-century house turned hotel, past the Ballance Street flats, and sharply up left to one of the finest view points of the city in front of Camden Crescent, designed by John Eveleigh in 1788, a couple of years before he did Somerset Place and a year after Palmer started Lansdown Crescent. Naturally he went Classical, which was still the prevailing or 'modern' style, but he also advertised that he could provide "Nobility, Gentry, and Builders with designs for Mansions, Villas, Dwellings, either Gothick or Modern", so presumably if the developers had wanted Gothick they would have got it. The crescent is named after Charles Pratt, Marquis Camden, judge, statesman, and Recorder of Bath from 1759–61, whose arms appear on the tympanum of the pediment and whose personal crest, an elephant, is carved on the keystone of every doorway.

Here, as in Somerset Place, Eveleigh combined the stepping up and down of doors and windows with a continual sweep of cornice, plat-band, and pediment but here he had to cope with a row of pilasters so that the mouldings at their base had to be wedge-shaped, a neat arrangement so well carried out that it is hardly noticeable. His central feature here, which is not in the middle because the eastern end of the crescent began to slip down the hill and had to be abandoned, has a triangular pediment above a plain architrave supported by five giant Corinthian attached columns—an odd number and therefore un-Palladian, which bothers the purists although it is doubtful if most people see anything strange about it. Its ground floor is rusticated, with arched windows and doorways. The end pavilions have similar features but without the pediments and with an even number of columns. The rest of the crescent is without rustication and has pilasters instead of columns. The doorways have Gibbs surrounds and straight pediments on consoles. The original balustrading to the roof has been removed, which gives a slightly unfinished look to the top.

Instability of the lower slopes below the crescent caused in the late nineteenth century the "Hedgemead Slip" and when attempts to rebuild were met with further slipping the ground was cleared and in 1906 was formed into Hedgemead Park over which the crescent appears to be floating in the trees.

We have now reached the end of the continuous Georgian expansion to the north so the complicated fan of road and streets and avenues to the east, lying between the Lansdown and London Roads will be considered later, but before looking at the other main Georgian bit, in Bathwick, there are one or two pieces along the London Road to consider and we might as well approach them up Walcot Street, much of which, however, is not Georgian.

5

Georgian Suburbs—
Walcot and Across the River

Walcot Street, which skirts the low-lying land along the river, is both from a physical and social view one of the most idiosyncratic bits of Bath and it is not surprising that when they made a TV programme they centred it on a mock Declaration of Independence.

Indeed, it is doubtful if Walcot ever considered itself part of Bath—after all its Saxon name probably means 'dwelling of the foreigners' (*wealas*, which later became 'Welsh'—typical Saxon cheek to call the natives foreigners). For a long time it lay outside the city walls, a small village until the eighteenth century introduced new terraces of houses with long gardens running down to the river on to which the nineteenth century introduced workshops, creating an amazing clutter behind the street frontages some of which were rebuilt in a curiously eclectic style which combined Classical cornice and parapet and occasional pediment with medieval stone mullions and transoms and provided purpose-built shop-fronts. Today there is still a long array of shops—second-hand furniture, books, and bric-à-brac, mostly Victorian and inter-war; antiques; food take-aways; car accessories; motor cycles; greengrocers; newsagents and so on—and a number of small industrial activities, including a foundry which the council has been trying to get moved.

There is too much variety to describe the street in detail but a number of the more unusual sites are worth considering, starting at the bottom end. The first feature is a church, St Michael's, which occupies the angle between Walcot Street and Broad Street. The present building was put up in 1835–7 to a design by George Philip Manners, replacing a previous rebuilding in 1742 by John Harvey which earned the deep scorn of John Wood whose own plans had been rejected. Harvey's church was in a Classical style whose bowed front had a pillared and pedimented porch flanked by round-headed windows. Rising above the middle of the church was a short tower with a cupola. Manners replaced this with a hall church (aisles the same height as the nave) in an Early English style with tall lancet windows, tall thin buttresses, and a tall thin spire rising above a tower and octagonal lantern. Sideways-on it makes a good eye-stopper to the end of Green Street, built in 1716 on the site of an old bowling-green. The church was St Michael's *extra muros* (outside the walls) as there was also a St Michael's *intra muros*. St Michael's is hardly great architecture but it has some character which is more than can be said for the packing-case style of the post-war Beaufort Hotel on the opposite side of Walcot Street, however comfortable and convenient it may be within.

Above St Michael's is the back of the Saracen's Head, a coaching inn built in 1713 and visited in 1853 by Charles Dickens, and opposite, behind a public lavatory, is the cattle market of 1810 whose stalls are occupied on Saturday by second-hand dealers in what is called rather grandly an antiques fair. The cattle come back once a week and for the rest of the time the place is used as a car-park. Beside it is the Corn Market, a three-storey Georgian building with a long single-storey exten-sion (1855) behind, with round-headed arches and a stone corbel table supporting rusting guttering. The city council has plans for this area, as it has for much of Walcot Street.

The next group of buildings is known as the Beehive Block because it once contained the Beehive Hotel selling "Fine Home Brewed Beers and Ales" and "Nutritive Oatmeal Stout" as well as "Foreign Wines and Spirits", and an opening gives access to the Beehive Yard where the South-West Electricity Board occupies the site of the old tramways electricity station and depot and has beside it the Bath Foundry of 1861—both in red brick. On the other side of the road, disused and crumbling, is a neo-Norman drinking fountain with granite columns, and next to the Beehive Block is St Michael's Church Hall, an Edwardian building in which an imaginative eye can see traces of Art Nouveau. Above the door St Michael stands in a rather unstable pose over a dragon and beside the hall is one of the numerous passages in Walcot Street which lead through to messy, but sometimes active, areas between the street frontage and the Avon.

Further up, a building now sadly abandoned still proclaims itself to be the Noted Red House Bread and Biscuit Manufactory. The Old Red House confectioner's and restaurant was in New Bond Street which is at this moment being knocked about monumentally for redevelopment. The bakery was founded by Alfred Taylor in 1798 but the factory building is of 1903, one of those strange mixtures of stone mullions and Palladian detailing, including a segmental pediment over the front door. The adjacent block, with ground-floor shops, has a similar mixture and is probably late nineteenth century.

The next passageway opens out on to a large open space and jumble of buildings where Walcot Reclamation sell stuff they have acquired from demolitions. At the other side of this entrance are the one-time offices of the building firm Hayward and Wooster, which was founded in the 1840s, and moved to Walcot in 1881. They bear a plaque stating that "Here lived Robert Southey b. 1774 d. 1865", but this refers to the Georgian house behind in which Southey, as a child, stayed for a time with his aunt. And next to this is the "Penitentiary Chapel", its name engraved below the cornice, which at the time of writing is havings its face washed. This is part of Ladymead House which was a female penitentiary for the reform of prostitutes and in 1816 attracted the attention of the energetic and charitable Mr Parish, a Hamburg merchant who had come to live in Bath. He extended the building to include a lock (i.e. isolation) hospital for venereal disease which in 1824 was converted into the chapel by the firm of Manners and Gill, although the present one is a rebuilding of 1845. In 1816–18 fifty-one women were admitted of whom seven were expelled for disorderly conduct, two "escaped", and three went into service "recovered and reformed". Later it became a home for old ladies and today the council have plans for it and it is being turned into twenty-nine flats for the elderly.

Beyond, Nos 114 and 116 are Georgian with a rather pleasant ground-floor concave addition in wood and stone, and opposite is the Bell Inn with big iron gates giving access to the back. The next road to the right is Chatham Row (called Pitt Street until the Great Commoner was elevated to the peerage), an eighteenth-century row which after being neglected for many years is at last being restored. The asking price of one of these restored houses is £49,500.

A little further up and lying back from the road are the nineteenth-century Walcot Schools, a large neo-Jacobean building, now auction rooms, and further up again is a disused burial-ground with an old mortuary chapel, a neo-Norman affair of 1849 which has been converted into Walcot Village (*sic*) Hall, at present the home of a drama society run by Bath Arts Workshop who have a shop nearby in a building with stone gable topped with a ball. The arts workshop has for many years been a lively and important part of the Walcot scene. Opposite the schools is a pleasant eighteenth-century row with a line of first-floor Venetian windows.

We are now coming up to the junction with the London Road and the top of the street is flanked on the right by two ranges of about 1900 which include the Hat and Feather pub, and on the left, by St Swithin's Church, a Classical composition of 1779 by John Palmer, enlarged in 1788, a new clock dial added in 1781, the little tower altered in 1790, and the whole repaired and redecorated in 1891. Basically it is a box decorated with giant Ionic pilasters and has a doorway set between engaged Doric columns and surmounted with a pediment. The altar is in a shallow bay projecting at the back and supported above the ground by a corbel table. In a grass patch on the east side are two tombstones of interest. One, a flat ground slab, is of Jane Austen's father, The Revd George Austen "who departed this life the 21st January 1805, aged 73 years", the other, a big block with a recumbent cross on it, of Fanny Burney, the novelist, who had married the Count d'Arblay, and of their son, The Revd Alexander Charles L. Prochard d'Arblay. She died in London in 1840, her son in 1916.

In London Street and past the Hat and Feather block is the fine, large and Classical Walcot Methodist Chapel of 1815 with its inscription "*Deo Sacrum*", Doric porch, Corinthian pilasters, arched windows, and triangular pediment. At the side are the entrances—separate for boys and girls—of the old Wesleyan Schools which occupied the basement. Down the side a passageway leads to the old organ factory which looks like another chapel and is now the headquarters of the Bath Canoe Club with a path leading to the riverside. Behind the chapel is a much overgrown graveyard.

London Street continues in terraced blocks, some eighteenth century, some nineteenth, while over the road and raised above it is Walcot Parade of about 1770 (Ison). Next are traffic lights and on the right Cleveland Place (1832—Peach), the approach to Henry Edmund Goodridge's Cleveland Bridge of 1827 with its sturdy little Greek Doric tollhouses. Cleveland Place and

Bridge were named after the Duke of Cleveland, Lord of the Manor, and Cleveland Place was designed by Goodridge although its variety indicates that others had a hand in the building, producing a mixture of sub-Palladian and neo-Greek. Of particular interest is the use of a pattern of incised lines on Cleveland Place West. An insertion, although designed by Goodridge, is the one-time dispensary of 1845 with its plaque to John Ellis "to whose persevering labour and munificent benefactions the Dispensary mainly owed its erection and pecuniary support". He died in 1856, aged eighty-six, and the tablet was erected in the following year. Dispensaries were private charities providing medicine for the poor who were recommended by subscribers, and Bath had several; this one, the Eastern, which was actually founded in 1832, the South-West of 1837 at No. 1 Albion Place on the Upper Bristol Road, and the South, now demolished, in Claverton Street, 1849.

On the opposite side of London Road is Anglo Terrace in a mock-medieval style with every dormer carrying a blank stone shield. Part was modified to give entrance to a malthouse behind which is now an antiques market. At the corner of the terrace is a pub and beyond the land was cleared after the war for the Snow Hill housing development which contains Bath's only point block. This area was once known as Long Acre so the new pub is called Longacre Tavern. It was in Long Acre in the nineteenth century that Mr Vezey had his well-known coach works. He got a mention at the Great Exhibition of 1851 for his "newly-designed sociable".

The pattern of terraces continues along the south side of the London Road, mostly with ground-floor shops, but there is a curious single-storey building, long and narrow, with an Ionic porch below a bust of Aesculapius, the Roman god of medicine. Today it is a funeral parlour but when built in 1837 it was the Bath Ear and Eye Infirmary. After a less tightly-built stretch we come back into the eighteenth century with Kensington Place (with its chapel) and Percy Place, both built in 1795-8 to designs by John Palmer. The chapel, now a warehouse, is a sturdy building with a rusticated ground floor and a first floor with three round-headed windows linked by a pattern of pilasters, entablature, and consoles, the whole front surmounted by a large pediment. The doors are at the side.

Further along, and set back from the main road, is the last major bit of Georgian Bath in this direction, Grosvenor Place, developed by John Eveleigh in 1791 as part of his project for a new Bath Vauxhall to rival Sydney Gardens, a scheme which brought him nothing but bankruptcy. In the centre of the range, bulging slightly forward in a curve, is the big building he put up in 1800 to be the hotel for the gardens. He certainly went to town on this and its decoration invokes varied responses—Ison thought it "one of the most exciting buildings in Bath", while Pevsner dismissed it as "vulgar and uninstructed", so whichever way you take it you are in good company. There is a big front porch with Doric columns and frieze with triglyphs, the ground floor is rusticated and the keystones of the round-headed windows have stalactite carving in the form of shadowy bearded faces. Above is a row of giant Ionic attached columns and two rows of wreaths continued on to them, and between them is a row of big medallions, some carved, some plain. At the top a heavy cornice advances and recedes in a series of right angles and above that is a balustrade. It's rather a lot for even a big building to carry.

It was never a hotel and was soon taken over as the Grosvenor College. In 1873 it was a ladies' college.

At the end of Grosvenor Place, Grosvenor Bridge Road leads down to a post-war housing development in what would have been Eveleigh's Vauxhall and which includes a pleasant group of houses and flats put up by a housing co-ownership society. The bridge itself, which was built as a suspension bridge in 1830 by Thomas Shew and rebuilt in concrete in 1929, leads to a footpath which takes us eventually to Hampton Row. Opposite Grosvenor, and separated by gardens from the main road, is the range of Beaufort East and beyond this lie Larkhall and Lambridge.

While the top Georgian layer was being added to the north another burst of building was going on in Bathwick over the river which was now made accessible by William Johnstone Pulteney's bridge, designed by Robert Adam and completed in 1774, taking the place of the ferries. The bridge is often compared to the Ponte Vecchio ('the old bridge') in Florence but about the only thing they have in common is being lined with shops. In the nineteenth century the shop frontages were considerably altered, but although the north side is still very much unlike the original careful cleaning and restoration of the south took place in 1975 organized by the Georgian Group (a national institution), with the assistance of the Colby Trust, the Bath

City Council, and a Government grant. The result is pleasant and brings out well the bridge's finest feature, a central Venetian window in a blind arch.

Pulteney got Adam to draw up plans for an urban development beyond the bridge but when the estate came to Pulteney's daughter, Henrietta Laura, whose name lives on in Henrietta Street and Laura Place, she employed Thomas Baldwin, who was cheaper, although his designs for the new layout were not completed as financial difficulties mounted, the Bath City Bank failed in 1793 and Baldwin went bankrupt. So the Grand Plan breaks down into *ad hoc* streets by other and later hands and what we have from Baldwin is Argyle Street, Laura Place, Great Pulteney Street and some side streets.

Argyle Street leads from Pulteney Bridge to Laura Place and is a short busy thoroughfare of shops and restaurants, with boxes tacked on to the ground floors to create shop-fronts, although one or two on the south side, such as No. 9, are original. Above can be seen the usual paraphernalia of cornices, pediments, and Vitruvian scrolls. Of a later date is the front of Argyle Chapel which was rebuilt in 1821 by Goodridge in a Grecian style with an Ionic portico but with wedge-shaped "Egyptian" doorways, even then, it was not left alone and now has an upper range with Corinthian attached columns. In the porch is a cast-iron fire-back dated 1734 and showing the Flight into Egypt, a gift from the Protestant church of St Ingbert, Germany. A plaque also proclaims that William Jay was minister from 1790 (when the chapel opened) to 1853, a stint of sixty-three years.

The origins of the chapel go back to 1791 when Lady Huntingdon sacked her minister for inviting laymen to preach in her chapel and he was followed into exile by five members of the congregation who then worshipped successively in Monmouth Street, Morford Street, which they had to leave when the Countess bought their premises, Hetling House, and St James's Parade where their new Tabernacle was opened in 1785 by their new minister The Revd Thomas Tuppen. Tuppen, however, was a sick man and his place was often taken by Jay, a young working mason, who gained a great reputation as "the boy preacher". When they moved to their new chapel in Argyle Street Tuppen was again ill and the first sermon was preached by Jay although he was not ordained until the following year. He was a fine preacher, although not greatly interested in pastoral work, and attracted a large and fashionable audience. He opposed the appointment of his successor, The Revd Dyer, and a splinter group formed. In consequence Jay's funeral, which "took place at Snow Hill in the Argyle burial ground during a snow storm" was conducted by the minister of the Countess of Huntingdon's chapel (she had died in 1791).

Near the end of Argyle Street, Grove Street descends to the riverside and continues as St John's Road along to Cleveland Bridge with Georgian rapidly giving way to nineteenth century except for a Palladian mansion which is now flats, was once a police barracks, and when originally built in 1772–3 was a new prison. It was designed by Atwood, once again frustrating Pulteney's attempts to employ Adam. Grove Street has been lowered and the rusticated ground floor of the old prison now hangs in the air. In 1842 a new jail was built at Twerton to designs by G. P. Manners. On the riverside of Grove Street (once known as Cheapside) developed a motley collection of workshops and warehouses which are being replaced, after considerable argument, by new structures which do not seem of any great distinction but will at least cut off one of the less inspiring views in Bath. On one refurbished building there is still to be seen the puzzling date 5792. The most likely explanation is that it is a Masonic date as the Freemasons' calendar starts from 4,000 BC and 5792 is therefore 1792. In the nineteenth century this became the poor area of Bathwick and the church ran a mission there from 1884–1914 with a host of good works— Bible classes, mothers' meetings, lending library, senior nightschool, penny-bank, provident society, lying-in charity, blanket charity, dispensary, children's school dinners, meat kitchen, and working men's club—a Welfare State in miniature.

Argyle Street leads to Laura Place with an insignificant fountain in the middle. This originally had a couple of basins, one above the other, and a Gothic top when it was put up in 1877 for the centenary of the Bath and West Society, but it lost its superstructure some years ago and was for a time turned into a flower bed. In 1805 the city proposed to have a Nelson's column there but they could not raise enough money and even when they proposed to change it to a 'Reform' column with a statue of William IV on top they could get no further than building the podium. Laura Place is a square set on a skew with a street at each corner. Its sides are formed of blocks of the same general pattern with fluted Corinthian pilasters, modillioned cornice, shallow parapet, and rusticated ground floor. First-floor windows have alternate triangular and straight pediments on consoles.

Coming off the south corner, Johnston Street is a cul-de-sac with an end view over the recreation ground to the new sports centre opened by Princess Anne in 1975. On the corner in No. 15, Pitt House, now the home of the Conservative Association, lived William Pitt from 1802–5. This was the Younger Pitt not his father, the Earl of Chatham, who had been MP for Bath and had died in 1778. Pitt lived from 1759 to 1806 and became Prime Minister at the age of twenty-four. "He is not a chip off the old block," said Burke, "he is the old block itself."

On the opposite side, past an octagonal Victorian post-box, Henrietta Street curves away towards Bathwick Street, with more round-headed ground-floor windows and doors and, as the ground drops, linked cornices, but this soon ends and then the road is lined with large nineteenth-century paired villas with the spreading eaves of the Italianate style and interspersed with some post-war building. While still in the 1790s development area we see on the right a passageway leading to Henrietta Mews and Henrietta Park made on land donated in 1890 by Captain F. W. Forester, and a little further an archway inscribed "Laura Chapel". The chapel, designed by Baldwin, was oval and, like the Octagon, had fireplaces. The roof fell in and the building was finally demolished in the early 1900s. The street is a mixture of houses, flats, and small hotels.

Great Pulteney Street is the widest in Bath, 100 feet between the buildings, and was obviously intended to be very grand, but it is too wide for comfort, too short for its width, and even if the surface modelling of the buildings was strong and the rhythm clearly evident, which it is not, the place would still look more like a parade-ground than a street—it is not surprising that it was chosen for the start of a motor rally, to the annoyance of some of the inhabitants. It was a bit better when it had its nineteenth-century trees but these were taken away and the present lines of parked cars add nothing of value to the scene. In No. 8 lived Sir Charles Napier the conqueror of the Indian province of Sind, who reported his success in a one-word telegram—"*Peccavi*" (I have sin(ne)d).

Many of the houses are now flats, although there are some hotels and offices and about half-way along the south side is a postal museum in the basement of No. 51. The result of local initiative, and organized as a trust, the museum has a fascinating and changing display of a whole variety of things relating to postal history in general and Bath in particular. As they point out, Bath is an appropriate place for such a museum as it was Bath's Ralph Allen who reformed the cross-posts, Bath's John Palmer who invented the mail-coach system, the Smith Brothers of Bath who published the first philatelic magazine, and the wife of a Bath postmaster who in 1840 posted the first letters with sticky stamps, the original Penny Blacks. Appropriately, there is another Victorian octagonal post-box on the pavement outside. Such post-boxes were called 'Penfolds' after the designer.

A few houses still retain their ironwork lampholders and it would be an improvement if they all had them. There are Corinthian pilasters an the occasional big triangular pediment, the middle one on the south side bearing the Pulteney arms; some windows have triangular pediments, some straight ones on consoles with pilaster strips below; there is a pattern in this but it takes some sorting out and the architectural message is not immediately clear as it is in the Circus and Royal Crescent. The whole street, has, however, benefited from recent cleaning and repair of the stonework.

It was a good address and handy for the town centre so quite a number of well-known people have lived there. One of the first houses was built for Hannah More, the eminent bluestocking and founder of Mendip schools and women's Friendly Societies, a lady whose monumental row with the parson at Blagdon started a pamphlet war, whose play *The Inflexible Captive* was first presented on the Bath stage, and who contributed a couple of pamphlets to the tracts published in Bath to counteract the influence of the French Revolution among the "lower orders". To Walpole she was "Holy Hannah" and "not only one of the cleverest of women, but one of the best" and the *Quarterly Review* said that "She did, perhaps, as much real good in her generation as any woman that ever held a pen". The house was held in the name of her sister Mary and they lived there from 1792 to 1802, although she was not fond of the city—"I hate Bath," she wrote—and she left in the year her friend William Wilberforce, the eminent social reformer, came to No. 36—he left in 1805. William Smith, the geologist whom we have already met, was at No. 27 in 1799, and Bulwer Lytton, the popular novelist now little read (when did you last read *The Last of the Barons*?) was at No. 2 in 1867 and 1872.

Louis XVIII was staying at No. 72 in 1813 the year before he was put on the French throne after the abdication of Napoleon; he numbered himself XVIII in 1795 on the death of his nephew whom he regarded as Louis XVII although he had never reigned. And at No. 55 in 1846 was Louis Napoleon, nephew of Bonaparte, who in 1848 was elected President of the French Republic and in 1852 took the title of Napoleon III and inaugurated the Second Empire. His living there is commemorated by a plaque but there is an alternative version that he stayed at the Sydney Hotel. In 1871 at the end of the Franco-Prussian War, disastrous for the French, he was captured near the Belgian border and a Republic was again proclaimed in France. The Empress fled to England (where else?) and was joined by her husband who died in 1873, once more an exile. Thomas Baldwin himself lived at No. 6 before he went bankrupt.

In No. 72 stayed Emma, Lady Hamilton, and in 1809 she was round the corner in No. 6 Edward Street. Nelson had died at Trafalgar in 1805, bequeathing, in a sense, Emma to the nation—which the nation found very embarrassing and so contrived to do nothing about it with the result that she died in 1815 at Calais in debt and rather poor accommodation. In her teens Emma had been an 'actress' who gained some success with her 'artistic poses' and in 1778 she was employed by a quack doctor, Graham, to demonstrate, as "Vesta, the Rosy Goddess of Health", his celestial bed whose magnets, he claimed, gave "charming springyness—that sweet, undulating, tittulating, vibratory, soul-dissolving, marrow-melting motion; which in certain critical and important occasions, is at once so necessary and pleasing". It wasn't a success. The tenuous link with Bath is that in the early seventies Dr Graham was practising the use of his "Balsamic Essences, and Aerial, Aetherial, Magnetic, and Electrical Appliances" in the city and in particular on the dotty Catherine Macaulay who lived at No. 2 Alfred Street and is not to be confused with Lord Macaulay (1800–59) although she too wrote a *History of England*. She married Graham's younger brother. A later inhabitant of Edward Street in the 1920s was the song writer, Frederick Wetherby, who had a 'Gothic' small-paned bow window inserted to make it difficult for people to peer in. It is still there on its carved wooden supports and, curiously enough, looks less out of place than the post-war block opposite that conscientiously endeavours to echo its Georgian idiom.

Forming a focus to Great Pulteney Street stands the Holburne of Menstrie Museum which was originally designed by Charles Harcourt Masters and started life as the hotel for the Sydney Gardens Vauxhall which had opened the previous year with "Horns and Clarionets every Wednesday evening—two Bowling Greens—two Swings (No swinging can be permitted on Sundays)". John Pinch the Younger added an attic storey in 1836 and when the hotel became a museum in 1915 the building was further adapted by Sir Reginald Blomfield (1856–1942), a pupil of Norman Shaw. Originally not a hotel in the modern sense but a suite of public rooms for the gardens it was in 1820 being advertised as providing "apartments replete with every accommodation as a Family Hotel". In 1878 it became the home of the newly founded Bath College but by the end of the century it had been abandoned, bought by a hotel company for £6,700 and left to rot, unused, until in 1907 people were writing angry letters to the paper about its condition. Originally there was a semicircular loggia at the back with bandstand above but this went in the reconstruction, as did the Sydney Tap, a basement pub. Next to it in the gardens were open-sided booths for private parties.

The gardens were a great success and superseded the Spring Gardens down by the river which had provided the main alfresco entertainment before and which were reached by a ferry. An advertisement of 1766 announced that "Spring Gardens are now open for the Summer season with breakfasting and Afternoon Tea, as usual—Hot Rolls and Spring Garden Cakes every morning from Half after Nine till Half after Ten, Sundays excepted—Musick will attend if required—Constant Attendance at the Passage-Boat leading from Orange Grove to the Gardens. A Commodious Pleasure Boat to be let." Spring Gardens had dancing as well and a poem in the newspaper of 1769 refers to

> The bold hurdy-gurdy; played by a man stout and sturdy,
> Of pleasure presents you the cream

And goes on to say that it was to this that

> Here, quite in her prime, Miss for the first time,
> Two very odd things puts together,
> Our own country-dance, and another from France,
> So jump'd you cannot tell whither.

Even Jane Austen liked Sydney Gardens although she added characteristically that one of the advantages was that being large they enabled her to get away from the music. The place acquired a labyrinth which was so puzzling that maps were sold, and in the middle was "a capital swing of Merlin's construction" which the proprietors claimed was so good for your health that they charged a three months' subscription of 5s. (25p) for its use. A typical gala was the one organized for the birthday of George III in 1806. Doors opened at 5 p.m., the resident band and the band of the Bath Forum Volunteer Corps played alternately from 5.30 to 7 and were followed by a concert of vocal and instrumental music. A fireworks display arranged by the "ingenious Signor Invetto" started at 10.30. Cold chicken, ham, tongue, and beef were available with wines, spirits, bottled porter, and cider. Tickets cost 2s. (10p) each but servants in livery were not admitted—presumably it was all right if they came in plain clothes. It doesn't sound wildly exciting but of course it leaves out the home-made fun which probably went on in the grottoes, labyrinth and bushes—the kind which got the London Vauxhall such a bad name. It was not unusual for well over a thousand people to attend a gala and the gardens kept their popularity up to the middle of the nineteenth century after which attendance began to fall off badly except at the occasional balloon ascent. In 1909 the corporation bought them and in 1913 they were made free to the public as a park. Today they are pleasant, with the usual grass, trees, flower beds, asphalt paths, tennis courts and bowling-green but the labyrinth, grottoes and swing have gone.

In 1800 the Kennet and Avon Canal, engineered by John Rennie and opened in 1810, came through the gardens with pleasant little iron bridges (advertised as 'Chineese") dated *Anno* 1800 and in 1841 came the GWR and more substantial bridges. In 1909 they commemorated the year of the great Bath Pageant in Victoria Park by building in Sydney Gardens a replica of the Roman Temple of Sul-Minerva. It still stands, although rather obscured by trees, giving quite a good impression of the front of the original, but its plain interior walls are an open invitation to graffiti, the more printable of which included, when last seen, "I hate the park: I hate park keepers", and "Fred is so interesting—and sociable—and such a bad loser at Monopoly".

The Holburne Museum, based on the collection made by Sir Thomas William Holburne in the middle of the nineteenth century, has a fine collection of silver, glass and paintings and also puts on special exhibitions on a variety of themes. Apart from this the rooms are a pleasure in themselves. Holburne was born in 1793; when he was only twelve he served at the Battle of Trafalgar and eventually became a commander. In 1829 his father died and he became the fifth, and last, baronet. He also inherited the family collection of silver, porcelain, books and pictures and continued to add to this during his life. Towards the end he lived with his three unmarried sisters at 10 Cavendish Crescent where he died in 1874, at the age of eighty-one. His youngest sister, Mary Anne Barbara, lasted another eight years and died in 1882, the last of the line. In that year she drew up a will in which she left their house, including the art collection and a legacy of £10,000, to a small committee with instructions to form it into a Holburne of Menstrie Museum. She had also started to negotiate the purchase of the Sydney Hotel as a home for the collection but she died before this was completed. The will was contested but declared valid and the committee formed into a trust, the museum opening in 1893, not in Camden Crescent, but in Charlotte Street, and the trustees did not acquire Sydney Hotel until 1915, the date on the drainheads at the back of the building which, as we have seen, they got Sir Reginald Blomfield to adapt.

The park is in the form of a rectangle with a triangular top and bottom but though it was originally intended to surround it with ranges of houses only the one on the west, Old Sydney Place, was erected to Baldwin's designs, and it was here at No. 4, now flats, that Jane Austen and her family lived from 1801-5. Her father, The Revd Austen, died in 1805 and was buried in Walcot church, where he had been married in 1764. He is buried in the crypt but his tombstone is in the garden beside the church, next to Fanny Burney's. The family left Bath and in 1808 Jane wrote to her sister Cassandra, "It will be two years tomorrow since we left Bath for Clifton, with what happy feelings of Escape!" The houses in Old Sydney Place, which are now flats, have round-headed doorways set in vermiculated (grooved like worm-tracks) rustication and the first-floor windows are grouped in threes, the centre ones decorated with swags and straight pediments on consoles—the common pattern. There is a triangular pediment at one end and another in the middle but the one at the far end has gone, replaced by a continuation of the parapet.

New Sydney Place on the east of the park is of 1808 to designs by Pinch and is an altogether more satisfactory composition—stronger and more clearly articulated and with a higher standard of decoration. The ends and middle come slightly forward and are crowned with triangular pediments, the central one bearing the arms of the Vane (Darlington) family, although sadly eroded, and the centre first-floor windows are enriched with straight pediments on double consoles and pilaster strips. All first-floor windows have iron balconies, those at ends and middle being combined to form verandas, and all ground-floor window and door openings are round-headed, the doors having delicate tracery in the fanlights, and in front of each door is a finely wrought throw-over. What, however, binds it all together are the strong horizontal mouldings—minor cornice, major cornice, string-courses below third-floor windows, Vitruvian scroll above the first floor and string-course below it (a string-course being a narrow moulding), and mouldings between the ground floor openings, giving the impression of piers from which the arches spring. Also, because the range slopes uphill, every one of these projecting lines is linked between the houses by a curve, giving a feeling both of cohesion and of movement as if the whole building were rippling up the hill.

The end walls have elegant double bows and Doric porches, the one at the east end surmounted by a very pleasant conservatory. Along from this is a fine Georgian wall and round the corner is Raby Mews, with gables, which is now mainly garages although there is an interesting conversion into flats with garages under—in most of the conversions of Georgian houses in Bath the lack of garages produces problems of on-street parking.

New Sydney Place was on the Darlington Estate and at the bottom is Darlington Street with a range of flat-faced late Georgian buildings, the house at the south end set slightly forward and with a rusticated ground floor. At the end of this is Vane Street where the rustication continues, first-floor windows have the centre of each group of three enriched and at the far end is a rather clumsy Victorian veranda.

Next to Raby Mews is St Mary's, Bathwick, the most prominent building in the area with its 125-foot tower, traceried, be-clocked, and be-pinnacled. Until the Pulteney development Bathwick was a hamlet on an estate which was bought by Sir William Pulteney who was created Earl of Bath in 1742 but who was not the Pulteney who started the development. This was Sir William Johnstone who married the Pulteney heiress and added her surname to his. Old Bathwick had a church, although nobody seems to know for certain where it was, but with the growth in population it was quite inadequate and plans were made to get a new one. Two Acts of Parliament were obtained and the Earl of Darlington, later Duke of Cleveland, gave a site at the foot of Bathwick Hill. It was in fact a double project because they were going to build a parish poorhouse as well and it is interesting to see that in the special parish rate which was raised for the project the Quakers were required to contribute to the poorhouse building but not to the church. In the event the poorhouse was never built. The architect for the church was John Pinch, the building was started in 1814 and the church was consecrated in 1820. It was in some ways, like the Houses of Parliament (1836), a contradiction in terms, Gothic clothing to a Classical box.

Outside, Pinch provided a good essay in Perpendicular Gothic with a 125-foot high tower and echoes of the abbey. Inside, however, he provided the conventional eighteenth-century preaching box with big galleries on three sides and big box pews which in this case all faced west towards a huge three-decker pulpit, the top stage of which was ten feet above ground and reached by a spiral staircase. Instead of the pillars supporting arches, which would have interfered with the view from the side galleries, they went straight up to the roof and had plain capitals. There was no chancel or choir stalls—they weren't used in those days—but instead a shallow apse with a small oak communion table with a big picture of the Nativity by Benjamin Barker which is now above the west gallery, and thirteen-foot high panels showing the Creed, Ten Commandments, and Lord's Prayer.

It is perhaps difficult for present-day churchgoers to realize how plain was a service and a church at the beginning of the nineteenth century—no altar, reredos, or chancel; the choir, if it existed, discreetly hidden away; no surplices or gaudier garments, no kneelings, no processions, no anthems, no festivals; no crosses, statues, or other symbols; no colour; the communion service read from the pulpit; no chanting and although there was some hymn singing, no *Hymns Ancient and Modern* until 1861. It all seemed rather dull and with little to offer in competition with the enthusiastic emotionalism of the Dissenters and the intellectual pride of the atheists. And then in the 1830s there appeared the Tracts of the Oxford Movement and the proselytizing zeal of the Cambridge Camden Society and its magazine *The Ecclesiologist*, started in 1841. Both the Tractarians and the Ecclesiologists were for bringing back life and colour and symbolic ritual into the Church of England—bringing back the gorgeous vestments, the processions, the images, the stained-glass windows, the chants, the High Altar, the painted walls, the full Catholic ritual (but not Roman Catholic—this caused a lot of problems, particularly with the more Protestant-minded bishops and congregations). And, of course, church design had to accommodate this, and, again of course, the Gothic was the only style for it, and preferably not late Perpendicular, which they considered debased, but the mid-period Decorated.

From 1841 to 1871 the Rector of St Mary's was Prebendary Scarth, an enthusiastic antiquary but not one to go overboard for the Tractarians—at his memorial service in 1890 he was described as "teaching Catholic truths, though undesirous of doing so by new methods". He did, however, in 1866 have the old pews and three-decker pulpit removed and replaced by a pulpit at the east end, with the new seating facing towards it. His successor, however, Prebendary Tugwell, small, immensely energetic, and member of a well-to-do Bath family, had unbounded enthusiasm for the new movement, and between 1871 and 1904 he transformed the interior.

In 1874 they got a new chancel instead of Pinch's apse. This was designed by George Edmund Street (1824–81), a High Church man much appreciated by the Camden Society, an apostle of the Gothic, and designer of the Law Courts in the Strand and the nave and west end of Bristol Cathedral as well as a host of other works. The style he used at St Mary's was, of course, a curvilinear Decorated (see the east window). He also designed wall decorations for the chancel and chancel arch which were done in 1881, the year of his death. In 1882 they got a reredos with side panels from a fifteenth-century Flemish triptych (still there) and in 1886 a new alabaster altar with a figure of the dead Christ in a kind of open-sided tomb under the top—"a revolting arrangement" said the *Church Times* in 1923 but greatly admired at the time; it is no longer visible. Tugwell disliked the contrast between the highly decorated chancel and the plain nave so in 1888 the latter got its painting. Finally, in 1894 the sacristy south of the chancel was transformed into a memorial chapel for his wife. It is perhaps the most remarkable feature in the church, mainly for its elaborate screen in brass and copper with scroll work, lilies, palm branches, rosettes, images, and cross, all made by Singer's of Frome. It has recently been done up and is worth seeing, whether you like it or not.

Tugwell's successor, Charles Hylton Stewart, while enthusiastic for the singing, was less fervent for the High Church ceremonial—linen vestments were re-introduced and incense no longer used (Tugwell had had some trouble with the Bishop over this). It was however in his time that another showy bit came into being when the bottom of the tower was turned into a baptistry in memory of The Revd Edward Handley who had served the church as an honorary priest. Its most remarkable feature, although it looks rather dingy without its lights on, is an electrolier of 1896 hung about with carbuncles and glass beads and brasswork. In 1916 there was a fire in the church and following it Pinch's Gothic plasterwork behind the galleries was taken off so that now we have bare walls there, and in 1963 there was a restoration which removed most of the painting from the church and substituted a much quieter scheme. In 1967 they added a church room designed by Beresford Smith.

By the church is a big roundabout from which Bathwick Street, here called Raby Place, a creation, both road and buildings, of the early nineteenth century, rises steeply up Bathwick Hill. The range of buildings in Raby Place (1825) is beautifully adapted to the slope with sweeping links along its two cornices and the vertical edge of each house in the terrace lightly defined by lesenes (pilaster strips without capitals). The ground floor is rusticated, or rather banded, for only the horizontal joints are grooved, a common feature of this period which makes for a lighter look. First-floor balconies and verandas add interest to the scene for they are apparent without being assertive. The railway tunnels beneath the top house and parallel to it is the Kennet and Avon Canal with its Sydney Wharf cut off from us by Regency and Victorian buildings. Continuing between them would take us back to Raby Mews here dominated by a large and graceless building on which South-West Gas has carved its name (with pride?).

Over the main road is Bathwick Terrace of about 1842 with its corner set at an angle and treated grandly with Ionic pillars and Doric pilasters supporting a plain entablature and triangular pediment. In contrast, the earlier George's Place (c. 1825) next door is quite plain, the ground floor converted by plate glass into shop-fronts, and its end rebuilt in a kind of post-war stripped Georgian. Beyond this in 1800 a bridge was made over the canal and beside it Pennant sandstone steps take you down to the towpath with a pleasant walk to the right, which we shall look at later, while to the left, an arch with baby stalactites gives access to what remains of Sydney Wharf where in summer passenger boats leave on pleasure trips.

A couple of opposing blocks, George Street (c. 1812) and Dunisford Place (c. 1825), both with stepped but not linked cornices, show a common feature of the Regency period, door-ways set in shallow round-headed depressions (depressed or blind arches), and then we are out of the Regency ranges and into villa country. Before this, however, a pleasant detour could be made by going along between Sydney Buildings (1821–32), a set of neat little rows of two-storey buildings with banded rustication, cornice and pediment, continuous sills, and little round windows beside the doorways, and the long range of Darlington Place (c. 1819–25) high up on the hill with gardens stretching down to a broad raised pavement. A little further on is an old malt-house, handily placed for the canal, which has been saved from ruin by conversion into an architect's office. The road goes on with fields on one side and on the other a set of pleasant two-storey, paired villas with ground-floor windows and doors set in depressed arches and roofs crowned with cornice and parapet. The surroundings are too pleasant not to have attracted further building and the road carries on between inter-war houses (one dated 1933) and some post-war infill.

The road then doubles back on itself, which is possibly why it is called Horseshoe Walk, and returns on the other side of the valley which is the bottom of Smallcombe Vale, and as we come back past a triangular green we see on the other side another of those ranges with linked cornices but with ground-floor bay windows which places it as later than the Regency examples.

Another feature is that above the paired doorways the end of the straight pediment and console of one rests on the beginning of its neighbour. This is Abbey View (1862–4 says Peach) and it takes us to the canal with a pleasurable walk back to the Bathwick Hill bridge. In this walk, which is thankfully provided with seats from which you can watch the ducks and moorhens, we pass the Classical chimney which is all that remains of a canal pumping-station, several locks restored by the Kennet and Avon Canal Trust, who deserve all the help they can get, and a little bridge labelled "Stothert" although, as Hugh Torrens has demonstrated in his book *The Evolution of a Family Firm*, these bridges were made in Coalbrookdale and only supplied by the Bath firm. Over the bridge is the Canal Information Centre. We are at Top Lock and beside it is the little Gothic Top Lodge Cottage and a little further is the back view of the malt-house advertising in faded black letters "Hugh Baird & Sons, Maltsters".

Without this detour we would go plodding up the hill past St Anne's Walk which leads to an inter-war development of vaguely Gothic semis, and, opposite, the bulk of post-war St Patrick's Court which tries by its stepped-up repeating pattern to fit the scene but does not really achieve it and sits uneasily with its Regency neighbour, Sion Place (*c.* 1826). Then there are the villas—big ones on the left, smaller ones on the right—but before looking at them we could make a foray down Cleveland Walk (1841) with big houses interspersed with inter- and post-war infill, or take the path opposite which goes back up behind the villa gardens and gives a fine view over Smallcombe Vale to the city from the abbey to the gasworks, including a green mushroom cloud formed by the tops of the trees in the Circus.

The change from streets, squares, and crescents to villas, either single or paired, set in their own grounds, which became the standard suburban pattern in the latter part of the nineteenth century and developed into the inter- and post-war 'estates', resulted from a change in life style, initially among the well-to-do who could afford their own carriages and so did not need to live near the centre of things. Basically it was part of an anti-urban movement and a growing Romanticism and Individualism and the reasons for it were various. Two with which we are still familiar were, firstly, a natural tendency to discard what had come to be regarded as conventional wisdom and, secondly, a distaste for the environmental consequences of an industrialized society. Artists and writers gave it energy, the new-found wealth of the rising commercial and professional upper middle class gave it substance. It eventually littered suburbia with High Victorian Gothic villas and gave Gothic trimmings to quite ordinary streets, greatly helped by the ability of industry to produce yards of identical Gothic mouldings. But in Bath the hold of Classicism lasted longer than in most and in any case the Bathwick development was early, with the result that most of the villas are Bath stone boxes with Classical trimmings, although there are bits of Greek revival or Gothic, possibly later 'improvements'—No. 3, for example, is basically Classical and has a Greek fret on the gateposts but also has an ogee-arched Gothic porch. Gothic is not much in evidence except in Priory Lodge which has all the paraphernalia of high-peaked gables and stone mullions and must surely be later. In some cases, possibly inspired by "England's Florence", there are wholly Italianate houses of which the most impressive is Bathwick Garage whose tall rectangular tower with its low-pitched spreading cap and round-headed windows rises above the trees. Another example is Fiesole (*sic*) where in 1850 lived the architect Henry Edmund Goodridge and which is now a youth hostel; it has the compulsory tower, spreading eaves on wooden brackets, loggia with balcony above, narrow round-headed windows, heavy stone brackets, and tall chimney-stacks. Another, ornately Italianate and big, is called Casa Bianca. Prominent, though low and non-Italianate, is Claverton Lodge, built, says Peach, by the Hon. Frederick Noel, Captain RN, in 1828 and "now" (1893) the residence of Mr and Mrs Ashworth Hallett—which is presumably why there is an H cut in the weather-vane and carved in a cartouche over the Doric porch. In the eighteenth century the Hon. Frederick would probably have bought or rented a house in the Crescent.

If we haven't got the strength to go up Bathwick Hill we could quite easily take a stroll round the perimeter of Sydney Gardens starting at New Sydney Place, and straight away we meet villas, Italianate and Gothic, with on the right a Palladian house which is now occupied by offices of the Department of Environment but which was once the local headquarters of the Kennet and Avon Canal Company. The canal runs underneath the building, its exit arch decorated with a swag of drapery running rather rakishly over a female head (on the next bridge it droops over a bearded male) and in the roof of the tunnel is a trapdoor through which messages could be passed. At the apex of the park North Road heads up the hill to meet Bathwick Hill near the university and along the contour goes the Warminster Road which was engineered in 1835 and passes between inter- and post-war housing. Back down the side of the gardens, past more Gothic Revival, takes us to Bathwick Street which originally went to a ferry but now leads to the Cleveland Bridge, designed by Goodridge and opened in 1827. This has two rather fine little Greek Revival tollhouses with Greek Doric pillars but they are not in use as the bridge, like several other Bath ones, was made free of its halfpenny toll following the Bath Act of 1925. In fact the bridge had to wait some time for this freedom and did not get it until 1935, as is stated on a plaque. Goodridge has also got his name on the bridge together with the date and the name of the contractor.

Bathwick Street is lined with ranges of late eighteenth- and early nineteenth-century buildings all in a Classical style but exhibiting a good deal of variety in detail, particularly in treatment of windows. Connecting through to Henrietta Gardens is Daniel Street, nearly all flats, with round-headed doorways and first-floor windows in depressed arches, but with a change at the far end near Sutton Street, where first-floor windows have triangular pediments and paired ground-floor windows are under a common arch. It is not at all grand but it shows how satisfactorily the Georgians could design their minor streets and how important such streets are to the general atmosphere of Bath. Near Cleveland Bridge is the inter-war fire station with arms of Bath flanked by helmets and hoses and, standing alone, a showy Jacobean-style archway of about 1800 known as "Pinch's Folly" which was the entrance to his builder's yard. The vase on top is a replacement of 1970. Also near the bridge, in St John's Road, is the church of St John the Baptist.

This is Bathwick's second church, built as the population continued to grow and originally intended for the "poorer brethren". Much less satisfactory from the outside, it hangs together better within, partly because of the absence of disrupting galleries. Again two architects were used. In 1861 C. E. Giles designed a small church with an apse-ended nave and three years later a tower and spire were added over the north porch. The church was enlarged in 1869–71 to designs by Sir Arthur Blomfield who turned the old nave into an aisle by knocking down the south wall and putting in pointed arches

supported by short pillars with foliage capitals, and built alongside a whacking big new nave and chancel, with hammer-beam
roof and lots of stained glass. Suiting the Anglo-Catholic ethos
of the church is a rood screen with a great cross above dating
from 1919 in memory of the Vicar, Father Dunn. Behind the
church is the old graveyard with the ruined remains of the
mortuary chapel which *may* be the site of the original church.
One tomb announces "This Grave is Full—1866", so presumably the graveyard was still being used after they got a new
cemetery at the top of Smallcombe Vale in 1856.

North-east of Bathwick Street the triangle between the road,
the river and the railway, once known as Villa Fields, was
developed for housing at the end of the nineteenth century (it is
not in the 1890 directory but is fully occupied in 1910) with
semi-detached or short-row housing predominantly in a simple
Gothic style with gables and bays but with some Arts and Crafts
wooden porches and some Classical touches—dentils and consoles, for instance. In Powlett Road is a blush of red brick,
simpler, with a touch of the Arts and Crafts, while down by the
river there is some post-war stuff such as the flats of Horton
House erected in 1968. At the end of Forester Road is the Bath
Boating Station from which you can hire a boat and get a swan's
eye view of Bath.

At the north-east corner, beyond the way down to the open-air
Cleveland Baths, first opened in 1815, is one of the sad sights of
Bath, a dying terrace—it may even have been demolished by the
time this book is published but it has been a long time going.
This is Hampton Row, a once-pleasant little terrace started in
1818 and built on a slope so steep that you go under the house to
get to the back garden. Views from the back are splendid but
from the front were rather spoilt when the railway came
through in 1841 and they built a great masonry wall to stop the
canal falling on it. At present there are still two or three houses
well looked after and with bright curtains up at the windows but
the rest are rotting, boarded up, with roofs falling in, and what
had been for so long homes are now in lifeless decay.

The early nineteenth-century work we have been looking at,
the tide-mark of the Georgian expansion, comes in a period
which elsewhere, Cheltenham or Brighton for example, would
be labelled Regency and it has some of the marks of that
period—bigger windows with, where they still exist, narrower
glazing bars; round-headed doorways with ornamental fan-

lights; bows; light surface mouldings—but it is sturdier and plainer than the more typical examples, as if the spirit of John Wood was still working on his successors and the term Regency is rarely used in relation to the early nineteenth-century architecture of Bath.

One further area which was developed during this period lies at the end of Pulteney Road called the New Road in 1840, a thoroughfare with later neo-Gothic and Italianate villas, and streets of Victorian housing leading off. This area contains the Dolemeads, the lower parts of Widcombe, the remains of Claverton Street and of Holloway, the old line of the Fosse Way.

Dolemeads is a low-lying area, so liable to flood that it was called "Mud Island", between Pulteney Road which runs along the slightly higher level of a river terrace and the banks of the Avon and is now all post-1900 except for the railway viaduct of 1841. In the map of 1803 there is nothing there and its development took place after the Kennet and Avon Canal came locking down past it to the river in 1810, after which it rapidly degenerated into a slum and was knocked down in 1900 to make way for Bath's first council housing following the Housing of the Working Classes Act of 1890. The ground level was raised, although this did not completely solve the flood problem, and red-brick terraces with stone trimmings were built and given hopeful names such as Excelsior or geographical ones such as Archway. There have been post-war modifications in a starker brick, with more prominent pointing and aluminium window frames, and in inter-war years council housing was extended, clad in Bath stone and to a more Arts and Crafts design. In 1856 the area got a church school, rebuilt in Jacobean style at the end of the century, and on 20th September 1821 a substantial Ebenezer chapel with Gothic-style Y tracery windows and battlements. This was extended to provide schoolrooms in 1910 and the new frontage on Pulteney Road bears the text "In place of the thorn shall come up the fir tree". The "thorn" was the Canal Tavern which was destroyed to make way for the new extension. The chapel, which has the texts on the roof already referred to, continues with vigour and has been extended at the back. The riverside road is called Spring Gardens in memory of the pleasure grounds which were there before the new Sydney Gardens Vauxhall killed them off and where the canal comes down to the river is a small stone building and chimney, Thimble Mill, the remains of a pumping-station which lifted river water to keep the canal topped up.

Near the chapel extension Pulteney Road turns sharp west to become Claverton Street where Widcombe Hill and Prior Park Road come into it. This end of Claverton Street forms the Widcombe shopping area and at the end of it Lyncombe Hill comes in but beyond that wholesale demolition, including the removal of the old gabled Cold Bath House designed by Thomas Greenway in 1704, was carried out after the war for road improvements. A new highway, Rossiter Road, was put through to Pulteney Road and a one-way system started which brought west-bound traffic through Widcombe, accelerated by the lack of a counter-flow. This the Widcombe Action Group objected to as it had a seriously detrimental effect on their shopping street and they campaigned to make Rossiter Street two-way, a proposal which was resisted by Avon County Council, the traffic authority, although Bath Planning Department in its document of 1978, "Save Bath", said that "it is considered that further investigation should be made into the practicability of the schemes, with a view to making further approaches to Avon County Council should they be justified". At present (1981) the traffic still thunders between the shops, creating noise, fumes, and vibration, and rendering road-crossing hazardous.

The buildings in this short stretch—mostly shops, with pubs and a post office—date mainly from the end of the eighteenth century (e.g. Widcombe Parade on the south side is dated 1780– 90 and is listed Grade II) and at present are mostly rather dilapidated.

Widcombe Hill is dominated at the bottom by the tower and spire of the Victorian church of St Matthew, built in 1846–7 for £7,000 and designed by the Bath firm of Manners and Gill. It is a large, if rather dull, hall church with nave and aisles of equal height and windows with Decorated tracery. Opposite it the church hall has changed function and a new one has been formed by blocking off the west end of the church. Further up the hill there are again villas but on the right and dating from about 1805 is the very attractive group of Widcombe Crescent and Terrace. The crescent has paired round-headed doorways set in wide depressed archways decorated with floral boss and festoons. Above each archway is a three-light window in which the centre one, although glazed, is a dummy as the party wall goes up behind. The roof line has a bold cornice and a parapet with stretches of balustrading. Sir James Brooke, the 'white Rajah' of Sarawak in Borneo, lived in No. 1 from 1831–4.

The broad pavement in front leads up to two imposing bows with Vitruvian scrolls which decorate the return end of Widcombe Terrace whose main front faces south and is set on a platform above the gardens, giving rather splendid views. The front is very pleasant with rusticated ground floor, round-headed doorways and first-floor windows set in depressed arches. There is a plat-band and a continuous sill course below the top windows, and the end houses are set slightly forward.

Opposite the crescent a side road, the Tyning, is lined with late nineteenth-century houses, and further up the hill Church Road branches off, leading past a seventeenth-century house with stone mullions and giving a view of Prior Park Mansion hanging against the green back-drop of the hill, to one of the most attractive and atmospheric settings in the city, the old parish church of St Thomas à Becket and the early eighteenth-century Widcombe Manor, set in beautiful grounds which merge into a green vista of trees and hedges and hills.

The manor, best seen from beside the simple churchyard gravestone of the novelist Horace Annesly Vachel (1881–1955) whose 'golden house' it once was, has an impressively decorated front with giant fluted Ionic pilasters, supporting an entablature with pulvinated frieze and heavy cornice, a triangular modillioned pediment with an oval window flanked by swags, and a parapet with sections of balustrading. Windows have keystones carved into grotesque masks. Above the doorway, which is set behind a Doric porch with pillars and triglyphs, and on either side of it, are round-headed windows. In front of the house is a bronze fountain decorated with delicate figures and said to be of late sixteenth-century Venetian origin, while in the grounds is a pleasant little orangery. Beyond the church is Manor Farm with a rather splendid octagonal dovecot and behind the manor is Widcombe Lodge, once the home of the novelist Henry Fielding and his sister Sarah. Fielding was befriended by Ralph Allen of Prior Park who is said to be the model for Squire Allworthy in *Tom Jones*. Opposite Manor Farm is the appropriately named Gothic Cottage of 1854 and a high wall bounding the gardens of Crowe Hall. Built for a lady named Crowe in about 1760 and considerably changed by the Tugwells in the nineteenth century, it suffered a bad fire in 1926 when it was occupied by the Mayoress, Madame Sarah Grand, but was subsequently restored. Also present at the time of the fire were Mr Tindall who had bought the house in 1919 for £15,000, his daughter, the cook, who died, and the maids, who were rescued from the roof. The Mayoress's chain of office was saved by a policeman.

In 1502 the old church was "by its great age obliged to be taken down" and Prior Cantlow of Bath Abbey caused a new one to be erected which is why a brass inside records that "Thys church floryschyd with foremosnste spectabyll Prior Cantlow hathe edydyfyde desyring you to pray for him with your prayer delectabyll to inhabylle hym in heavnn ever to abyde"; a tower battlement bears a mitre, and the key and sword of Sts Peter and Paul appear on the wall above the porch. It is a sturdy little building with tower, nave and chancel, all battlemented, although the chancel ones are more ornate. There is a fine Perpendicular window at the east end and a fat golden cockerel on the tower top. The bells were taken away to St Matthew's, under considerable local protest, and St Thomas's got what was considered a very unfair exchange, the bell from the Ebenezer chapel which was at that time in Church hands, before being acquired as a Baptist chapel in 1849 by a splinter group from the Providence Chapel, Lower Bristol Road.

Back down at the Claverton Road end of Widcombe Hill there is a corner pub whose emblem, a statue of a White Hart, is said to have originally adorned the old White Hart in Stall Street from which Elezear Pickwick ran his coaches, and on its other side a second road, Prior Park, runs back up the hill. Stretching back from this bottom corner is an early eighteenth-century three-storey row designed by Wood and built for Ralph Allen's stonemasons and so known as Ralph Allen's Row. For years they have been under planning blight, due to proposals to demolish them for road widening, and for a long time were boarded up and in a state of extreme dilapidation. They are now being restored. It was a classic case of conflict in environmental interests. The buildings were of considerable historical interest yet there was undoubtedly a traffic problem.

At their end a side road goes up past the once derelict Prior Park Cottages and a house called Good Hope, and a late Georgian row. Happily, the cottages and Good Hope have been restored. Opposite Good Hope and facing the road is the long range of Prior Park Buildings of 1820 with a central pediment rather overpowered by a high attic on each side, and with an attractive strip of garden along the whole front which flanks a canalized mill-stream with grass and trees. This garden is now looked after by the council. At the far end a steep little road, Forfield Rise, takes us past a new development and a nine-teenth-century brick row, Forfield Terrace, to link with the third of the uphill roads, Lyncombe Hill, which has a fascinating collection of Regency Classical on one side and Victorian neo-Gothic on the other, notably Augusta Place, with stepped cornice and lesenes, round-headed fanlights and thin glazing bars, and the neo-Gothic Priory with buttressed porch, battlements, thick pinnacles, and a cross on a shield.

Prior Park Road continues up the hill past the abbey cemetery which was paid for by Lord Middleton when he was the Honourable and Reverend W. J. Brodrick, Rector of Bath. Laid out by John Loudon (1783–1843), the eminent landscape gardener, with a Norman-style chapel by Manners, it was consecrated in 1844. Next to it in 1862 was consecrated the Roman Catholic cemetery with a chapel by C. F. Hansom. The road now changes its name to Ralph Allen's Drive and goes up past Prior Park Mansion to Combe Down where Ralph Allen had his quarries which provided much of the stone for the building of eighteenth-century Bath and down which he constructed his tramway which, by means of gravity and pulleys, brought great blocks down to his riverside wharf. There it was loaded on to barges by Mr Padmore's crane which Wood described as "allowed by the Curious to be a Masterpiece of Mechanism". The tramway, said Wood, cut the price of stone at the wharf by a quarter.

Bath stone at the time did not have a very good reputation and Allen had not been very successful in selling it in London. By using it for his great mansion his intention was not only to provide himself with a country house befitting his newly earned wealth but also, according to Wood who designed it for him, "to exhibit the stone in a Seat which he had determined to build for himself near his Works, to much greater Advantage, and in a much greater Variety of Uses than had ever appeared in any other Structure." The mansion was built between 1735 and 1750 but Wood appears to have had a difference of opinion with Allen and the building was completed, not entirely to Wood's plan, by Allen's Clerk of Works, Richard Jones.

It has a superb site, sloping down northwards so that the rusticated basement forms a platform out from the hillside linked by an arcaded walkway to the wings, which have, however, been greatly modified. The two-storeyed frontages have attached Ionic columns on the north face and on the south a great portico with giant Corinthian columns supporting a plain pediment and a modillioned triangular pediment with plain tympanum. The roof-line is marked by a modillioned cornice and balustraded parapet. Ground-floor windows have alternating segmental and triangular pediments and the central doorway is round-headed.

In the original plans the basement contained the domestic offices—small beer and strong beer cellars and a wine vault, laundry, kitchen, scullery, bakehouse, larder, and pantry, rooms for the butler and housekeeper, servants' hall, and WCs; on the ground floor there were the great entrance hall, a chapel running up through both storeys, dining- and drawing-rooms, and a bedchamber; on the top floor were five bedrooms with dressing-rooms and closets, a servant's room, and a long gallery along the front of the house. It was in this great mansion that Allen entertained such notables as Pope, Fielding, Pitt, Smollett, Gay and Gainsborough. The friendship with Pope suffered a setback when the poet brought his 'friend' Martha Blount with him. Mrs Allen did not approve and the poet left in a huff. In spite of Allen's attempts at reconciliation, relations remained strained and Pope struck back from the grave by insultingly leaving Allen £150 in his will as "being, to the best of my calculations, the account of what I have received from him". Allen remarked drily that Pope had always been bad at arithmetic and would have been nearer the mark if he had added another nought, and gave the £150 to the Bath Hospital. There is a footpath from the cemeteries up to the top of the drive which is known as Pope's Walk although it is uncertain whether he actually used it. Down in the ground of the house fish-ponds were created and over one end was erected the famous Palladian bridge, its roof supported by Ionic columns, similar to the one at Wilton House.

When Allen died in 1764 they buried him under a pyramid in Claverton churchyard over the hill and the house went to William Warburton, Bishop of Gloucester, who had been a frequent visitor and had married Allen's favourite niece the lively Gertrude in 1745 when she was eighteen and he was forty-seven. Warburton died in 1779 and his widow married his chaplain. On her death in 1796 the house went, in accordance with Allen's will, to another niece who was then succeeded by her son and afterwards his half-brother on whose death the property was bought by a Mr Brown and then by a Bristol Quaker, John Thomas, who was active in promoting the Kennet and Avon Canal. In 1829 it was bought for £22,000 (which today would get you a small terrace house) by Bishop Baines who turned it into a Roman Catholic theological college (1829 was the year of the Catholic Emancipation Act) and in 1836 he employed H. E. Goodridge to design an impressive Baroque outside staircase to the north front. The same year there was a disastrous fire which gutted the interior, although sparing the chapel, and the interior was redecorated, much material coming from the demolition of the eighteenth-century Hunstrete House near Marksbury, including sculpture now seen in the east wing pediment. Bishop Baines died in 1843, the college closed in 1856, and the house was put up for auction. In 1867 it was repurchased for the Catholics by Bishop Clifford for £23,000 and in 1924 became a boys' boarding-school. In 1844–63 a new church was built in the west wing and although it is a rather fine building it disturbs, by its size, the balance of the original composition. Prior Park is still a school although in 1980 it encountered severe financial problems which were only alleviated by a splendid response from old scholars and friends of the college.

Prior Park is one of the architectural glories of Bath and yet it is not part of the close-knit fabric of the city, and when it was built it was not in the city at all but a gentleman's country residence, one of those Palladian new houses which were built in the country by business men of the *nouveaux riches*. Indeed its owner's influence in Bath has probably been exaggerated. He was active in founding the hospital, he had some connection with improving the roads, and was responsible for building the New Bridge in 1744, he supplied much of the stone, he was for a time on the council, although most notable for excuses for absence, was Mayor for a year, and secured (and lost) Pitt as MP for the city, but he was primarily a national figure, though modest and retiring, and removed, as was his great house, from the giddy social whirl of eighteenth-century Bath. An intensely private person, though very generous, this quiet Cornishman came to Bath in 1710 when he was seventeen as assistant to the postmistress and by sheer business acumen and organizing ability made himself two fortunes, one from organizing the cross-posts which were nationally in chaos, and the second from the quarries which he acquired through his marriage with Elizabeth Holder in 1736 (his second marriage). His probity and lack of ostentation, no less than his great wealth, won him great respect.

At the top of the hill Ralph Allen's Drive joins the plateau—top road which links the upland villages which are now part of the city although not part of its Georgian development. Eastward the road curves north past the university and gives a choice of descent between North Road, Bathwick Hill, and Widcombe Hill, while westward it is tapped by Wellsway (the old Fosse Way), Bloomfield Road, Englishcombe Lane, and the Hollow.

Wellsway swoops down the hill and then levels out for a short distance at Bear Flat which has nothing to do with bears in spite of the big ursine statue over the door of the Bear Inn with one paw dangling down as if to scoop up customers. The name was originally Berewick, the barley farm. At this point Bloomfield Road comes in with a neat row of late Georgian buildings of varying heights but with the usual features of cornice, parapet, plat-band, Doric pilasters, and banded rustication. This has been continued in a post-war block of flats which fits quite well with the scene. Opposite, however, are nineteenth-century villas of which No. 1, Whelley Lodge, has a huge hanging lantern over the door and a thick-traceried window on the side. None of these villas is on the 1860 map and they are probably of the High Victorian period of the 1880s.

In fact most of the development round here is late nineteenth and early twentieth century particularly in what is known as Poet's Corner whose street names run from Chaucer to Kipling and, presumably as an Anglo-American gesture, include Longfellow. Up in the corner Byron and Shelley are surely uneasy neighbours and it is perhaps not surprising that Milton and Longfellow present their backsides to each other. In 1860 these were the fields of Holloway Farm and Milton Avenue runs up an old hedge line. These Edwardian ranges exhibit a considerable variety of decorative detail and make a happy hunting-ground for seekers after eclecticism—Classical and Gothic capitals, gables with imitation beams, bays with peaked caps crowned with spiky metal finials, plain glass and stained glass, ceramic tiles, carved keystones, and so on. For a contrast between Regency (1804) and Edwardian see Longfellow Avenue where flat-fronted houses with round-headed doorways, stepped cornices and pediments, and Venetian windows face bays with foliaged capitals, eaves supported on brackets, and rectangular fanlights. Incidentally, most of the Regency houses have now turned their backs on the street and have their front doors behind, in Devonshire Buildings. In Shakespeare Avenue is a Methodist church with a big Perpendicular-style window and a strange tower with angular mouldings and a spire. The extension to the back is in a different style and dated 1912.

Beyond Poet's Corner the Wellsway takes a sharp bend but this was a later improvement of 1851 and the old road continued straight on down Holloway which is probably just what it says, a sunken or hollow road, although some prefer to explain it as a Holy Way on the pilgrimage route to distant Glastonbury, basing their belief on the presence of a hospice in the eleventh century associated with the church of St Mary Magdalen which was first built in 1096. The hospice later became a leper hospital and, after the dissolution of the abbey, a hospital for mentally handicapped children (they called them lunatics in those days) until it was moved to Rockhill House at Combe Down. The hospital, which is now the church caretaker's house was rebuilt in 1761, as a plaque testifies, but has pointed windows which Pevsner thinks cannot be so early though there are other examples of Georgian Gothic as early as this and the rebuilders may well have wished to signify the antiquity of the establishment.

The church, with its stumpy little battlemented and pinnacled tower, was another Cantlow effort and had a tablet in the porch similar to that at St Thomas à Becket—"This chapell florysched wt formosyte spectabyll in the Honoure of M. Magdalene Prior Cantlow hath edytde desyring yow to pray for him wt yowre prayers delectabyll that sche will inhabit him in hevyn ther evyr to abyde." Outside the south wall is a Judas-tree (*Cercis siliquastrum*) which blooms purple in the spring; Judas was supposed to have hanged himself from such a tree, in mark of which it blossoms bloodily at Lent.

A side turning, Magdalen Road, takes us down to Magdalen Avenue which has no exit except for steps down to the Wells Road. This is a little Edwardian development, well kept up, pleasant and quiet, left over from the post-war clearing away of streets, and affording a view at the end of the Georgian range of St Mary's Buildings whose bold upsweeps of parapet, cornice, and plat-band threw Peter Smithson into an ecstasy of appreciation in his *Bath: Walks Within the Wall*—indeed it was the possibility of their demolition which gave him the idea of recording these walks. It is quite pleasant.

A little further down from the old hospital is Paradise House, now a hotel, mid-eighteenth century (Pevsner) with strongly moulded Venetian windows, pedimented doorway, mullioned cornice and fine stone vases to the gate piers. It is flanked by two other buildings, the one on the left having a Venetian Gothic two-light window with a central marble shaft with flowery capital and a polychrome pointed arch above.

Holloway has a rural air with its few houses and a flagged high pavement with railings facing a stone wall and a steep wooded slope through which one can make a toilsome climb up steps to the top of Beechen Cliff which was acquired by the city in 1860 for £150. At the bottom of the road we come into a post-war housing development of artificial Bath stone and grey brick which replaced an area of grey terraces which had got rather run down in the nineteenth century and tended to be classed with Dolemeads and Avon Street as a rather unsavoury neighbourhood. The council owned the land but could not afford to develop it profitably on the basis of council-house rents so it was handed over to a private developer who put up houses for sale. These rows, running along the contour and connected by flights of steps, doubtless provide better accommodation than the previous houses but the stark whiteness of the artificial Bath stone does not blend with the landscape as did the old grey streets and contrasts strongly with the genuine Bath stone of St Mark's Church which was opened in 1832 to serve the district. Designed by G. P. Manners it is a chunky building in a simple Perpendicular style with battlemented and pinnacled tower and a polygonal chancel with Decorated tracery added in 1883. It became redundant in 1972 and is now a social centre used by numerous clubs and organizations. The adjoining church school has become an outpost of the technical college.

Beyond the church, St Mark's Road has the now familiar pattern of a Georgian row on one side and late Victorian (post-1860) paired villas with Italianate eaves on the other but where it comes down to Claverton Street the corner site is occupied by the Temperance Hall of 1847, a simple Classical temple with Doric pilasters and a plain pediment, which became the Church of the Nazarene in 1946, following a successful evangelical campaign held in the recreation ground in 1944. We are now at

Cork Street, a typical Bath-stone faced, bay-windowed, Victorian street.

Newbridge Towers, a Victorian villa with outside stairs and veranda.

Avon, bridge, and cabinet works. The works are housed in a large, red-brick building.

Herman Miller Factory—a modern and award-winning design.

Wellington Buildings, a nineteenth-century range in Weston village, for comparison with the post-war range.

Post-war range near Wellington Buildings. Note the change in style and materials.

Avondale Road. This shows a Victorian usage of chequered brickwork and terracotta ornaments for quite small houses.

St Alphege's Church, a Catholic church in the Roman basilican style by Sir Giles Gilbert Scott in 1929.

Innox Road—typical inter-war council housing.

Twerton—post-war high-density housing.

South Twerton Junior School, originally Ascension School of 1893.

Mr Dredge's patent suspension bridge. The crane behind belongs to Stothert and Pitt.

Bath University—a general view of this low-slung structure.

Gospel Hall, Claverton Down.

Holy Trinity Church, Combe Down, 1835, by Goodridge, and rather strange.

Ralph Allen's Cottages, Combe Down. The centre one with the pediment was the foreman's cottage. It also has a sundial and is called Dial House.

the foot of Lyncombe Hill and a few steps up will take us to Southcot Place (1817—Peach), three storeyed, with a plat-band and round-headed doorways with keystones, and a new range on the southern uphill side.

6

Fringe Benefits—
North of the River

If, with no very great stretch of the imagination, we think of Bath as a fried egg then the Georgian heart forms a rather off-centre yoke and the white is a broad skirt of buildings, mainly of the nineteenth and twentieth centuries with little specks of yolk which are the hearts of old villages which have been engulfed in urban sprawl. Unlike a fried egg it does not lie flat but rises to the north and south and then flattens out on the plateau tops. Even then the white is not complete for there are quite large areas to the north and south which are still fields.

It is a complicated pattern but for description it may be divided into three quadrants and the southern plateau. The quadrants are the north-east between the Lansdown and London Roads, including Beacon Hill and the old villages of Lambridge, Larkhall and Lower Swainswick (though scarcely recognizable for what they once were); the north-west between the Upper Bristol and Lansdown Roads, including the old village of Weston; and the south-west, south of the Lower Bristol Road and including Oldfield Park and Twerton. The southern plateau has an arc of building running through Claverton Down, Combe Down, Odd Down, Sladebrook and the latest addition of Whiteway. Nothing very ancient remains in any of these areas as they have been extensively re-modelled and added to from the eighteenth century onwards and the majority of the architecture is Victorian with inter- and post-war infill and addition, leading to such a bewildering variety that only the main points can be picked out.

The North-East Quadrant

If we climb up Lansdown Road to St Stephen's Church, where the road forks, we find ourselves on a narrow plateau with Beacon Hill off to our right beyond which the land slopes quite steeply, but not steeply enough to prevent building, down to the

Lam Brook (or Charlcombe Brook as it is otherwise called). Much of this valley is filled with post-war housing, engulfing a few nineteenth-century rows and some inter-war semis and lying in a horseshoe round two post-war schools, one an infants' school of 1967, the other the Diocesan School for Girls which opened there in 1965 and is changing its name to St Mark's now it has started to take boys as well, although one wonders why the girls couldn't also have a saint. The southern edge of Beacon Hill, however, where it looks down towards the London Road is precipitous and wooded in its upper part before the slope eases sufficiently to be built on. Northward the plateau slopes down to the Charlcombe valley over open fields. Basically, therefore, there are three sub-regions—the plateau top and Beacon Hill, the Lam Brook valley, and the longitudinal stretch from the wooded slope to the London Road.

This last area has a spine road running north-east from the end of Camden Crescent called for most of its length Camden Road although towards the end it becomes Claremont Road, veering to the right and descending to join London Road via St Saviour's Road. This route takes us through a representative selection of the housing of the region, starting with a three-storey, flat-faced Victorian range with narrow linked plat-bands, stone shelfs under first-floor windows, and doorways surmounted by flat pediments on brackets. The party-walls between the houses rise above the roof, a feature which usually dates from the by-laws made after the Public Health Act of 1875 and which is widespread in Bath by-law building. Straight pediments on brackets also feature in Berkeley Place but here the ground floor has banded rustication and there is a cornice and parapet—this is nineteenth century but the Classical details show how the ghosts of Georgian builders were still nudging the Victorian designers at a time when elsewhere they would be going neo-Gothic, which makes nineteenth-century dating by style difficult in Bath. That most of the building in the north-east quadrant is nineteenth century and later is shown by a map of 1800 when there is hardly a building in the area.

On the left, raised up, Upper Camden Place has eighteenth-century detailing although many of the houses have been altered and the end one has a triangular pediment with a corroded coat of arms in the tympanum. On the right is Lower Camden Place at whose end a building break gives a view of a notice which states the house is (or, rather, was) an "Asylum for

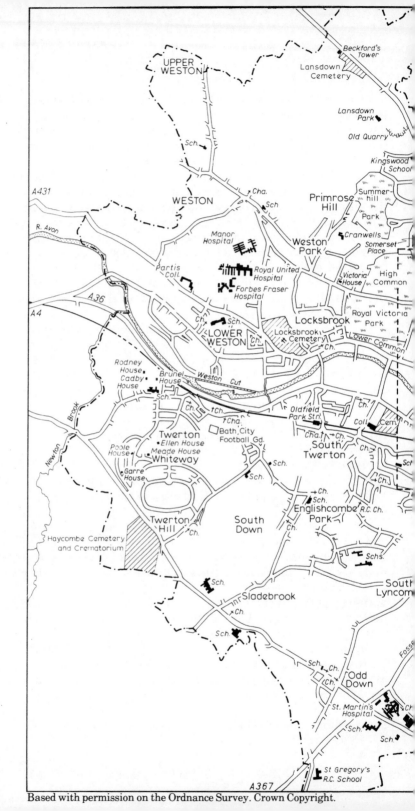

Based with permission on the Ordnance Survey. Crown Copyright.

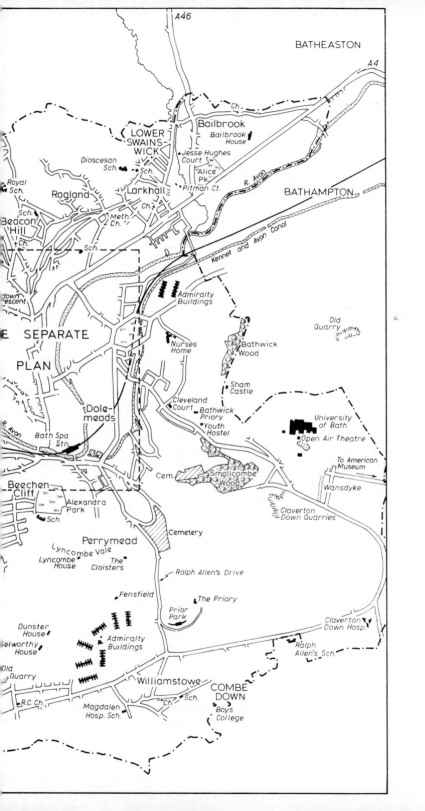

Teaching Young Females Household Work". It has been flats and is now being done up and is reached from Gay's Hill, off which runs Belgrave Crescent, a pleasant layout with architraves and keystones to the windows, straight pediments to the doorways, plat-band, and the usual raised party-walls. It curves up to rejoin Camden Road and then comes Belgrave Terrace, a large range dated 1874–6. At each end is a segmented gable, in the middle a rectangular one, and between end and middle, on each side, four triangular gables, a striking, if rather idiosyncratic, composition. Opposite, Ivythorn Villa is a plain house with battlements added, and beyond the terrace are Malvern Villas, a set of large Victorian gabled neo-Gothic semis and Malvern Terrace which is also Victorian but with Classical overtones.

Beyond the end of Bennet Lane, which leads down to the post-war, green-roofed Snow Hill development, there is open ground on the right, with views, and on the left a short Victorian terrace in Pennant sandstone and Bath stone, with bay windows and—wait for it!—raised party-walls. Further along, Claremont Place has a set of Greek Revival paired villas of 1817 ending at South View 1 and 2 dated 1897 but still with straight pediments and plat-bands. On the left Rivers Street, now a cul-de-sac, leads back up to Perfect View, a long two-storey range of painted stone houses with plat-band, string-course, and—you'll never guess!—raised party-walls. It has, indeed, a perfect view over the city and the hills to the south. At the top end you can take a field path on to St Stephen's Road or climb steps for a short walk through the woods to some new housing around Summerfield Road and then back down through the woods to the other end of Perfect View where there is a welcoming seat.

Back on Camden Road we pass the end of Frankley Road dropping sharply down the hill and lined on one side with Regency-style houses, the centre one more elaborate with a triangular pediment and the name Frankley Buildings; the style changes at the bottom where it is dated 1897. On the main road are more nineteenth-century buildings with shops and a pub and then Claremont Methodist Church with porch, buttresses, round window, and turrets, and now Claremont Road begins to run downhill through Eastbourne Avenue, inter-war on the left with gables and leaded lights, Victorian on the right (1889). Round to the right is more Victoriana, Beaufort Villas of

1889, Eastville of 1881, Belgrave Road with large nineteenth-century villas and some inter-war infill, and finally on the left Grosvenor Villas, a set of semis dated 1927 (Vernacular Arts and Crafts), 1878, 1892, 1891 (twice), and 1890. And now we are in St Saviour's Road and can turn left to look at the church.

This is a big one with a pinnacled west tower, pierced parapets, Perpendicular-style windows, and a fondness for ogee arches. It was designed by John Pinch junior, whose father had designed St Mary's, Bathwick, the foundation stone was laid in 1829 and the church consecrated in 1832, dedicated to St Saviour.

In 1882 a chancel with a fine east window was added to designs of Charles Edward Davis, the City Architect. There is an elaborate reredos, big galleries, and plaster vaulting—fan in the chancel, tierceron elsewhere. As in so many of Bath's churches there are masses of wall tablets.

Opposite are Beaufort Mews and Beaufort Place, which looks Georgian, and then a small shopping centre with post office, ironmonger, a couple of newsagents, a couple of greengrocers, a couple of butchers, electronics, fish and chips, ladies' hairdresser, and up in Salisbury Road an establishment which at the time of writing is labelled "Wool Shop" and sells pine furniture. There are also public lavatories and the Larkhall Inn (Larkhall, incidentally, means the corner frequented by larks). A little further on are early nineteenth-century rows in Dafford's Place and Dafford's Buildings, leading to Eden Terrace with bays and gables and opposite Elmcroft, dated 1896, and a curious medley of Classical and Gothic with a touch of Arts and Crafts. St Saviour's Road crosses the Lam Brook to continue as Deadmill Lane to meet the Gloucester Road.

Before the bridge Ferndale Road goes up steeply to the right past a Victorian terrace to long post-war ranges in artificial stone and wood panels, set parallel to the Gloucester Road. Beyond the bridge is the stone bulk of Deadmill, once a corn mill powered by water taken from the brook. It was gutted by fire in 1900 shortly after the owner had re-equipped it with "the newest roller system" but it now looks much as it did before except that the water-wheel has gone. According to Peach, who is not always reliable, Dead Mill is a corruption of the name of a past owner, Dedemulle.

Deadmill Lane joins the Gloucester Road at the city boundary and we can come back towards Bath and turn off left into

Bailbrook Lane which becomes excessively narrow as it goes past the single terrace of houses which is Bailbrook village at the end of which stands a one-time mission church made of rusting corrugated iron with a small tower and Gothic windows. In 1978 planning permission was given, against some local opposition, to turn it into an artist's studio. Below the road is a large market garden, a farm, and the grounds of Bailbrook House, a large Georgian building of before 1791, attributed to Eveleigh, consisting of two blocks joined by a entrance hall and decorated with Ionic pilasters. It became a mental hospital, then a nurses' home, and is now, with much additional building at the back, a residential college.

Near the junction of Bailbrook Lane and the London Road is Batheaston Villa, now in a rather sorry condition. A big, four-square, Georgian house, with an Ionic porch, a niche in the side wall with a draped female figure which at the time of writing was decorated with plastic flowers, and round the back a large two-storey bow with battlements and a big iron balcony on iron supports and two wooden Corinthian pillars. It was here in 1775 that Lady Miller started her highly popular poetry contests in which her guests competed in writing verses which were deposited in a vase which the Millers had brought back from Italy. Some of the verses were published in 1776 as *Poetical Amusements at a Villa Near Bath*. The book was very success-ful in spite of the poorness of the poetry—as Horace Walpole wrote,

> The collection is printed, published—yes, on my faith! there are *bouts-rimés* on a buttered muffin by Her Grace the Duchess of Northumberland, recipes to make them by Corydon the venerable, alias (George Pitt); others very pretty by Lord P(almerston), some by Lord C(armarthen), many by Mrs. M(iller) herself that have no thought but wanting metre; and immortality promised to her without end or measure. In short, since folly, which never ripens to madness but in this climate, ran distracted, there never was any-thing so entertaining or so dull.

If, instead of pursuing our relentless way up St Saviour Road, we had turned off at the shops up Salisbury Road we would have come to the Diocesan School and the modern developments of Fairfield Park, Larkhall, and Raglands, a mixture of recent terraces, inter-war semis, and here and there the nineteenth-century rows such as Worcester Park which must have looked rather lost in the days when they were surrounded by fields.

There still remains a good deal of open space, including a large recreation ground, and the green hills lie around, around . . .!

Working westward again and towards the higher ground we would come to Beacon Hill and its common, a big triangle of grass with a few swings and a roundabout, with a long, early nineteenth-century row on one side and on the other a late Victorian red-brick row with stone trimmings and (dare we mention it?) raised party-walls. Next to this is a successful design of flats in brick which fits in quite nicely and beyond that is the grey St Stephen's Junior School which bears the dates 1891, 1903, and 1905. From here runs Richmond Place with eighteenth-century rows of flat-faced houses with cornices and pediment, leading to Richmond Road with the Royal School and St Stephen's Church.

The school was designed in 1856 by James Wilson, a local architect, who also did the Wesleyan Kingswood Boys' School, for the Lansdown Proprietary School for Boys but this went bankrupt in 1865 and the buildings were taken over by the Royal School for Daughters of Officers of the Army, founded after the Crimean War, which it still is although entry is now less restricted and everyone just calls it the Royal. The style is more Jacobean than the full-blooded Gothic Wilson used for Kingswood or the Early English he used for St Stephen's, but the feature which makes it a landmark is the tower with a corner turret pointing like a finger to heaven.

Lansdown was in the parish of Walcot, the second largest in England, and as population spread northward it became evident that a new church was needed so in 1840 the foundation stone was laid by the Rector of Walcot. Owing to the nature of the site, the church was aligned north-south so that the altar was at the north end instead of the more conventional east. The bishop didn't like this and refused to consecrate the church although it was licensed for public worship in 1845. To meet the orientation objection they altered the plans to include two shallow recesses on the east and west sides so that the altar could be on the east although it made the church an extremely awkward shape and they couldn't really afford the alteration—work stopped for four years while they tried to raise the extra money and when the job was completed the church was still in debt so it still couldn't be consecrated. However, things picked up and in 1883 they added an apse by Wilcox at the north end, put the altar in that and persuaded the new bishop, Lord Harvey,

to consecrate the church at last, as a tablet in the chancel
records.

From 1845–81 the church was served by assistant curates
from St Swithin's but in 1881 the last assistant, The Revd
Hilton Bothamley, became the first vicar of the new parish and
served it until 1911. He was very active and his memorial tablet
(he died in 1919) reminds us that "by his untiring effort and
munificent gifts ... the church [was] enlarged and transformed". Much of this was in the way of decoration, but a major
transformation was a new ceiling to the nave in 1886, largely
paid for by George Stuckey Lean. On a cross-beam is carved the
quotation "Behold I see the Heavens opening", a reference to the
martyrdom of St Stephen, who was stoned to death.

Bothamley's wife Mary was also much appreciated and when
she died at the age of fifty-four a wall panel in ceramics was put
up in her memory by her husband, and her friends, "chiefly the
women of the parish", donated a bell to the tower.

Beyond the place originally made for the altar is a kind of
shallow transept which was added in 1866 for use by the girls of
the Royal School and on the front pew is carved, between linen-
fold panelling, the school motto "The Lord Giveth Wisdom", and
there are memorial windows to two headmistresses. One is to
Emelie Maria Kingdom who was the first Head from 1863 to
1882 and the other to Mary Walker who was Head from 1882 to
1898. There is a second set of windows to Mary Kington on the
side wall. These were given by her sisters and are labelled
"Fortitude", "Caritas", "Fides", and "Pax". In the "Caritas"
(Charity) window a pelican appears. It was believed that if a
pelican had no food for its children it would peck its breast and
feed them with its blood and the medieval church took this as a
symbol of Christ's sacrifices for the world.

Indeed, the church has many picture windows, including one
where the distinctive tower of the Royal appears in a Jerusalem
street scene, several murals, including a large one on the back
wall behind the gallery, many inscriptions, and a twinkling
reredos. The latest window, put in after the war, shows St
Francis with a leper, St Telemachus intervening between two
gladiators (which cost him his life), St Alphege, Prior of Bath
and Bishop of Winchester, being killed by Danes with ox-bones,
St Boniface, one-time Bishop of Crediton who went to convert
Germany and is shown chopping down Thor's oak in the Forest
of Hesse, and, a nice counterweight to male chauvinism,

Elizabeth Fry the eighteenth-century Quakeress and prison reformer. Modern modifications to the entrance have provided a pleasant small hall with coffee bar and toilets.

Outside, the church looks solid and rather graceless, with stumpy buttresses and thick pinnacles, but the tower is remarkable, rising in three stages, the top two with high pinnacles and flying buttresses. Pevsner called it "crazy", Bryan Little wrote that it was "brilliantly original" with a "fanciful, pagoda-like quality". It is certainly striking, a well-known landmark and, seen from a distance in the right light, beautiful.

If we go up the other side of St Stephen's, following Lansdown Road we find on the left, around Sion Road (originally Alma Road and completed in 1858), and Hamilton Road an area of large detached houses, some from the end of the nineteenth century, others inter-war and some modern. On the right is the massive entry to the Royal School, with heads of Victoria and Albert, and further up on the left, hidden by trees is the neo-Gothic bulk of Kingswood School, with some recent additions. Peeping over a high wall in College Road, beyond where Hamilton Road comes in, is a rather severe rectangular tower with a modillioned cornice and a balustrade. This was erected in 1880 by Sir Robert Blanes, Mayor of Bath in 1872 and its MP in 1885, to relieve unemployment in the building trade. Blanes was either a genuine philanthropist or a good vote-catcher for he also organized parties at his house for the working classes and arranged excursions for them to the seaside.

Kingswood School was opened by John Wesley in 1748 at Kingswood, Bristol, and moved to Bath in 1852. It was for some time, though not at first, restricted to the sons of Methodist preachers but gradually "lay boys", as they were called, began to be accepted (there were 37 in 1928 and 145 in 1946). Entry is not now restricted and they even take some girls. For a long time the school had two Heads, one for the teaching side and the other, the Governor, for administration.

The first Kingswood opened for fifty boarders aged six to twelve who were subjected to a Spartan regime. They got up at five in the morning, went to bed at eight at night, and had no playtime—"He that plays when he is a child," wrote Wesley, "will play when he is a man." The curriculum consisted of arithmetic, English, French, Latin, Greek, Hebrew, history, geography, chronology, rhetoric, logic, ethics, geometry, algebra, physics and music, and all the books originally used were written by Wesley himself. Later, at Bristol, boys were allowed to stay on to receive, as Wesley said, as good or better education than they would have had at Oxford or Cambridge. However, there were times when the rules were not kept to very strictly and Wesley often grieved for the state of his school.

The new school at Bath, designed by Wilson, cost, with the land, £16,000, but the sale of the old school fetched only £1,000. The new building was heated, quite unsuccessfully, by a hot-air system with "valvular gratings" in the skirtings. Built in an H form in Perpendicular Gothic which the Methodists tended to adopt for their later chapels, with a central tower and oriel window, it was considerably enlarged in the 1880s by the addition of a long, four-storey extension at right angles to the back. Originally it had no chapel and the boys had to walk into Bath for services at Walcot and King Street. It did have a swimming-bath, but this was done away with in the 1870s to make way for classrooms and laboratories; a new bath, steam-heated, was provided in 1909. Since the war, extra buildings, including a sixth form block, have been added. Several houses around have been taken for boarding accommodation and there are playing-fields up on Lansdown opposite Beckford's Tower.

The North-West Quadrant

Just as nineteenth-century speculators covered up the green fields of the north-east, so also they laid their busy building hands on the north-west although here they were more strongly imbued with the spirit of the Italianate and the Gothic Revival. They left quite a lot of open land, however, some of which has since been infilled with inter- and post-war housing although even today there are large tracts of farmland in the north which are still within the city boundary. In addition, embedded in the north-west, is the ancient village of Weston, the *tun*, or settlement, to the west of Bath.

The eastern boundary starts in the north with Lansdown Road but then deviates west down Cavendish Road and Marlborough Lane which mark the western edge of Georgian Bath. The area fans out to the west and is traversed by four spine roads—Weston Road/Weston Lane/Weston High Street in the north; Upper Bristol Road/Newbridge Hill/Kelston Road in the centre; Newbridge Road, which was engineered by John Macadam for the Bath Turnpike Trust in the 1830s as an improvement on Newbridge Hill; and down towards the river the old line of Locksbrook Road and Brassmill Lane. These are all linked by a north-south route through Combe Park (1860s), Chelsea Road (1880s), and Station Road.

To make a generalization (which is always dangerous) it may be said that these east-west routes each traverse differing nineteenth-century developments, for there is a change from north to south. At the top, near the hills, there grew up after about 1840 an affluent area of large villas in their own often considerable grounds, in the centre were semi-detached houses, often quite large, and in the south were built ranges of more modest two-storey houses, although even here the bigger semis are to be seen as well. The whole of the north and middle seems to have been a good address in Victorian times for if we look at late nineteenth-century street directories which include the occupations of the working classes but not of the middle or upper we find that in most of this area names are given but not occupations.

The northern area was definitely the most affluent and begins with the big villas, Gothic and Italianate, at the top of Park Lane opposite the Royal Victoria Park—Stratton House, combining Classical, Italianate, and Gothic, its chimney-stacks linked by an arch; Abbey Rectory (No. 17) very Gothic with curly gables, pierced parapet, and an angel; No. 18, Italianate; No. 20, now a private hotel, Jacobean of 1835—and up on Weston Road Ormond Lodge with Venetian windows, cornice, parapet, and pilasters, looking late eighteenth and early nineteenth century, Fairlands and Onslow House, both big behind trees, and then a little pair of two-storey houses interestingly named Moravian Cottages. There had been a Moravian chapel in Bath in Princes Street in the 1760s until 1845 when they built the big chapel with Corinthian columns at the top of Charlotte Street to a design by James Wilson. This was taken over by Christian Scientists in 1907 and the Moravians moved to a red-brick chapel in Coronation Avenue, South Twerton, until 1955 when they added an impressive new church at the end of Weston High Street.

Moravia in central Czechoslovakia, between Bohemia and Ruthenia, and there in the fifteenth century was established the Church of the Brethren (later known as Moravians) who broke away from the papacy and were so savagely persecuted that after the Thirty Years War in the early seventeenth century they ceased to exist as an organized body. They were revived in the eighteenth century by Count von Zinzendorf (1700–60) of Saxony who brought members of the Brethren to his estate and devoted his life to developing the community and spreading its ideas to America and England. It was in 1736 on a voyage to America that John Wesley met a group of Moravian emigrants and their pastor, Gottlieb Spangenberg, who made a deep impression on him. Back in England in 1738, John and his brother Charles sought advice from another Moravian, Peter Böhler, and it is very likely that their earnest discussions contributed to John Wesley's sudden conversion to a deep and abiding belief in the saving grace of personal faith in Jesus Christ. Methodism is not Moravianism but there is little doubt that Wesley owed a great deal to his contact with the Moravians.

Back to the buildings! All of Weston is not, of course, Victorian—opposite the cottages, for example, is Cranwells Park, a pleasant new development which took a slice off the grounds of the house Cranwells which was built in about 1849 (Peach) for Jerome Murch, seven times Mayor of Bath. Further along on the left, two imposing stone gateposts are inscribed "Park Gardens" and lead to a private nineteenth-century development with big villas, vaguely Classical or Italianate, but with an infill of smaller inter- and post-war housing. At the end of Park Gardens, Audley Park Road leads one way to Victoria Park and the other way turns back to Weston Road with new housing on either side and a view over the Lock's Brook valley and Locksbrook cemetery. It joins Weston Lane near the junction with Weston Park and by the Park School (private preparatory) and the low Italianate building which is now the Bell School of Languages.

Weston Park was a development which started about 1845. Once again there are big villas, Italianate, Jacobean, Gothic, or so eclectic as to defy classification, set in big grounds planted with trees and bushes. They were the homes of the well-to-do; Weston Park House, for example, was built in the 1870s and inhabited by Handel Cossham, who made a fortune from the Bristol coal mines and was for some years MP for Bath. Today these houses are schools or nursing homes or doctors' co-operatives or student hostels or offices or, more rarely, flats; parts of the grounds have gone for more recent housing whose artificial Bath stone and aluminium-framed windows do not always sit well in the environment. Fortunately, many of the trees planted in the nineteenth century still remain—it is a leafy place.

Weston Park East and West, roads which run up to the north, never joined up although there is a footpath between them and further paths take off into the fields and up the hill. Summerfield, built about 1808 for Sir R. S. Blair (Peach) with lots of boxy buildings added behind, is now an Avon County Special School, with a playing-field over the road. The old house still presents a pedimented front decorated with Ionic pilasters.

And now Weston Park takes us into the High Street of Weston village, but not by car as the street is one way in the opposite direction, and a good thing too! This is by the war memorial which, in addition to the two World Wars, commemorates Private R. Eacott who died in Korea in 1953. In medieval times Weston Manor was mainly important for wool production from the sheep which grazed on the sleights (slopes) and top of Lansdown. Some of the wool would be spun and woven in the village and a will of 1524 refers to two "stocks" or fulling mills, but most of the fleeces went to Bath as the manor was owned by the Bath monastery up to the Dissolution in 1539. By the eighteenth century the industry had died out in Bath and the wool would have had to be sent further afield, and in the nineteenth century cattle and grain began to be more important—there were two breweries in Weston in Trafalgar Road. Farming still plays its part but improvements in communication, and particularly the increase in car ownership, has filled in around the old village with inter- and post-war housing so that most of the inhabitants are commuters—although of course there has been an increase in shops and garages. In 1950 Weston village was incorporated into Bath.

A new industry, still there, came to the parish, though not the village, in 1898 when Cedric Chivers moved his bookbinding business out of Bath to a house called Portway in Combe Park. Apparently the inhabitants of the new house would only allow a factory if they could not see it and to this day it remains discreetly hidden. Previously Portway had been a "Middle Class School" with fees of nine guineas for the older boys and five for those under nine years of age. Later it became a girls' school before Cedric Chivers bought it. On one side is the Homestead, built for the headmaster of the National School in Weston village who retired there in 1891. On the other side is the ground of Lansdown Cricket Club which in the nineteenth century was used for county matches in which W. G. Grace often played. Beyond that is the big scatter of buildings which is the Royal United Hospital, including single-storey brick buildings from the First World War, bigger buildings of Bath stone for the move out from the city in 1932, and a good deal of post-war building including the new maternity unit opened by a pregnant Princess Anne in 1981. Although Bath is in Avon the hospital comes under the West Wilts Area Health Authority as it draws many of its patients from that region. The rest of Combe Park consists of big Victorian semis with gables and bays, mostly in Bath stone but one or two brick-fronted with stone trimmings, and inter-war housing.

In the nineteenth century Weston village was well supplied with streams and the brook (now underground in a pipe) ran along the main street. Industries included not only the breweries but also a paper mill and a flour mill. The water supply may account for the fact that there were so many laundrywomen in the village in the nineteenth century—as late as 1865 the Bath Directory noted sixty-five laundresses in Weston and in 1876 *The Church Rambler* reported that "the Village was simply the wash house of Bath . . . only the women worked during the week, the men on Saturday when they took the baskets home, and then on Monday there was a general orgy on the proceeds." In hard times the money from laundry work was important as the vicar noted in 1895—"The distress has been very serious in Bath, and Weston would have been very badly off had it not been for the wives and sisters whose laundry work has saved us."

A lot of changes took place in the fabric of the village in the nineteenth century. In the High Street a long, simple building still bears the inscription "Village School in Unity with the National Society 1817". It was extended in 1895. Another school, which is now the church hall was also built further along the High Street, largely due to the efforts of the Vicar, The Revd John Bond who also founded a men's club and reading-room in the Batch. In 1876 the parish presented him with an inkstand and erected a granite drinking-fountain in the High Street where it still stands although the inscription is almost indecipherable. However, in spite of the efforts of school, church, and chapel Weston was reckoned a pretty rough place in the nineteenth century.

In 1802 there was a new vicarage by the church to designs by the Bath architect Thomas Baldwin. It is a graceful building with cornice, parapet, Corinthian-type pilasters, and a couple of medallions. The church itself is nineteenth century apart from the tower, with a nave of 1832 by John Pinch and transepts and chancel of 1893. There are battlements and corner buttresses and the window style is Perpendicular although the porch door-way is decorated with a double-curved ogee arch, a character-istic of the Decorated period. The church has a rather heavy, stumpy look and *The Church Rambler* found it disappointing. In the churchyard is the tomb designed by Baldwin for his old boss, Thomas Warr Atwood, big, with an urn on top (the tomb, that is). Another commemorates the Oliver family, of whom the most famous was Dr William Oliver who was an excellent physician and helped to found the Bath Hospital but is best remembered for having 'invented' a biscuit. He bought property in Weston in 1759 and it remained in the family until about 1880 when it was bought by William Carr, the Twerton industrialist. Dr Oliver lived in Bath in Queen Square, died in 1764 and was buried at Weston.

Much of the old Weston village was rebuilt and modernized in the nineteenth century (Victoria Terrace, for instance had a Victorian face put on a seventeenth-century body), and new terraces were added, but some of the old remains. Prospect House, for example, is of about 1702, and there are buildings whose stone mullions and dripstones suggest a sixteenth- or seventeenth-century date. Trafalgar Road (the Battle of Trafalgar was 1805), which contains the Countess of Hunting-don's church, a replacement for an older one which stood behind the present Co-op., is nineteenth century, as are Waterloo Buildings at the top. A pleasant development in Church Street with a Georgian flavour is by the Avondown Housing Associ-ation and shows that all modern change is not necessarily 'modern'.

At the end of the High Street the road turns sharply right to climb the hill past modern housing to Lansdown ('the long hill'), much of which was bought in 1690–1701 by William Blathwayt, Secretary of State to William and Mary, who lived at Dyrham House. The one-time Star Inn by the racecourse was rebuilt after the war and renamed the Blathwayt Arms. In the early part of the nineteenth century the horse races were run from Beckford's Tower to Lansdown Lane but after about 1830 the annual race meeting was moved to the present site. Beckford's Tower (up Lansdown Lane and right at the junction, or approach along Lansdown Road) was designed in 1825–6 by Henry Edmund Goodridge for the eccentric William Beckford who lived in Lansdown Crescent. It is now administered by the Beckford Tower Trust, formed in 1977 and given and endowment by the tower's new owners, Dr and Mrs L. T. Hilliard. The tower is open on Saturdays and Sundays, April to October, from two to five p.m., and you can climb the 154 stone steps, which in Beckford's time were richly carpeted, to the belvedere where there are splendid views of Bath and the surrounding countryside, a little interrupted by the stonework between the windows.

William Beckford was born in 1760, the year George III came to the throne, and died at the age of eighty-four in 1844, in the seventh year of Victoria's reign. He inherited a great fortune, largely made from a sugar plantation in Jamaica, from his father, Alderman William Beckford, twice Lord Mayor of London, and Byron called him "England's wealthiest son". Much of his money he spent on travel, a remarkable collection of books, art, furniture, and other art work—and on building.

His first great structure was at Fonthill in Wiltshire where he pulled down most of his father's Palladian mansion and from 1797 to 1812, with the spasmodic aid of the architect James Wyatt (1747–1813) built an incredible neo-Gothic abbey with a central octagon tower 290 feet high, a hall 120 feet long, and two wings 400 feet long and 25 feet broad. Originally the tower had a spire, but this fell down. In 1819 the south-west tower where Beckford was living had to be rebuilt; then the price of sugar fell and Beckford lost money, and in 1822 he sold the abbey for £33,000 and moved to Bath—first to No. 66 Pulteney Street and then in 1833 to No. 20 Lansdown Crescent. He also bought No. 1 Lansdown Place West and joined the two houses by a bridge although later he sold No. 1 and bought No. 19, turning 19 and 20 into one house. In 1825 the centre tower of Fonthill Abbey collapsed.

On Lansdown, Beckford built himself a new tower completed in 1827, using a local architect, Henry Edmund Goodridge, and it was from there, while it was building, that he noticed that his abbey tower had disappeared. For his new edifice he abandoned the Gothic entirely and set up a severe Italianate building with a tower capped by a bit of neo-Greek fantasy based on two Greek monuments—the Tower of the Winds and the Choragic Monument of Lysicrates in Athens, drawings of which had been published in 1762 in *Antiquities of Athens* by Stuart and Revett.

It has eight cast-iron columns and a cast-iron roof. Other modern features were a central-heating furnace which sent warm air up the tower, and a pump which drew up water from a well.

On the ground floor was the Scarlet Drawing-Room and Vestibule, and in the Annexe were the kitchen and offices. On the first floor was the Sanctuary, with a statue of St Anthony of Padua whom Beckford had adopted as his patron saint, the Crimson Drawing-Room, half of which is now part of the museum, and the Etruscan Library. Between the crescent and the tower Beckford landscaped the ground and planted trees and bushes, all now gone. In this he worked with his gardener, Vincent, who lived in the cottage by the entrance to the tower which later fell into disrepair but has now been renovated and renamed Beckford Cottage.

Beckford left the tower and grounds to his daughter, the Duchess of Hamilton, who sold it in 1847 to a publican who turned it into a beer garden so she bought it back and gave it to the Rector of Walcot as a burial-ground on the condition that her father's body should be brought from the abbey cemetery and reinterred by the tower, where he had wanted to be buried. His tomb is now there, in polished granite with a coat of arms and beneath it the inscription—

Eternal Power,
Grant me through obvious clouds one transient gleam,
Of thy bright essence in my dying hour.

It stands in an oval enclosure surrounded by a ditch. Goodridge, who was also employed to design the 'Byzantine' entry gates and wall to the new cemetery, is buried not far away with his wife and daughters and other Goodridges up to 1900. The Scarlet Drawing-Room became the funeral chapel and the tower and grounds were consecrated in 1848. Repairs to the tower took place in 1884 and 1898 and then in 1931 a mysterious fire destroyed much of the interior and the Rector started an appeal for restoration. More funds were called for in 1954 when the stairs had become unsafe and in 1957 a donation from the Hilliards enabled external repairs to the lantern to be made.

In 1970 the Church Commissioners declared the cemetery and chapel redundant, the place went up for sale, and in 1971 they approved a proposal from the Hilliards and sold them the freehold. Now the tower is a residence and a museum, much renovation has taken place, and the steps and terrace, which were turned into a ramp for funerals, restored. The place is well worth visiting, not only for the fine views but also for an interesting collection of items relating to Beckford, including a model of Fonthill.

Beckford, who was both eccentric and egocentric, lived under something of a cloud socially as he was reputed to be homosexual. In 1784 he formed a close relationship with his cousin William Courtenay which was rumoured, though not proved, as being somewhat more than Platonic. Courtenay was certainly homosexual and to avoid arrest for this he fled to France in 1811 where he died in obscurity. Beckford wrote to his tutor, "I have little hope that scandal is exhausted and fear its venom will poison your peace of mind much more than my own." In 1783 Beckford married Lady Margaret Gordon, whom he adored. She gave him two girl children and then died in 1786, a loss from which he never recovered. For most of his time at Bath he was a recluse, seldom seen, but he was given a magnificent funeral and the local newspaper reported that twenty thousand people lined the route to the abbey.

As well as being a great collector and builder Beckford also had some reputation as an author, his works including an 'Eastern' novel, *Vathek*, which he originally wrote in French; *Biographical Memoirs of Extraordinary Painters* (1780), which was a joke as none of the painters had existed; *Italy: With Sketches of Spain and Portugal* (1834), which was a great success; and *Recollections of an Excursion to the Monasteries of Alcobaca and Batalha* (1835), also a success. Fonthill was partly based on the Portuguese monastery of Batalha.

Near the racecourse, on the opposite side of the road, was the fifteenth-century chapel of St Lawrence, part of which is incorporated in Chapel Farm House.

It was on Lansdown in 1643 that the Royalists attacking Bath and the Parliamentarians defending it fought each other to a standstill. At the replay at Roundway Down near Devizes the Royalists won and returned to take Bath and Bristol. In the Lansdown battle the Cornish leader, Sir Bevil Grenville, was mortally wounded (he died later at Cold Ashton) and this is commemorated by the Lansdown Monument of 1720 set up by Lord Lansdown, Grenville's grandson.

The middle section of the north-west sector begins with a big blob of open space beside Marlborough Lane, named not after the great Duke but by a corruption of Marl Brook. The open space is Victoria Park which in its lower part becomes Lower Common which is shared between allotments and a children's grassy play space where there are things for swinging and sliding and climbing and falling off.

The Royal Victoria Park, green and leafy, is in two parts separated by Marlborough Lane and the eastern entrance from Queen's Parade is between two gate piers surmounted by lions given by Mr Geary, each with one paw resting lightly on an orb. Immediately inside is an Italian vase with chubby cherubs, presented by "a resident" in 1910 and to its left, hidden below hedges, are tennis courts, a superb bowling-green, and tea-rooms. Further on the left is a fine bandstand with a classically-styled stone carcasse and a semi-domed roof, with a small central dome, supported on iron pillars and ornamental brackets. It is flanked on either side by a pair of vases almost hidden by rampant rose bushes and set under flat canopies on four short pillars. An inscription tells us that these vases were given by Napoleon to his Empress Josephine (there is a 'J' visible on one of them), were brought to England by a Colonel Page and in 1874 by the will of Joseph Fuller of 19 Lansdown Crescent were given to the park, to be later "restored" (they still have bits missing) and "protected" by a Captain Huth in 1914.

It is all very pleasant and reasonably informal, with serpentine paths, big trees, shrubs, flowers, and broad stretches of grass and the sweep of the Royal Crescent above, although the chief thoroughfare, the Royal Avenue, is somewhat spoilt by being used as a linear car-park. At the far end we pass between two gateposts surmounted by sphinxes, the gifts, respectively, of Mr Reeves and L. Williams Esq. (is there a social comment here?).

The other part, over the road, is more varied and starts off with the whacking great Victoria Obelisk, triangular in section and guarded by three stone lions, each with a different expression on its face (one looks rather bored). Originally erected by "the inhabitants and visitors of Bath" for Princess Victoria's coming of age in 1837 they continued to chart her progress with further inscriptions. On the front is a medallion showing the young Queen in profile and recording her marriage to H.R.H. Prince Albert of Saxe-Coburg and Gotha, then on one side the death of "Albert the Good" in 1861, and finally on the other side "Her Majesty Queen Victoria and Empress of India, born May

1819, died 1901 aged 81, and reigned 63 years". It is a fine monument and was designed by George P. Manners, the City Architect.

The obelisk became a centre of celebration at Queen Victoria's coronation on the 18th June 1838. A great procession set out from the Guildhall and wound its way through Union Street, Milsom Street, and George Street, and then down to and round Queen Square, back up to the park and along the Royal Avenue to the obelisk. It was led and followed by the yeomanry, had three bands at intervals, and contained the Mayor and council, the Coronation Committee (which had twenty-five members), gentry and citizens, and school children marching six abreast. At the obelisk the Chairman of the Committee presented the Mayor with a goblet from which he drank the Queen's health and then the children sang "God Save the Queen" and were each presented with a plum cake and a coronation medal with ribbons—there is some confusion about this as another arrangement was that the medals were to be sent to the schools so that they could be worn in the procession and the plum cakes were to be distributed in Pulteney Street where the children assembled. Main streets and crescents were illuminated but private illuminations were discouraged by the council. Also no party political banners were allowed in the procession.

Up in the north-west corner of the park are the rather fine botanical gardens with trees, bushes, and flowers, many labelled, seats, and pleasant areas of grass (on which you are not supposed to picnic or sit). There is also a tiny waterfall feeding a pond—the water from this goes on to fill a rectangular pond for sailing model boats and further down a lake with ducks beside the Victoria Vase put there in 1880. Above the waterfall is a Classical summer-house with Aquae Sulis cut into the pediment and three round-headed entrance arches on double Doric pillars. It was originally part of Bath's contribution to the British Empire Exhibition at Wembley in 1924 and was moved to the gardens in 1926.

Inside the gardens is an unusual sundial in the form of a small, chunky, inclined cross, the shadow of whose arms marks the time on the sides.

Opposite the northern entrance to the gardens are two pieces of stonework. One, a huge head of Jupiter, rises above the bushes and, as I was told by a friendly park-keeper, has been well known to Bath couples who did their courting "behind

Jupiter". The other is a Classical block by Charles Edward Davis, whose father first laid out the park, and was put up in 1936 to commemorate Shakespeare's birthday. Inscribed on it is a quotation from *Hamlet*—

> . . . Take him all in all
> We shall not see his like again.

The Royal Victoria Park is a very pleasant place and Bath owes a debt to the commoners who refused to sell the land for building and to those whose enterprise and hard work gave Bath such a fine open place so near the heart of the city.

Then, on the north side of the Upper Bristol Road, comes a little web of late nineteenth-century streets with bays and raised party-walls, which we shall try not to mention again as they are found all over the area. Nice examples are tidy Edward Street, stepping up the hill to the inter-war housing of Audley Park, and Cork Street of the 1890s whose quite elaborate window decorations are repeated in Cork Place at the top. Cork Street, however, is pedimented and faced with Bath stone while Cork Place has barge-boarded gables and a Pennant front with oolite trimmings so that the one echoes something of the Classical spirit of Bath while the other reflects the Romantic spirit of the Gothic Revival. Cork Place is in Tennyson Street— and you can't get more Victorian than that!

All this lies opposite the great gasworks complex which started in a modest way in open fields in 1818 and, like Topsy, "just growed", with great gasholders, still there, across the river. Much has been demolished but there still stand the offices designed by G. P. Manners in 1888, bearing the inscription "Bath Gas Light and Coke Company". The coke used to come up the river and was the last post-war load carried on the Avon Navigation. Also opposite the gasworks is the Victorian church of St John the Evangelist (1837–8, the first years of Victoria's reign), apse-ended and with a big transept and a porch over which is inscribed the invitation "Abide with us for it is towards evening and the day is far spent". When visited, it was locked.

A little further on are Ashley and Shaftesbury Avenues, named after Antony Ashley Cooper, seventh Earl of Shaftesbury (1801–35), the great social reformer, and opposite is Locksbrook Cemetery with its forest of headstones in marble, granite, and peeling Pennant, and a fine pair of mortuary chapels linked to a commanding central spire, all designed in 1861–2 by the

City Architect, Charles Edward Davis. The chapels have good detailing and it is sad that they have lost most of their little columns and angels' heads. A bench affords a view of the gas-works.

Opposite the cemetery stands a building now labelled Bath City Council Supplies but whose earlier inscription shows that it was once the "Girls' and Infants' School" of 1876, and at the corner of Ashley Avenue, and still bearing its Cyclists' Touring Club insignia, is the Weston Hotel in Jacobean style and inscribed at the back with "George Biggs 1890".

The Upper Bristol Road now forks and we follow Newbridge Hill with the cemetery wall on one side and a set of Victorian semis on the other before we come to the pub at the top of Chelsea Road, a street of shops with one range dated 1888. To the west of Chelsea Road is a small Victorian development with behind it Horstman's Gear Works.

Gustav Horstmann (the company dropped the Germanic final 'n' after the First World War) came from Germany in 1848, married a Somerset girl, and settled in Bath as a clock-maker in Bladud Buildings. He was an enterprising man who in 1879 patented a self-winding clock. In 1900 his son Otto was selling bicycles and optical goods in Rivers Street, and in Union Street was the optician's shop of Horstmann and Sons. In 1904 the sons—Otto, Albert, Sidney, and Hermann set up a company at 13 Union Street to sell a patent gear invented by Sidney. It was not a great success but when they came up with an automatic switching device for gas lamps they were on to a winner. Sidney, however, was still inventing, and in 1908 he set up a factory in James Street West (sold in 1979) to make a car he had designed. Production continued, with a break for the First World War, until 1927, producing some 3,000 at the rate of about eight a week. In 1915 they built the nucleus of the present Newbridge Works on what was then Ashman's Farm. They also occupied the Albion Works on the Upper Bristol Road, which, although phased out, still bears their name; in 1969 they bought a company at Newport and in 1974 another at Poole; in 1967 they set up factories in Australia and India. In the following year their new factory in Brassmill Lane, all 35,000 square feet of it, was opened by Anthony Wedgewood Benn who was then Minister of Technology and Power.

In 1976 their proposal to extend the Newbridge Works pro-duced a storm of protest from the local residents. Bath Council approved the plans but Avon County at first rejected them although they later changed their mind after some modification had been made. The affair dragged on until a public inquiry was held and the Secretary of State for the Environment gave his approval. *The Times* made allegations of local collusion and had to retract, apologize, and pay damages. In 1981 Horstman's, ever forward-looking, moved into the microchip business at Newbridge. By then, however, they were not alone but had become part of the Simms group of companies, whoever *they* are.

Horstman's make a wide range of precision goods but the heart of the enterprise is still concerned with the control of electrical and gas systems and their system for switching motorway lighting has a lineage that goes back to that early invention that did away with the street lighters with their bicycles and long poles.

Newbridge Hill is for the most part lined with big semi-detached Victorian villas in quite large gardens and it shows a variety of building materials—Bath stone, Pennant, and brick—and styles—bays under little hats, barge-boarded gables, verandas, spreading Italianate eaves, sash windows, stone mullions, fruit-and-foliage stone capitals, Venetian Gothic and polychrome banding and arches. At the west end is one of the wilder houses of Bath, Newbridge Towers, a building of red brick with a turreted angle tower, big wooden balconies, barge-boarded gables with stone beamwork, windows with stone mullions and transoms and battlemented bays. It suggests a kind of Bavarian Balmoral and is impressive. One quiet building in this road, in Regency style with cornice, parapet, and depressed arches, shows in faded lettering that it was once a "School for Young Ladies".

The most monumental building, on the north side at the west end, can hardly be seen for trees although its name, carved on the wings, is visible from the road—"Partis College 1825". The college is not an educational establishment but a kind of superior almshouse which owed its inscription to the efforts and money of Fletcher Partis. To be eligible for entry the ladies had to have an income of not less than twenty-five pounds a year, be in good health, Church of England, and daughters or widows of clergymen, professional men, or "others of corresponding rank". The building was designed by Flood Page, a London architect, and is in Greek Revival style with a long, low centre stretching on either side of a portico with Ionic pillars and triangular

pediment, and two wings at right angles, decorated with Doric
pilasters. It is an impressive, if somewhat austere building, but
rather far from the shops.

Several short streets branch off Newbridge Hill, some of them
leading to new housing. Apsley Road, for example, takes off next
to the Apsley Garden House Hotel with its Italianate tower and
spreading eaves and continues between inter-war buildings
with shallow bays and little gables, down to Emmanuel Church,
a low, stone building with good ironwork screens to the foyer
and doors and a strange little separate bell tower at the side.
Copper was used on the roof ridges and front canopy and this is
now a bright green. The church was opened in 1956 on the site of
the old Mission Church of 1909 and was designed by James
Carpenter and built by the old Bath firm of Hayward and
Wooster. It cost £9,832, which today would not even buy a small
flat, and was paid for out of war damage compensation funds
which totalled some £100,000 for destruction by air raids of
churches in Bath.

On the north, Evelyn Road leads past imposing Victorian
houses with bays and gables to Forbes Fraser Hospital, single
storeyed with veranda round three sides of a grass quadrangle
and typical of inter-war cottage hospital design. It was named
after an eminent Bath surgeon and opened in 1924 as the Royal
United Private Hospital.

A little further west, Penn Lea Road, which was originally a
short street of big Victorian houses, has had an infill at its south
end of two post-war blocks with panels of green slate-hanging
and now leads to a post-war housing development, a pleasant
area which stretches from the hospital ground to Penn Hill Road
on the far side of Partis College, leading to Weston High Street.
Opposite Partis College Old Newbridge Hill turns down to join
Newbridge Road and it was this steep and difficult hill which
caused the Turnpike Trust to engineer the new broad and level
Newbridge Road at the lower level. Newbridge Hill itself continues westward as Kelston Road for about another three-
quarters of a mile to the city boundary and open country,
passing the post-war Oldfield Girls' School on the right.

Newbridge Road is quite impressive. Broad and gently
curving, it is lined for the most part with late Victorian houses,
detached, semi-detached, and in short ranges, some vaguely
Classical, but most neo-Gothic with a considerable variety of
decorative detail. Most are faced in Bath stone but in some this

is used as trimming for the darker Pennant. The western part of the road, on the south side, was not completed in the nineteenth century and has a long run of pleasant inter-war housing, rather Arts and Crafts with a lot of white-painted woodwork and quoins, part of an estate which stretches behind around Westfield Park and Homelea Park down to Brassmills Lane and bordering an area of one-time farmland developed between the wars as a council estate, Rudloe Park, low-density with a long grassy centre on which "organized games" are forbidden.

Another inter-war insertion is on the north along and between Newbridge Gardens and Yomede Park. Other northern roads such as Lyme Gardens, Lyme Road, Rosslyn Road and Charmouth Road are small Victorian developments, the last one leading up to the typical post-war school buildings, with lots of glass, of Newbridge Junior and Infants' Schools, well-provided with playgrounds and a field round which a path leads to Newbridge Hill.

Newbridge Road carries on over the eighteenth-century (later lengthened) New Bridge which is now, after the rebuilding of the old bridge at the end of Southgate Street, the oldest bridge in Bath.

Locksbrook Road and Brassmill Lane are another world with small terraced housing, neat and tidy enough, a variety of industrial and warehouse buildings, the river, and a canal, the Weston Cut. Locksbrook Road goes south past a range of stone, two-storeyed, bayed buildings to the old LMS railway station, now a small industrial undertaking, and then dives under a railway bridge past a coal yard to the Horstman factory, single-storeyed with a flat roof, and on the award-winning Herman Miller furniture factory, a big curved-edged box of light yellow plastic and reflective glass. Then comes a junction with Station Road and down to the left a road to a footbridge leading to Bath Cabinet Works (now Arkana) and the Lower Bristol Road, and built as a toll-bridge in the 1860s by the Twerton and Weston Bridge Co. Ltd. to connect Twerton to Weston Station. From the bridge we can see upstream the Weston Cut which created a mid-stream island, crammed with industrial buildings although a gap has been created as the old Carr's Mill has just burnt down. It was known as Dutch Island because of Dutch workers in the brass mills. By the river is a trading estate, a bunch of warehouses.

Locksbrook Road continues on one side with brick houses and

a chapel, now industrial, and on the other an earlier row of
flat-faced stone houses. Then more industrial buildings on the
left—Mark House, Dolamco, Power Movement, Anglian
Windows—and opposite a yard crammed with Post Office Tele-
communications vans, followed on the left by Chivers Book
Sales, Lythway Publishing, and Firecrest Publishing—with
opposite a joinery factory and electronic and radio distributors—or at least that is how it was at the time of writing—
places do tend to change hands.

Next to Chivers etc. is the Dolphin Inn, built in rubble with a
double saddleback roof, higher towards the Cut at the back
where the original frontage was. Down one side is a track
leading to a humped bridge over the Cut, from which we get a
view of the lock and one of the nineteenth-century mills on the
island.

A little further and leading up the hill is one of the most
amazingly decorated Victorian streets in Bath—Avondale
Road. It could well serve as a catalogue illustration for terracotta for here among chequered brickwork are terracotta panels
in many varieties, terracotta capitals beside the windows,
terracotta quoins and lesenes, terracotta battlements. Some
people might think it overdone, but it is certainly striking. At
the top the road turns left and we can either cross the disused
railway by a brick bridge and go out on Newbridge Road by a
shop or go back down Osborne Road with quietly pleasant stone
Victorian houses on one side and on the other the big red-brick
bulk and crazy roofs of A.B.M. (Associated British Maltsters) on
the other, and back to where Locksbrook Road becomes Brassmill Lane—not that there are brass mills any more. Nor, for
that matter, the lime kilns which are marked on earlier maps,
although up on Newbridge Road a large garage is fitted into the
remains of a limestone quarry.

The red-brick building is mid-nineteenth century and was
originally built as a brewery maltings which were acquired by
A.B.M. about 1930. They added a silo block in 1952. Production
of malt ended in 1980 and this big building is now used simply as
a barley store.

There is more industry on our right with an engineering
works and a yard full of pipes and Mixconcrete who do just that
and send it off twirling round to be delivered to sites. Opposite is
the Lock House, now flats, next to a grassy space with swing and
slide before we come to the extraordinary roof of Rotork, a firm

founded after the war and producing mechanical valves. This building got an award. The last industrial area is the Brassmills Trading Estate which is more concerned with warehousing and distribution than manufacture. It consists of a set of boxes in artificial Bath stone and at the end, surrounded by fencing and rolls of cable, is the box occupied by the Telephone Engineering Centre. A welcome diversion is a little green notice by a track leading to the disused railway which tells us, on behalf of Cyclebag, the excellent cycling organization, that "this path has been built and is maintained by volunteers" and says "Please look after it; Cyclists ring bells for walkers; Do not let dogs foul the path". Once you get up on the track you can walk or cycle to Bitton, about three and a half miles away—and very pleasant the trip is, too.

Back in Brassmills Lane it is hedge and grass on the left and the inter-war council estate on the right, followed by some later development and then, as we approach the main road, the latest, Selbourne Close, which is a mixture of one- and two-storey housing and looks much better from this side than from the main road. Opposite and well concealed is a site for touring caravans (no tents) with notices in English, French and German (hard luck if you are Italian) telling you not to park in the roads if the site is full as the police have power to tow you away. The caravan park itself is very well laid out with hard standing and electric power points and is pleasantly landscaped with trees and shrubs. The proposal for its establishment was hotly opposed by local residents who cannot have realized that cara-vanners are, in the main, tidy, well-organized people.

7

Fringe Benefits—
South of the River

The South-West Quadrant

Here again is the familiar Victorian scene of big villas, detached
or paired, and two-storey terraces with raised party-walls.
Ubiquitous bays present themselves, castellated, parapeted, or
under their own little roofs, their corners either plain or heavily
decorated with carved capitals. Occasional terraces still have
plat-bands and straight pediments. Barge-boarded gables peak
up from some of the big houses while others have the wide-
spreading eaves of the Italianate style. Buildings are mostly
faced in Bath stone, but there is some Pennant and occasional
brick and artificial stone appears where gaps left by the
Victorian and Edwardian developers have been filled with
inter- and, mainly, post-war housing, but there is still a
good deal of open space, including allotments. The nineteenth-century development repeats the pattern of the more
opulent housing occupying the higher ground and changing
to smaller, though still substantial, terraces on the lower
slopes.

The old GWR railway runs, still working, through the
northern edge of the area, there is a short length of the disused
LMS line of 1869, and a longer stretch of the one-time Somerset
and Dorset which tunnelled under Combe Down in 1874 and is
now a linear park—a rather grand name for a footpath. The
railways were not only routes but barriers and many a street
stops abruptly as it reaches the tracks. Between the GWR and
the river are Westmoreland and East Twerton; between the
GWR and the S and D is Oldfield Park; and south and west of the
S and D are Bloomfield, South Twerton, and Twerton. The only
major east-west route is the Lower Bristol Road, which used to
be called Lower Place and skirts the northern edge. The other
main routes run down from the southern hills, the chief ones
being the Hollow, Southdown Road, Englishcombe Lane, and

Bloomfield Road, while marking the eastern edge are Wellsway and the Wells Road.

The big stuff, some of it very big, is found in the south-east from Wellsway westward around Bloomfield Avenue and Oldfield Park. Some is Italianate with notable examples in Oldfield Road such as St Catherine's, now a nursing home, set up by the Sisters of Charity in 1934, but most of it is in a kind of eclectic Gothic showing a variety of decorative detail in a single building and with a preference for a kind of Jacobean. Highly decorated examples may be found in Bloomfield Avenue which runs round a central open space with bowling-greens and allotments; one house which backs on to the end of the green has stone swags and is dated 1893. Upper Oldfield Park has more big houses of various 'neo' types on to one of which was built the inter-war City of Bath Girls' Grammar School, now Hayesfield Comprehensive School for Girls (Bath maintained its tradition of single-sex schools when it re-organized into a comprehensive secondary system). The school's roadside wall has big brick panels and the stone gateposts carry rusty iron plates which bear the legend "Oldfield Park". There are later accretions—a wooden hall, huts in the grounds, a modern bit built on to the back of the house. The house itself is amazing, with a massive porch and above it a big stained-glass window divided by stone mullions and transom and with a centre door which opens on to the top of the porch. Above the window is a shell hood and above that a curly gable with a window in it.

In order to get the size for a comprehensive the school had added unto it the previous Arts Secondary school (boys) half a mile away over the railway in Brougham Hayes, a simple nineteenth-century building with a later block added when it was a domestic science college. Brougham Hayes itself is in the terraced area and has down one side an early flat-faced range faced in Bath stone, although at present much of the stone is painted which would offend the purists but makes it look quite jolly. On the other side of Brougham Hayes was a big drill hall which has been demolished and its site used for naval and police vehicles, and beyond that St James's Cemetery with a dismal neo-Gothic lodge behind a neo-Gothic arch, and in the grounds two apse-ended, neo-Gothic (Decorated) chapels united to a curious centre stump. At the moment the chapels are surrounded by palings and there are notices saying "Dangerous Walls—Keep Clear".

Another comprehensive made by cobbling together two separate schools is Beechen Cliff for Boys. The upper school is the previous City of Bath Boys' Grammar, a 1932 building up behind those poets' streets, and the lower is the previous boys' secondary modern which combined a large house on the Wells Road with a group of three buildings down by the railway which were originally board schools, the whole linked by paths and stairs.

At the end of Oldfield Road, in Junction Avenue, is the church of St Bartholomew, first built in 1938, wrecked by bombing and then rebuilt in 1951–2. Of simple design with clerestory windows, a large Perpendicular-style window at one end, and buttresses; the south end as just been completed in 1981 in a rather austere style with buttresses and a cross-shaped window to a design by Vivian and Mathieson of Bath. With the closing of St Mark's in 1970, St Bartholomew's became a parish church.

South of Oldfield Park, across the old railway line, the lower slopes of the hillside are carpeted with low-density, post-war housing built in artificial Bath stone and arranged in ranges and blocks, with occasional interruptions of inter-war building. Roughly in the middle sit Moorlands Junior and Infants' Schools with plenty of playground space and next door to the schools is a large house with a strange, big castellated tower beyond which are trees and a recreation ground. The northern limit of this development is bounded by Englishcombe Lane beyond which are fields before the top layer of building around Odd Down is reached.

Through the western end of Moorlands runs Monksdale Road which crosses the linear park near a children's small playground where a stream runs in a concrete bed. Monksdale joins Oldfield Lane beside a red-brick factory now occupied by Clark's the shoe manufacturers of Street, and up on the left towers an old mill which is now a Co-op. dairy depot. Joining Oldfield Lane and sounding American but looking thoroughly British are First, Second and Third Avenue, streets of sturdy Victorian terraces, and opposite the pub on the corner of Second Avenue is a building of considerable worth, the Roman Catholic church of Our Lady and St Alphege, designed in 1929 by Sir Giles Gilbert Scott (1880–1960). Wholly Italian in concept, basilican in form with deep eaves, round-headed arches, and simple capitals, it has a sturdy charm and sits with dignity and neighbourliness in its Victorian setting. Next to it is the church hall and an outpost of St John's Roman Catholic Junior School.

To the north are quite wide streets lined with respectable late Victorian terraces stretching to the Lower Bristol Road with a zone of interruption formed by the GWR line of 1840 which was there first. One of these streets, Moorland Road, has been converted for shopping with about thirty shops covering a wide range of products, mainly convenience goods, and including a Woolworth's, banks, post office, library, laundrette, betting shop, and pub. Round the corner the Scala Cinema has become a discount store run by the Co-op.

It is often said that by-law housing is so uniform as to be boring. This is not the case in this area for although the roads are of a standard width and the terraced houses of a standard size there is considerable variety in materials and design. This variety sometimes occurs in a single street where one side may be different from the other, the style may change from one end of the street to the other, or individual houses may be idiosyncratic. For example, Denmark Street is flat-faced on one side, with cornice, parapet, and depressed arches while the opposite side has single-storey bays; and while Triangle East has one-storey bays and quite elaborate ornamentation round the upstairs windows and under the eaves, Triangle North, into which it runs, has two-storey bays and less ornament. Both are faced with Pennant with Bath stone trimmings whereas Crandale Road which runs into Triangle North is faced entirely in Bath stone—and sometimes the Bath stone is in form of large blocks and sometimes small. Some streets such as Crandale and Caledonian Roads lack bays and are flat-faced, a form which is more common north of the railway. Another feature is that the area is threaded with pathways passing between the backs of the houses.

At the point of the Triangle, near the bridge over the GWR by the unmanned Oldfield Park Station where trains occasionally stop, is a clutch of chapels—Methodist, Baptist, and Jehovah's Witness. The Oldfield Park Methodist Church has a commanding position and is a two-storey hall church, rock-faced and gabled, with an entry porch approached by steps. Beside it is a corrugated-iron hall looking quite elegant in green and white paint. Opposite, in Triangle North, are the two blocks of the Oldfield Baptist Church built respectively in 1902 and 1929 although the chapel was founded in 1828. Both are in a satisfactory Classical style although the older, larger, block with its Ionic pilasters and impressive front is the more showy. Kingdom Hall for the Jehovah's Witnesses shares a building with a firm who make blinds. The other major church is St Peter's on the Lower Bristol Road by the end of Dorset Street which has the Sunday School and Parish Room of 1888 and the Twerton Schools of 1878, now East Twerton Infants' School. St Peter's, consecrated in 1880 and designed by Charles Edward Davis, is an apse-ended hall church in an Early English style. Beside the church is a laundry (cleanliness next to godliness?) and between them flows a stream; opposite is a pub (thirst after righteousness?).

Opposite the school is a play area labelled "for children under 12" and westward from here runs Denmark Street with a church or chapel at the end converted to industrial use. Round the corner in Stuart Place is the old gaol designed in 1842 by George P. Manners, the City Architect—a bulky, gloomy building, heavily Classical with parapet and bracketed cornice, heavy architraves, banded rustication, and Doric pilasters. It closed in 1878 and was taken over by a firm which manufactured confectionery; today it is occupied by an engineering firm. Various sites had been suggested for the new gaol to replace the one in Grove Street, but eventually in 1837 they bought the twelve-acre Twerton site for £768.15s. from a Mr Hale. The way to it from the Turnpike (Lower Bristol) Road was narrow and tortuous and the council had a lot of trouble in acquiring the land to make a better approach. Manners's plans were submitted to the Prison Inspectorate who altered them, requiring amongst other things, a higher wall and a WC for each cell which would not, they said, make for smelly cells and would save the staff a lot of trouble. The Gaol Regulations of 1866 show that the treatment you got depended on what you were in for. Persons awaiting trial were fairly accessible to visitors who could bring them little extras, and they were allowed to wear their own clothes unless these were so scruffy that they had to be given a prison suit, in which case it was a different colour from that worn by convicted prisoners. The ones with the easiest time were the debtors. They were allowed to be provided with, or buy, food, wine, malt liquor, clothing, bedding, and "other accessories". They could pay someone to clean out their cell and they were allowed to practise their trade while in prison as long as they provided the tools. They also had daily exercise in the open air while the others only got it as the surgeon required "on grounds of health".

There were some recognition of conscience—Jews were not to work on their Sabbath; no hard labour was to be done on Sundays, Christmas Day, and "days appointed for public feasts or thanksgiving"; persons who were not C. of E. could not be forced to attend chapel or religious instruction but could be visited by their own minister. No one was to be put in irons except "by urgent necessity". Female prisoners were attended only by female warders and their cells had different locks from men's. If they were visited by the gaoler, the matron or some other female member of staff had to be present. Both gaoler and matron had to make daily rounds and also at night at "an uncertain hour".

Every prisoner had to wash every day and have a bath once a month (not in the presence of another prisoner). Clean personal linen was provided once a week and sheets washed once a month. There were three meals a day, two of which were hot. The surgeon had to visit at least once a week and had to keep a journal "in the English language" and also had to visit daily anyone in solitary confinement—the gaoler was empowered to order up to three days of this with a diet of bread and water, while the Visiting Justices could order up to a month. This could be for breaking rules, swearing, assault, indecent behaviour, irreverent behaviour in chapel, absence from chapel without permission, idleness or negligence, or "wilful mismanagement of work". There was also corporal punishment which had to be attended by the gaoler and the surgeon, the latter to "give such orders for preventing injury to health as he may deem necessary".

There was to be no tipping and no smoking and the debtors were not allowed to sell any of their little extras to the other inmates.

Other industrial/commercial buildings are the long range of Pitman Press (1913–30), Bath stone facing the Lower Bristol Road, brick behind, and up in Bellot's Road two, big, imitation Bath stone boxes with brown, vertically ribbed upper parts, one a Cash and Carry, the other William Cowlin, Builders, while at the end of the road are the older buildings occupied by Bell Engineering Services. By these a path leads past a pleasantly laid out cemetery to where Bellot's Road and the old S and D cross the GWR line on parallel bridges. Here we may join the linear park.

This East Twerton, Lower Oldfield Park area has nothing grand about it but it is nevertheless pleasant, well cared-for, well supplied with shops, human in scale, and interesting in detail. To complete the picture we must go over the linear park into Twerton itself.

Here the nineteenth-century development was smaller, with Lymore Avenue leading on to Shophouse Road and Twerton High Street, a few side roads, and terraced fingers pointing up the hill as Coronation Avenue (presumably Edward VII's in 1901), Ivy Avenue, and Southdown Road. Even so there is still variety—some bays, some flat-faced fronts, sometimes with plat-bands, string-courses, and straight pediments, some houses faced in Bath stone, others in Pennant. There is not much industry as this was down by the river and on the island, although one side of Lymore Gardens is lined with a brick building into which a number of firms has settled, and the bigger buildings are schools and churches. There is also a good deal of open space.

Where Lymore Avenue and Coronation Avenue meet in Lymore Terrace is South Twerton Junior School of 1893, originally Ascension School, a Jacobean-style structure with Classical pediments over the doors and a remarkable corner turret with a copper-clad gently curving top, and down the other end of Lymore Avenue is a starkly Jacobean-style school which is now part of another of those far-flung Bath comprehensives, Culverhay, but has a foundation stone laid in 1910 by Jonathan Carr, the Twerton mill-owner. From the beginning the Carrs had an interest in education. Thomas Carr bought the woollen mills in 1847 and the following year opened in them a school for children he employed although he could get no Government money for it. After a few years, in 1853, the Vicar of Twerton sent a memorandum to the Education Committee of the Privy Council proposing "a school for 150 boys and 150 girls, with two houses for the Master and Mistress, in connection with the Church of England, but open to all Dissenters" and this opened in 1854 on the Lower Bristol Road. The Master's salary was £40 a year and the Mistresses's £20.10s.

Round the corner and up the Hollow another part of Culverhay has been Oldfield Girls' until they moved out to Weston but is older than that as it bears the dates 1897 and 1898. By South Twerton Junior School is the Church of the Ascension built in 1970–71 with a vicarage behind of 1959, and half way up Coronation Avenue is the red-brick Moravian church of 1906 looking vaguely Central European with its curious little spirelet and overhanging upper storey.

Opposite the school in the Hollow, in Innox Road and around, is an inter-war council estate in which many of the houses have hipped, mansard roofs although the lower roof slopes are really tile-clad upper storeys. To the west is Innox Park, steep and grassy, and behind and beyond stretch grass, hedges and trees. At the other end of the park, Freeview Road is presumably so called because it overlooks Bath City Football Ground which separates it from the High Street and is surrounded by flood-lights on stands looking like huge spectators from another world. Below the football ground is a home for old people, Marjorie Whimster House, whose roof shape gives it a vaguely Chinese look.

To the west, up Dominion Road, is a post-war housing development which includes Quebec, a pleasant group of single-storey buildings whose centre bears the Bath City Arms, set around three sides of a grassy quadrangle with a plaque which tells us it was "unveiled by Sir George Wilkinson Bart., Lord Mayor of London 1940–41 at the official opening on the 25th October 1952" and that "these bungalows . . . called Quebec were erected for aged persons with the aid of a grant from the Lord Mayor of London's National Air Raid Fund to which the people of the Commonwealth generously contributed".

The inter-war and immediately post-war housing is at a low density with plenty of grassy spaces and trees and reasonably sized gardens but the latest stuff, of which there are several chunks in Twerton, is crammed in closely with small gardens behind heavy plank fences, small windows, single-pitch roofs, and artificial Bath stone walls with long runs of dark wood panelling, all set in asphalt and connected by stairways. The effect seems claustrophobic although it reflects the rapid increase in land prices and the reaction against the 'prairie planning' of the fifties.

The more open planning is seen to the west, but before looking at it we may take a brief view of the High Street, the heart and indeed almost the whole of the old village. Here there is post-war reconstruction and infill, both residential and commercial, including a parade similar to the one in Weston village. There are two nineteenth-century chapels, as we may expect in an industrial village, the Zion Methodist Free Chapel of 1853 with

Bath stone front and rubble sides, and, in Mill Lane, the Twerton Baptist Church with an addition of 1928. Then there are eighteenth- and nineteenth-century ranges and individual houses, including Nelson House, three-storey with cornice and pediment. Nothing is regular, heights vary, and the building line steps forward and back, and yet, or perhaps because of this, the effect is pleasant and is enhanced by the curve of the street which affords serial vision. Originally the High Street was part of the main road out of Bath but when the GWR came in 1840 its high embankment cut off the High Street, giving access only by narrow arches, and the railway company was required to construct a new road to the north of the line, cutting Twerton off from the main traffic stream. Between the High Street and the railway was a farm with old buildings but these are now being demolished to make way for a small housing development.

In 1888 Twerton pioneered the Co-operative movement in the Bath area, largely due to the initiative of a Midland Railway goods guard, Benjamin Colbourne, and the encouragement of Jonathan Carr, and on the floor of the doorway of a shop at the east end of the High Street can still be seen the initials T.C.S. By 1914 they had three branches, a coal depot, a choral society and education committee, and had in 1894 organized a co-operative cabinet-makers' business which lasted for several years. Meanwhile Bath had formed its own society and in 1922 the two were amalgamated. Today the Co-op. in Twerton occupies a post-war, box-like building.

At the end of High Street is the church of St Michael, originally Norman (in 1086 Twerton was held by the Bishop of Coutances, sublet to Nigel de Gourney, and had 200 sheep, two mills, and fifteen acres of meadow). It was rebuilt in 1839 and again in 1886 when it was enlarged with financial help from the Carrs. They kept the Perpendicular tower, and moved the Norman doorway to the north porch where it stands, round-headed and decorative, the capitals of its pillars carved as beasts' heads. Next door is the neo-Jacobean rectory paid for by the 3,000 guineas compensation from the GWR for putting the railway through the garden of the old vicarage, now Clyde House, in the High Street. Over the road, in Watery Lane, is Poolemead, a big Victorian house with a massive towered porch, whose grounds are at this moment being covered with new building for the Royal National Institute for the Deaf.

The High Street continues westward to become Newton Road

past new housing in the grounds of the old Carr House, now demolished and the land used for low-rise blocks of flats, and Twerton C. of E. Junior School, single storey with a lot of glass, which opened in 1954 as a replacement for the old school which had been bombed. Later an infants' school was built higher up the hill. Beyond the school is the loop of Day Crescent lined with 'Cornish' houses so-called because the building blocks were made from the waste from Cornish china-clay workings. This was an expedient adopted in the early post-war years when there was a shortage of building materials, as was also the use of prefabricated metal panels found on the other side of the road.

Newton Road comes out into the valley of the Newton Brook to join a main road at the bottom of Pennyquick Hill whose strange name probably started as Penna—cu-wick, Penna's cow pasture or dairy farm. Here by the stream is a big, flat-topped mound with bramble-infested slopes which is a 'dirt batch' or pile of waste from a coal mine. Batch is a common Somerset word for a small hill, or slope, and derives from the Old English *baec*, a 'back' or ridge. These mines in the bottom of the Newton Valley were operating until the 1890s and supplied Twerton with coal.

South of Newton Road a post-war council development stretches up the hillside to Pennyquick and Whiteway, meeting up with an inter-war council estate around North Way at the top, where the houses are similar to those we have seen on Innox Road. On the hillside, however, there is a good deal of variety— blocks of four- to six-storey flats, semi-detached two-storey houses, and short ranges. The higher blocks have flat roofs, the rest low-pitched; some houses have porches or door hoods, others have neither. Most of the walling is in smooth artificial stone blocks but in some cases they are left rough, in others the pointing is emphasized, and a few include panels of wood. The infants' school is two tiered with roofs either green or white, and opposite is a modern pub, the Centurion, while up at the top end is a clubhouse or institute next door to an asphalt, flood-lit football pitch. There are no shops, but a bus service threads its way through. The views are marvellous and as building density is low there is a lot of open grassland and plenty of garden space. Those who like plenty of space will never agree with others who believe that closeness encourages community spirit and that there is a special urban 'feel' engendered by packing houses tightly together. One problem is that like many developments of this period it is under-provided with garages and the roads tend to be choked by parked cars. There are two recreation grounds, the one at the top, with iron gates and rugby posts, being encircled by Haycombe Drive.

The long, narrow belt by the Lower Bristol Road between the river and the railway embankment, stretching from the Churchill Bridge to the Newbridge junction, is a diversified, somewhat chaotic area which forms, as we have seen, Bath's main industrial zone, although there still exist, mainly on the south side, nineteenth-century ranges of shops and houses. Westmoreland Terrace, for example, was built as a Victorian shopping range and still has its Corinthian piers separating the shops, with two-light windows above under segmental pediments. Another range is quite elaborate with a three-storey centre with its windows under a triangular pediment and surrounded by a quite elaborate architrave while the two-storey flanks have segmental pediments and Doric pilasters—it is noticeable that the Classical influence was still strong in this area. At the moment the shops are occupied by floor coverings, hardware and electrics.

Another long block on the north is Victoria Buildings which in spite of its name still exhibits Classical characteristics. It starts with three storeys at the east end and then descends to two. The high end has a plat-band, cornice, parapet, and pilasters, the lower is flat-faced with straight pediments and raised party-walls. Shop-front boxes have been added to one end and contain a second-hand shop, fruit and vegetables, fish and chips (and Chinese take-away), newsagent, and the Liberal Club. Others, such as Vernon Terrace further along on the south side, have single-storey bays and eaves cornices on brackets. Vernon Terrace is further distinguished by a couple of bands of polychrome brickwork and decorative dog-tooth work under the lintels.

The occasional large detached houses, all on the north side, have been taken over as offices, of which examples are Albert Villa, now the offices of Hayward and Wooster (today members of the local Joseph Cartwright Group), with a fairly companionable extension opened in 1978 by the Mayor, and The Woodlands, now the home of Walter Lawrence, Civil Engineers. The prestige front of the Woodlands, the one facing the road, has been cleaned up and is rather pleasant, although the metal-framed windows are anachronistic, but the side and back have simply been given a coat of plaster.

Some businesses have come here because the carcasses of defunct nineteenth-century mills were available. The Peter Simper Organization, for example, who are concerned with amusement machines, took over Camden Mills whose tall stone walls with segmental-headed windows and projecting wooden hoist covers rear up not far from the Churchill Bridge, and Bishop's Move, a removals firm, occupies another of these stone buildings. Most, however, have purpose-built structures which vary in style according to their age and give a rather jumbled look to the roadside.

Charles Bayer and Co., corset manufacturers, for example, occupy a tall red-brick building with Bath stone trimmings and brick lesenes. The big windows have curved tops and on the ground floor have heavily rusticated stone surrounds. Charles Bayer was one of those enterprising German immigrants and he not only made a fortune out of Victorian ladies' passion for unyielding corsetry but also invented the safety pin although he did not patent it. He built his factory in 1892 and went on to develop factories and warehouses throughout Britain. Hit by the Great Depression the company sold off many of its branches in 1929 and was re-formed in 1931. Today it is part of a larger organization, the Vantona group, and while still making substantial foundation garments it also goes in for the less restraining and skimpier styles demanded by present fashion.

Another name which keeps cropping up in the Lower Bristol Road region is C. H. Beazer. Beazer's, as builders, have contributed a good deal to private, post-war housing development in Bath, to the extent that some areas are known to the natives as "Beazerland", but they have also diversified and extended their activities outside the city. There is even a Beazer Garden, a flat area of grass and flagged paths near the Pulteney Weir, opened by Sir Charles Chancellor, Chairman of the Bath Preservation Trust in 1973. Up Westmoreland Road we come to C. H. Beazer (Plant Sales) in a large modern building of no great distinction in whose entrance hangs a wooden sign of 1897, "J. H. Beazer, Builder, Carpenter, and Undertaker". Below it a smaller sign says "C. Beazer, Builder and Contractor, 1934", and below that a whole string of names—"C. H. Beazer (Holdings), C. H. Beazer and Sons, E. Mortimer and Son Ltd., Bath Plant Hire Services Ltd., Bath Cast Stone Ltd., A. Wills & Son Ltd., Blackford & Son (Calne) Ltd., Bath Plastering Ltd., and Argyle Electrical

Installation Ltd." Opposite, another long box contains Bath Wholesale Meat Traders, Smith Engineering, Devon Savouries, and Avery (scales). Further along the Lower Bristol Road where Midland Bridge Road comes in is Beazer Supplies, selling household equipment in a rather graceless, angular, modern building. Further out where a widened road leads to the new bridge is C. H. Beazer (Construction) Ltd, which now houses the head offices, and if we follow the road down to the bridge we find on our right Bath Waste Disposal (part of the Beazer Group). Also on this road, to the left, is a big modern warehouse for Littlewood's.

Two other roads lead northward to river bridges. Victoria Bridge Road takes us past big corrugated-iron buildings of Stothert and Pitt to Mr Dredge's patent suspension bridge (pedestrianized) which we have already looked at when we went down Nelson Place, and Midland Road takes us past the old gasworks to a road bridge with traffic lights. Here several of the old red-brick gasworks buildings have been taken over by the Bath Council Engineering Department, while at the beginning of the road is Red Bridge House, a modern cuboid building whose front part is more impressive than the back and which houses the offices of H.M. Inspector of Taxes. Further west a road leads past the tall, red-brick building of the old Bath Cabinet Works, still making furniture but now part of the Arkana group, to the footbridge we saw from Locksbrook Road. On the main road by this is a large, single-storey, box-like structure belonging to Herman Miller whose new factory over the river we have already noted.

Beazer's has mushroomed since the war but the Stothert and Pitt story goes back to the eighteenth century and has been thoroughly researched and engagingly presented by Hugh Torrens in his book *The Evolution of a Family Firm* (1978) from which most of my information about them comes. In 1815, the year of Waterloo, the Stothert family partnership of father and son, both Georges, with an ironmongery business in Horse Street (now Southgate) was dissolved and the son set up a foundry at No. 17 which in 1826 moved to a site in nearby Philip Street and in 1830 was renamed the Newark Foundry; the site is now occupied by the bus station.

Originally they produced castings for mainly domestic purposes—furnaces, cisterns, boilers, pipes, and the like, although they also advertised "wheels and machinery", but later they began to go in for bigger stuff and at the Great Exhibition of 1851 in the Crystal Palace they exhibited a crane. In the 1830s they took on Robert Pitt as an apprentice and in 1844 the firm became Stothert, Rayno and Pitt (George Rayno had been Henry Stothert's chief engineer) and in 1855 when Rayno retired it became Stothert and Pitt. Their products had always been diverse and to the output of cranes may be added tanning machinery, agricultural machinery, concrete mixers, pumps, and steam engines. A particular post-war development has been the production of vibratory rollers for compacting materials laid for roads and runways. It was for cranes, however, including the massive Titans and Goliaths, that Stothert and Pitt became best known and their products are to be found at docksides all over the world. In the 1850s they produced their first steam cranes, one of which won a silver medal at the Paris Exhibition of 1867, and in 1893 they provided the first electric wharf cranes in use in Britain, installed at Southampton.

In 1857 they opened their new factory, still confusingly called Newark, in the Lower Bristol Road. This massive frontage with its big blocks of Pennant ground-floor, segmental-headed windows, and top storey of Bath stone with Doric pilasters, was designed by Thomas Fuller (1820–98) who was born in Bath and later emigrated to Canada where he designed the neo-Gothic Parliament House at Ottawa (1816–17); later he moved to the USA. This original factory was extended at both ends and then in 1916 they added a big, double-gabled block with large depressed arches which at present are painted a reddish-brown and look rather fine; the big entrance has, however, been filled in. More extensions follow westward. Their offices opposite are the standard, uninspiring, rectilinear, post-war style stuck up on little legs which create parking spaces. The middle section, however, comes down to earth or how otherwise would people get in—rope ladders?

Further west is Stothert's canteen, single storey with lots of glass, and near it the Longmead Gospel Chapel, also single storey but with clerestory windows. Then much further along on the north side is Stothert and Pitt (Parts and Services), post-war and big with a lot of reinforced glass, which at the time of writing is up for sale. The extent of Stothert and Pitt's is not, however, fully shown by the building frontages for the works have spread along the riverside behind and cover a considerable area.

A flat area handy for river, road, and rail is attractive to more than manufacturing enterprises and particularly to those who require large storage spaces—for example Hill Leigh and Co., Timber Importers, who have big sheds crammed with timber and open yards with "No Smoking" notices, or Guest Road Services Ltd who need space to park their fleet of vans, or the side-by-side Tinknell Fuel Ltd (Shell distributors) and Cotswold Petroleum Ltd (Esso distributors) who need room for their fuel tanks, or at the far end of the Lower Bristol Road G. W. Sparrow and Sons Ltd the international crane-hire specialists who need somewhere to put their cranes. Sparrow's started from small beginnings after the war and have had a remarkable growth rate. They have advertised their head office as being in Georgian Bath but its location, as we have seen, is in surroundings far removed from the Georgian image—although if you are hiring a crane are you going to bother where the firm is situated? In fact the offices are in one of those modern bug-eyed monster buildings which have been likened to stacked television sets.

The only available open land on the south side was the old GWR goods station and sidings. The low Pennant building still carries in white letters the legend "Great Western Railway Goods Station and Bonded Store" but today it is "Pickford's Enquiries" and the goods yard is covered with tarmac and Pickford vans. After the war the newly formed Wessex Water Authority had Bath offices built north of the Lower Bristol Road, off Westmoreland Street, but on 1st April 1981 these were closed and they transferred to more recent ones by the riverside where there was also a yard for their vehicles and they could keep a watchful eye on their self-regulating radial sluice. They call it the Twerton Office.

We have by no means exhausted the list of enterprises located along the Lower Bristol Road which include J. V. Hydraulics, Regency Cleaners, Bath Panel Beaters (in a strictly utilitarian building), George Yeo (builders and DIY shop), Hygate Gears, Cobb's Bakery (up Jews Lane), Copy Consultants (Western) Ltd (agents for a Japanese plain paper copier), Drainage Castings, Huggett Electrical Ltd, and a bookbinding works, Period Binders. One fairly recent and unusual enterprise is the Morris Minor Centre where they buy old speciments, do them up, and resell them—they also have an office in the old Twerton railway station which sticks out from the side of the embankment. Of the remaining enterprises probably the best known outside Bath is the Pitman Press which has a long Classical-type Bath stone frontage on to the Lower Bristol Road and on the opposite side a modern warehouse and loading bay with a cantilevered canopy.

The old factory front, started in 1913, has cornice and parapet (with a sloping clerestory peeping above), rusticated lesenes, and fluted Doric columns flanking the main entrance, with a clock above flanked by what look like ice-cream cones but are in fact torches. A second door has Doric pilasters and a wreath above. The Classical effect, which is un-Palladian, is a little spoilt by the large metal-framed windows, but it is, as Bryan Little wrote, "not undignified", and certainly has more individual character than much post-war, anonymous 'packing-case' office architecture.

We have dealt, as a portrait should, with the present scene, but there was already development by the end of the nineteenth century as the Ordnance Survey map of 1886 shows. Stothert and Pitt's Newark Foundry (Iron and Brass) is there of course, as are the gasworks and the Camden Flour Mills, but at the end of the Camden Mills is the Bath City Iron and Brass Foundry and scattered along the river bank are two saw mills, a cabinet works, five malthouses, a chemical works, and, at the west end, a woollen mill. There were a number of reasons for this development. The river provided water, sometimes power (though most of the factories ran on steam), and acted as a drain and a transport artery; the turnpike road ran south of the works, and after 1840 there was a railway. There was flat land for building, even if it tended to flood. Perhaps the most important factor was that nobody seemed to want to live down there so that the land was left open as Bath spread and there was little competition for it. A map of 1803 shows nothing in this area but gardens and fields with one or two isolated houses and this open country stretches as far as Twerton; another map of 1820 shows the addition of no more than four short ranges of buildings. One of the major problems of developing industry further in Bath is that there is hardly any suitable land left within the city boundaries.

The Southern Plateau

North Road, Bathwick Hill, and Widcombe Hill all climb up to converge in a triangle of roads at the eastern end of the plateau and then continue as the single Claverton Down Road. At this eastern end a very considerable area of farmland lies within the city boundaries, brought in by the Bath Extensions Act of 1950, and very pleasant it is with its fields and hedges and woods and farms. The road triangle made by Copseland, Oakley and Claverton Down Road forms a nucleus for a small group of buildings, mostly nineteenth century, which include, facing Claverton Down Road, a rather pleasant little Gospel Hall, once Anglican and now Nonconformist, in a vernacular style with a touch of Art Nouveau—sloping walls, mullioned windows, and a couple of angels draped with scrolls—"Glory to God" and "Good Will to Men". To the north of the triangle lies Bath University on land which had previously been Norwood Playing-Fields, a change of use which did not meet with universal approval.

The university started life as the Bristol Trade School in 1856 under the patronage of the Bristol Merchant Adventurers' Society and got its first name-change in 1885 when it became the Merchant Venturers' Technical College in an elaborately neo-Gothic building in Unity Street. In 1949 it was taken over by Bristol Education Authority as Bristol College of Technology and then in 1960, as Bristol College of Science and Technology, it became one of the country's ten CATs (Colleges of Advanced Technology) administered by the Ministry of Education. In the 1960s CATs were converted to universities and the Bristol one got its charter in 1966. Meanwhile it had in the 1950s moved out of its old buildings to occupy the now vacant complex of the old Muller Orphanages at Ashley Down, Bristol. This was considered inadequate for the new university and in 1961 it was decided to move to an area based on Kings Weston House (now occupied by the police) in the west of Bristol. Planning permission was given and then withdrawn when the size of the undertaking was realized so in 1963 the university-to-be had to look elsewhere. In that year they were offered the Norwood site by Bath City Council, accepted early in 1964 and received Government approval in June of that year.

Unlike the building of eighteenth-century Bath where individual architect/developers worked for individual clients, the design of the new university was a committee effort with a team of architects (about twenty in 1965) from Robert Matthews, Johnson-Marshall and Partners, in consultation with cost consultants, consulting civil engineers, traffic consultants

(Buchanan) and the university's seven-member Academic Advisory Committee. They also had to work within changing requirements laid down successively by the Ministry of Education, the Department of Education and Science (DES—1964), and from April 1965 the University Grants Committee.

There are numerous ways in which a university can be designed, but it was decided that the new building must ensure: (a) a close mix of functions—academic, administrative, and social, and (b) ability to expand. A linear design was therefore adopted with an ability to expand at each end and at right angles to the main spine, a design somewhat reminiscent of the central feature of the 'new town' of Cumbernauld. Thus the main university road runs through the heart of the complex at ground level with buildings rising up on either side and the heart of the university is a second-storey parade with rectangular openings letting light down to the road below and affording glimpses of trees rising from the ground level. At each end of the promenade are cross-blocks for residence and along the sides are lecture halls and rooms, laboratories and workshops, library, bookshop, common-rooms, dining-rooms, banks and shops. A sound piece of planning carried out in aluminium, plastic panels, glass, and walls of concrete fashionably bearing the marks of its wooden shuttering and also some rather bad staining. Not everything is, however, contained in the central linear block—there is more residence to the north and other buildings are dotted about the campus, although a large area has been left for splendid playing-fields. The main entrance to the university is from Claverton Down Road although it can also be approached from North Road. Water supply to the university was helped by the fact that on the hill behind there was already a Water Board reservoir.

Because of the need to build quickly, because of the technological image, and because of financial restriction, it was necessary to use prefabricated materials and modern building techniques with the result that the buildings have simple, rectangular forms and the overall impression is one of low, slabby blocks with a couple of vertical slabs (the student accommodation, happily relieved by coloured curtains). It is not, however, an obtrusive structure. Originally it was to have a tall cylindrical accommodation block rather like the Post Office Tower, but this never got built.

Although 'Technology' was dropped from the title there is still a strong emphasis on science and technology and a good deal of important technological research is carried out. Many students follow a 'sandwich course' where they spend some time in industry.

To the south of the main building there runs from west to east the tree-lined Avenue which leads out of the city to the American Museum in Claverton Manor. The medieval manor house was down towards the river in the village of Claverton but early in the nineteenth century this was pulled down and all that remains is a broad flight of steps leading to nothing. The new house was built in 1819–20 at the top of the hill to designs by Sir Jeffry Wyatville (1776–1840) who is best known for his remodelling of Windsor Castle for George IV during which he changed his name, with the King's consent, from the less grandiloquent Wyatt—not a bad thing for us as there are a number of other architectural Wyatts. The house has been adapted inside into a set of rooms furnished to illustrate authentically various stages of American history. Other themes, such as Indians, and a colonial kitchen, are illustrated. It is well worth a visit but it is as well to remember that they charge you twice—once to get into the grounds and again to enter the house.

From the university Claverton Down Road continues eastward through countryside, turns south, and then loops back westward past Claverton Down Hospital, where Brassknocker Hill comes in. It carries on past the Civil Service Sports Ground and the post-war Ralph Allen School, until it hits Combe Down, or rather that part of it known as Williamstowe, and then we are in a built-up region through Combe Down, Southdown, Rush Hill as far as Twerton Hill from which the road runs down the west side of the Whiteway-Twerton development which we have already looked at.

This is an area which it is very difficult either to make broad generalizations about or to resolve into regions for it is a mosaic of building, mostly developed since the end of the eighteenth century so that we find in close juxtaposition early nineteenth-century mansions in the Classical tradition, nineteenth-century, two-storey ranges, inter-war private and council building, and new post-war developments. Although there are patches with common features, inter-war council housing for example, they often contain relict buildings from an earlier period while elsewhere modern buildings have been popped into gaps in a matrix of nineteenth-century development. Even shops and pubs do not appear to obey any strong locational principles except, perhaps, that most are found along the main road. This part of the portrait will therefore tend to be rather more selective, starting with churches.

Combe Down Church is, appropriately, in Church Street and the present building dates from 1835—the date is over the tower door along with the text "This is none other than the house of God"—and was designed by H. E. Goodridge. It looks rather lumpy with its heavy pinnacles, octagonal tower, and spire. At the far end, however, at the corner of the angular apse is inscribed "This stone was laid by Mrs. Gore Langton of Newton Park, July 31st 1883" and this refers to the aisles and chancel which are less showy. Next to the church is the old vicarage, a big neo-Jacobean job of 1838, set in an old quarry, and round the corner at the end of the Avenue is the four-square church hall of 1897 with string-courses and mullions.

A more remarkable building is the Roman Catholic church of Saints Peter and Paul designed by a local architect, Martin Fisher, and built in 1965 where Entry Hill comes in. Constructed in stone, concrete, and wood, it has a large, cool interior with flagged floor, ground-level windows, and a tent-like roof with a skylight through which light comes down to the altar. On the wall by the entrance the two saints sit back-to-back, St Peter with his keys, St Paul with a book in his lap; they look rather uncomfortable. The church and the playing-fields opposite occupy old quarries which ceased production in about 1904. Down Entry Hill a bit and along Hawthorn Grove on the right we find St Andrew's Anglican Church, consecrated by the Bishop of Bath and Wells in 1957. Here they have gone Classical with a Venetian window and broken pediment although the curved line of carving over the porch adds an alien and interesting touch. The church is part of a small complex which serves as a church centre.

More new churches were built further west. Near the traffic lights where Bloomfield Road crosses Frome Road, which is what Claverton Down Road has now become, is St Philip's and St James's. It used to be simply St Philip's and quite small, but after the war the church sold the site of bombed St James's to Woolworth's, used the money to enlarge St Philip's and tacked on the extra saint. Over the entrance is not a text but "Licensed for music, singing, dancing and any other entertainment of the like kind" and this is because the building includes the church hall. It has a big tower and plain windows. Next door, mainly in Victorian buildings, is St Philip's C. of E. Junior School, on the other side, by the corner, is the now boarded-up Odd Down Congregational Institute, established in 1802 and enlarged in 1913, while opposite is the single-storey United Reformed Church with at right angles a long extension for social purposes. The United Reformed Church came into being in 1972 by the amalgamation of the Presbyterians and Congregationalists.

Down Rush Hill we come to Englishcombe Lane, off which is Mount Road, and in Mount Road is St Barnabas's Church with a foundation stone laid by the Bishop Suffragan of Taunton in 1957, the year before the building was consecrated. It is a modern hall church, towerless but with a great big bell on one outside wall, aisle windows in plain glass, nave ones coloured and rather fine, and a long church hall at the side which is being extended. The altar in the Lady Chapel was taken from the ruins of bombed Holy Trinity Church in James Street West, part of whose war damage compensation was used in building St Barnabas's. Nearly opposite is the Sladebrook Gospel Hall of 1904, now a joinery workshop, and if we carry on down to the Hollow and turn up left we come to the Methodist church of 1959, long and low with a broad, squat, pyramid-capped tower. A Bath architect, Beresford-Smith, was the designer and it cost £23,000 to build.

All this church building was a consequence of the growth of population on the plateau and so too was the increase in the number of schools. Odd Down had its old-established junior school of St Philip's, and Combe Down also had an old school, still functioning, on whose roadside wall is a commemorative stone tablet to The Revd William Batchellor "for 26 years a liberal friend to Combe Down", who died in 1856. There are, in addition, several more recent schools including Southdown Junior (c. 1930) and Infants', Fosseway Junior (c. 1930) and Infants' (1950) and Culverhay Comprehensive which was originally built in 1953 as West Hill Secondary Modern.

The Culverhay site is called Barrow Mead and was of archaeo-logical interest, with evidence of occupancy from the Iron Age to the fourteenth century; in other words it was a deserted hamlet, probably the Bergh mentioned in the fourteenth century as a hamlet of Twerton. It is possible that the 'Barrow' was a *Burh*, a Saxon reference to an Iron Age hill fort on the spur of land above, but this cannot be proved as Barrow House was built on the site and the land around it landscaped. If the hill fort existed then the settlement was outside its walls. A trial excavation in 1950 showed Iron Age gullies, early medieval buildings, and an eighteenth-century house. A rescue dig in 1953, done while the school was building, was made by Philip Rahtz and Ernest Greenfield. This revealed two curving hollow ways, at least two minor buildings, and a large house which began as a timber building in the twelfth century and was rebuilt in the thirteenth in half-timbering on stone footings; one half was paved but clean, the other contained a hearth and oven. There was a lot of pottery, and other finds included spindle-whorls, hones, keys and buckles. It was reported by Rahtz in *A North Somerset Miscellany* published by the Bath and Camerton Archaeological Society in 1956.

Another school which has changed its nature and name is out near the Wellsway just inside the city boundary. This was opened in 1961 as the Cardinal Newman School for Boys but in 1979, with a rearrangement of Roman Catholic schooling in the area, it became a comprehensive and its name was changed to St Gregory's. St Gregory was Pope from 590 to 604 and sent Augustine on his missionary visit to Britain. The school is a pleasant-looking building in brick with grey and blue panels and has a three-storey, central block with single-storey wings.

The development of Combe Down as a settlement began in 1726 when Ralph Allen began to acquire and develop the quarries which supplied most of the stone for the building of eighteenth-century Bath, a process greatly helped in 1730 when he engaged John Padmore to construct a tramway down the line of the present Ralph Allen's Drive and Prior Park Road to the riverside quay. Even then development was slow and Edmund Rack, Secretary of the Bath and West Society, wrote in 1780 that "the entire village of Combe Down consists of 11 houses built by Ralph Allen in 1729 for his quarrymen".

The main quarry lay behind a road now called The Firs where the back gardens of the late nineteenth-century ranges run up to the face into which the tunnels were driven—most of the stone was mined, not cut from an open face, and Combe Down is honeycombed with tunnels. There are several other quarries in the area, some of which have been used as sites for housing; one, by the main road, is occupied by a café, The Rockery, and if we follow an asphalt path from the end of de Montalt Road past Monkton Combe Junior School and its pleasant playing-fields, we come to a large quarry on the left which is being filled in and another on the right where they make blocks of artificial stone.[1]

Some of the cottages and big houses date from the late eighteenth century but the rest is mainly nineteenth century with some twentieth-century infills—and this at a time when the quarrywork was declining. A new industry which started in 1805 was the de Montalt paper mills (it became a laundry in 1854), water-powered from a tributary of the Midford Brook—some remains still stand down in Horsecombe Vale (ST 713619). Earl de Montalt, who had married Ralph Allen's niece, renovated and enlarged Allen's cottages which were renamed de Montalt Place, and was partly responsible for founding the mill. The road pattern of the village is a little confusing, with paths threading off in all directions and houses placed at a variety of angles.

A pleasant feature is the triangular Firs Field bought for £750 as a war memorial, with the main road on one side, The Firs on the west and the Avenue, tree-lined, on the east which comes out at the end of de Montalt Road by a big Regency-looking bank with "Bank" carved on a plaque high up on the front wall. A little further along are the Ralph Allen row of cottages, two-storey and looking Classical, some with parapets, some without. The centre one, reputed to be the foreman's house and office, has a triangular pediment with a ball, and a sundial above the porch—which is presumably why it is called Dial House. A little further along is the Union Chapel and schoolroom of 1815 set up by the Argyle Chapel and Somerset Street Baptists of Bath. Further east, beyond the school, the road is lined on one side with large Italianate houses and on the right at the end of a drive is The Brow, built in 1834. More Italianate houses are down Belmont Road, including one at the bottom with a remarkable collection of angular oriels. Belmont takes us into Summer Lane which goes up past a row of cottages set in a quarry to a mushroom farm at the top with big white-painted concrete sheds and back to Church Road. Turning left up Combe Road which has the New Church, a single-storey, modern building, we come to the King William, past which a road goes down to Rock Hill House, a big, asymmetrical stone building in Jacobean style but with a Classical front doorway with attached columns and entablature on whose frieze is carved "Magdalen

[1] For details of the quarries see "The Stone Industry of Bath" by Philip Wooster in Vol. 11, 1972 BIAS (Bristol Industrial Archaeology Society Journal).

Hospital School". This refers to the building being used in 1846 as a "House for Imbecile Children" in place of the one next to the church of St Mary Magdalen in Holloway. In 1924 it had twenty girls and eighteen boys. Today it is a hospital.

On the other side of the main highway, here called North Road, lies the big expanse of the Admiralty establishment with low brick blocks and wooden hutments, all set in grass, surrounded by a link fence and flanked by two mainly post-war housing areas, semi-detached or in short rows but with a few four-storey blocks of flats such as Bradford Park, and a parade of 'Cornish' houses in Queen's Drive. It is all low-density and quite pleasant. A little further to the west, Hansford Square seems a typical bit of inter-war suburbia.

And now we come to the triangle of roads in which sits the complex which today is St Martin's Hospital but was originally built in 1837–8 as the Bath Union Workhouse, or Frome Road House, with accommodation for five hundred paupers which rose to over a thousand with the building extensions of 1842, '55 and '65. One of the most remarkable of the inmates was John Plass who at the age of seventy-two laid all the stone, inside and out, of the workhouse chapel which was designed by G. P. Manners and opened in 1846, the date over the door. It is a gaunt building with buttresses, simple pinnacles, a bell-cote, and tall lancet windows. Inside is a gallery and memorial tablets to officers of the union, including Probationer Nurse Rachel Snelgrove who fell ill "in the performance of her duty" and died. She was only twenty-two.

A picture of John Plass and a commemorative tablet are in the porch. The plaque records that he died in 1849, aged eighty-two, and was buried in the adjoining ground which the bishop had consecrated in 1847 to save, according to the newspaper report, "the inconvenience of carrying the bodies to different parishes". After the workhouse had been running for a year, one of the guardians wrote a furious pamphlet criticizing his fellow guardians and claiming that the clerk had absconded with £800 of the parish poor-rate, with the connivance of the medical officer, and hinting darkly at other misdoings—"Time will not permit me to describe at any length the unpleasant disclosures made by the schoolmaster, Mr. Harris, respecting the person who was the Matron." Well—perhaps—although the workhouse seems on the whole to have been well run. There was, however, an incident in 1857 which strikes an unpleasant note. The manager of the Theatre Royal in Bath offered the workhouse children a free matinée of *Jack and the Beanstalk* but when they arrived for their treat they were turned away as the guardians had changed their minds and decided that the children were not to be put to the risk of acquiring "the habits of early dissipation". Makes you sick, doesn't it?

It is interesting to note that in 1858 by far the biggest amounts spent on paupers was for Walcot, followed by Lyncombe/Widcombe and St James's and yet these contributed most to the poor-rate, an indication that the parishes were not social monoliths but had a mixture of rich and very poor. The union, incidentally, included both Bath and the surrounding parishes, stretching as far south as Hinton Charterhouse. The workhouse buildings are gaunt, but the centre of the front has a triangular pediment with a clock on it and windows with straight pediments on consoles. Further ranges stretch out to the back, there is a tall red-brick flue, and several groups of buildings have been added to give the extra facilities required by a hospital. The workhouses were set up to reduce the amount of outdoor relief. They were ended by the National Insurance Act of 1948 and now we all pay a poor-rate (National Insurance contributions) and are eligible for outdoor relief (Social Security benefits).

Up the west side of the hospital runs the Wellsway, the old Fosse Way, and this continues, through a roundabout, south towards Radstock. Beyond the Wellsway we are into Odd Down, so-called not because of any peculiarities but probably after some old Saxon Odda, an area which has been built over in this century. To the south is a triangular network of streets, most lined with 1930s council housing, but some with private building, and including a pub whose signpost shows a Saxon warrior uneasily holding spear and shield in one hand and a drinking bowl in the other, a shopping parade, one or two separate shops, and a youth club in Odin's Road. The geologically named Oolite Road is on a quarry site. To the north is a mixture of inter-war and post-war housing with Corston View at its western edge where, after the war, was a patch of prefabs which was destroyed to make way for more substantial building. In some ways this was a pity, for the prefab, although too small for a family house, was a brilliant piece of design, was cheap, could be turned out in quantities and, once the infrastructure of drains and electric cables and water and the concrete pads had been installed, a house would roll up on a couple of transporters and be erected by a small labour force in a very short space of time. They were only meant to last for seven years but there are places where people are still living in them very comfortably.

At the top of Rush Hill is one of Clark's shoe factories and at the bottom, past Culverhay School, we cross Englishcombe Lane which goes in one direction south-west to Englishcombe village and in the other direction runs between two patches of housing, Sladebrook to the east and Southdown to the west, both mixed in character. Southdown, for example, has an inter-war shopping parade in brick and a number of inter-war houses and bungalows as well as a considerable post-war development.

Dominating South Down is High Barrow Hill, known locally as the Round Hill and kept as an open recreation area. At the top is a concrete Ordnance Survey triangulation pillar, its top fitted with metal grooves to take the levelling screws of a theodolite, and at the bottom are public lavatories. Between them is a grassy slope where people can stroll, exercise their dogs, and do their courting. The views in all directions are very fine and there is a splendid outlook over the city of Bath.

Skirting the west side of the Round Hill, Rush Hill has become Whiteway Road and takes us sharply down past housing on the right which we have already looked at and open fields on the left with Haycombe Cemetery and Crematorium at the top. At the bottom, Newton Road goes off to the right towards Twerton, and the main road crosses the Newton Brook and takes us out of the city of Bath.

Even this little rural corner of Bath has not escaped change. The large field to the south of the main road is in fact a grassed-over rubbish tip, and even as this is being written the machines have moved in between Newton Road and the brook to landscape the area for a new camping site while beside the Newton Road a large single-storey council depot has been erected.

And so we leave our portrait of hill-girt Bath with its Roman and medieval heart, its Georgian streets and squares and crescents, its Victorian mansions and acres of tidy, by-law housing, its inter-war, neo-Georgian and low-density council housing, and its post-war, cuboid erections faced in reconstituted Bath stone. There it lies, waiting for its conservation and traffic problems to be solved, waiting to define its present-day economic base. Does its future lie in marketing, or tourism, or education, or medicine, or industry, or its revival as a spa—or in a combination of these things? Or perhaps there will be something as new and unexpected as that sudden and unprecedented acceleration of activity which gave us the Georgian city which is so greatly admired.

One thing its history shows us is that Bath is a survivor—out of a marsh rose a Roman city—out of the ruins of that city rose a Saxon monastic town to which the Middle Ages added fairs and markets and a cloth industry—in the eighteenth century came the phenomenal spread of building for the new social life of the city—in the nineteenth it became a residential and service centre with the beginnings of modern industry—and in the twentieth the industry has been further developed, new small housing has spread and infilled, and the city has acquired a university and a college of higher education as well as expanding its technical college and its hospital service and developing its tourist industry. Today, Bath has blocks of flats, and offices, and multi-storey car-parks, and a new shopping precinct. It has department stores and supermarkets, hotels and cafés and pizza parlours, Chinese, Indian, and Italian restaurants. Any idea that Bath has its feet so firmly embedded in the eighteenth century that she cannot move should be abandoned, although it must be admitted that much of the new architecture sits rather uneasily in and around the Georgian beauty of the centre—of which a great deal more remains than some people would have us believe.

Bath is beautiful, and varied, and famous—and is a living city, not a museum or a 'sleeping Princess'. Long may she flourish!

Index